Wetumka

Wetumka

A Centennial History

B. J. OSBORN

Writers Club Press

San Jose New York Lincoln Shanghai

Wetumka
A Centennial History

Writers Club Press
an imprint of iUniverse, Inc.

For information address:
iUniverse, Inc.
5220 S. 16th St., Suite 200
Lincoln, NE 68512
www.iuniverse.com

ISBN: 0-595-21464-9

Printed in the United States of America

For
My Parents

Darl Garrison Osborn (1911-1954)
Beatrice Smith Osborn Kennedy (1919-1997)
And My Brother
Bobby Gene Osborn (1940-2001)

Contents

Preface

The personal relevance of this history is obvious as I am a native Wetumkan. I mined the public record to try to understand the wrenching accounts of hard times that I heard often as I was growing up. I wanted to confront the actual contours of Wetumka's ordeal.

Several outstanding citizens who once lived at Wetumka told me that they had long harbored the ambition of writing down their own history of the area, but, that they had not had sufficient drive or that another part of their lives had gotten in the way. I would certainly like to read other historical accounts of the area and have left plenty of room for anyone who would like to write their own version of Wetumka's history.

I used only primary sources (created at the time of the events described) in my research. Every assertion is faithfully derived from the record. I took it upon myself to create databases, make calculations and devise my own interpretations. This is the true responsibility of the historian.

Most of all I tried not to sound overly academic. Everything is written in very common language; and, when the publisher's representative presented me with proofs of the chapters, I declined to correct every little error or continue to tinker with word placements.

This endeavor occupied a few minutes to a few hours of nearly every day during the last two years. It was, indeed, satisfying.

Modesto and Twain Harte, California, December 2001

1

The New Wetumka

WETUMKA, in its Centennial Year, strikes the visitor as a prime example of an original Oklahoma town with a distinctive central business district of "double buildings" of native rock and "fancy brick" fronts. The founding generation of Wetumkans completed most of these buildings in little more than a decade. By 1903, there were already thirty brick-front buildings in town and several others were under construction. A full year before Oklahoma achieved statehood, three Wetumka banks, with highly optimistic business expectations, were open for business on the west side of Main Street. (No other state had ever had as much population or had been so richly supplied by railroads when it was launched as Oklahoma had been in 1907. Every town envisioned itself as the beginning of a wealthy metropolis in the new Century.) Wetumka's early population growth was very rapid according to the National Census. Within its boundaries the increase was from an uncounted handful in 1900 to 1,190 in 1910.

Some of the early settlers said they had had the sensation of being on special trains full of new settlers hurrying to Oklahoma and getting off at stations to join friends and kinfolks. Others were stopping at destinations suggested by the railroad. For some of them their first stop was at a tent city south of Wetumka. Several counties had their "Ragtown" and Hughes was one of them.

At the end of 1911, the first two blocks of Main Street had been converted from the first primitive fire-prone wood structures (that had been hastily moved from Old Wetumka) into these sturdy, handsome stone buildings. In that year, the combination two story Town Hall and fraternal lodge was constructed. The site of the first and present city municipal buildings was first occupied by a small frame hotel owned by Mr. Kirkpatrick who, of necessity became a grocer when it burned down. Mr. Kirkpatrick was the manager of the grocery department at The Coin Strore during the last 28 years of his life. (The Chowins Brothers built the first Town Hall, the first High School ten years later and were active in city construction for decades.) The second elementary school (Mingo School in the Mingo Addition) was ready at the north end of Main Street in 1911.

Also, in 1911, the whole block between The First National Bank and The Old Brick Hotel on West Broadway was complete. C. J. Dickerson had this area constructed at a cost of $4,000. Dickerson's General Store had just been completed across the alley. This is the building that for decades was known as The Farmers' Exchange. Other than for paint and the addition of an awning, very little has been done to alter its appearance.

The man most familiarly remembered as the owner of this business was Argie Taylor who moved to Wetumka from Sapulpa in 1938 and acquired the building and stock. He stated that there would be only one change which he thought was overdue. He wanted the spelling corrected from "X-Change."

The American National Bank was located on the southwest corner of Main Street and Broadway. (The building is presently used by an insurance agency.) The First National Bank was in rented space where the Coast-to-Coast store is now located. The Bank of Commerce was first located in the stately two story building next to the present Hughes County Times building. (This building still houses the original bank safe and the second floor provided office space for some of the best known doctors and lawyers in early Wetumka.) The American National Bank building, arguably the most attractive building in Wetumka, was the last finished as its completion was delayed because the elaborate limestone trim had to be brought by rail from a distant quarry.

Wetumkans endured dirt streets through their business district for nearly 25 years. It was a tremendous hardship and the businessmen often complained of their loss of good merchandise to the dust. Whenever the wind picked up, they would all rush to close their doors and windows. Starting in 1908, a man was contracted to haul water all day and constantly water the streets. His wagon had a huge tub in front of a sloping bed. He rigged up a valve that allowed water to sheet out the back of the wagon. Some of the merchants balked at paying their share of the $65 monthly expense.

The original sidewalks were of planks sawn from native timber. Concrete and rock crossings at the main intersections made it possible to cross. The dust was considered a greater menace than the mud. It was part of normal life all year when the streets were busiest. Rain would often keep people from coming to town. By 1909 the town council had started putting in concrete sidewalks in the business district. The first twenty-five blocks were done by Roy Chowins.

Weleetka was never able to pave its streets. The railroad hauled slate to partially surface some of its streets. The town finally got a hard surfaced Main Street with Highway 75 in 1930. Dustin had dirt streets until 1952 when the State Highway Department paved 1100 feet of their Main Street in conjunction with the paving of SH 9.

During the oil boom of the mid-1920s, three corners of Main Street and Broadway were taken up by these rival banks which had filled in the gaps by building formidable annexes and renting them as office space. (The new and final location of The Bank of Commerce included large office complexes on both Main and Broadway. The annex on Main Street was for many years the T-P Mercantile Company (for Tomlinson and Parsley; from the late 1930s it was the home of the R. L. Meadors and Son Department Store which had been moved from Dustin. Robert Lee Meadors or to me as a customer "Uncle Bob" was

Turner's brother.) The other corner was the site of the two-story Meadors Brothers and Busey Building. It was a general merchandise store with a huge warehouse in back that stocked everything from farm implements to fine clothing. Turner Meadors had lived in Holdenville from its founding in 1898. He moved his business interests to Wetumka in 1903. The Meadors Building also provided space for a doctor, a lawyer and other professionals. (Dr. Gille, the pioneer dentist, first had his office in the Meadors Building. In the 1920s, he relocated in an apartment house he owned opposite his Main Street residence. From there he moved to the new Bank of Commerce building downtown. It should be noted that Dr. Gille's daughter, Helen, married Turner Meadors' son Ray, in 1921.)

When Turner Meadors died at his home in Oklahoma City in February, 1941, his obituary was carried by all of the major newspapers. He was recalled as one of the most extensive landowners in eastern Oklahoma and as a philanthropist who gave freely to his causes. The current Turner Meadors reminds me that his grandparents were "Big Baptists." Indeed, they were and were always important benefactors to the church in Wetumka. Frank Meadors, so fondly remembered by many Wetumkans, moved to Oklahoma City in 1929 at about the time that his father had. Frank was a homebuilder and his investment focus was more "town oriented" while his brother Ray looked after the extensive Meadors farming interests. There had been a Meadors Motors Company in Wetumka for a long time. Frank established Downtown Chevrolet in Oklahoma City and he was in the process of creating a chain of dealerships when he died of a heart attack on September 5, 1945. He was only 56 and barely survived his father by five years.

The most important and credible source of information about Wetumka's earliest days is in the written accounts left by Dr. D. V. Berry who moved to Okmulgee after his retirement from medicine. Dr. Berry, in his own words, built the first "business house" and the first new residence in Wetumka. (Dr. Berry's residence was on Grand Avenue which became Highway 75.)

The doctor had lived in the area for ten years before the new Wetumka was laid out by the railroad. He had ministered to the desperate health needs of the Indians and was listed as one of the staff doctors at The Wetumka Boarding School for Indian Children two miles east of town near the North Canadian river.

Dr. Berry was very much an insider as he'd gained the trust of important Indian leaders. He wrote that the railhead at Wewoka was very well established and the railroad which came through this part of the future Hughes County at the turn of the century was originally surveyed to go through Wewoka. Dr. Berry saw survey crews at work and he sensed that something big was in the works. He knew the Seminole Chief, John F. Brown, since he'd spent many a night at his residence during his medical travels. (The Chief had a big house at Sasakaw which became known as the White House of the Seminole Nation. Construction on this building began in 1897 and continued for decades. It was dismantled in 1952 and the lumber was shipped to Ada. It was not unusual that the chief's father was white. Chief John Brown held his office for 34 years.)

The Seminole Chief and his lawyer, a former governor of Kansas, were called to St. Louis. At a meeting there, the railroad contract with the Seminoles was bought out for $25,000. The surveyors had determined that the terrain favored the route of a railroad through the future Wetumka and the considerable sum of $400,000 could thus be saved. Dr. Berry stated, "that's how Holdenville got the railroad."

Dr. Berry, blunt in his pronouncements, said that he'd come to Indian Territory because there were no particular medical standards in effect. His medical training consisted of reading medical texts "with an old doctor" and attending lectures for two years in St. Louis. He was comfortable working alongside the Indian medicine man as he performed his own time honored native rituals.

When railroad surveyors staked out the grid which would be Wetumka, the Indians in the area hastened to plant corn over the entire area. This obscured the streets somewhat but when the lumber arrived, the workmen hewed out a road through the corn to the lots that Dr. Berry had selected. Dr. Berry set up his medical practice in a drugstore. The first business in the new town was "The Wetumka Drug Company." In 1909 Walter Jarret opened the sixth drug store in Wetumka.

Dr. Berry's son, Homer, was one Wetumka's most famous sons. He had been a poor student in the schools of Wetumka but was a renowned aviator in both World Wars. His flying career was brief in the first World War but during the second he was an officer in both the British and American air forces. He was very important in getting American planes to Britain under the "lend lease" arrangement and later he was recalled as a Lieutenant Colonel by his own government to evaluate the capabilities of captured planes and to make recommendations to improve America's air arsenal. He was even on the cover of TIME magazine.

Colonel Bert Shaber, Jr., U. S. Army Retired, reminds me that his father and grandfather were grocers in Wetumka since the founding. I was acquainted with Mr. Bert Shaber when he operated his store near The Coin. He was a fountain of reliable information about the ways of the Indians who lived in the area.

Witnesses to the founding of Wetumka agree that the town actually took shape during the terrible winter of 1900-1901. James King, the second town marshal of Wetumka and Hughes County's first elected sheriff was one of the earliest citizens of the new town. He said that his job was not so difficult as it consisted mainly in breaking up fist-fights. He recalled helping pull up corn stalks in the streets.

Sheriff James King served two terms as the first sheriff of Hughes County. Tommy Townsend, an early farmer in the Lawnwood area east of Wetumka was acquainted with Mr. King. (Mr. Townsend and his wife were married in Wetumka in 1905). Mr. Townsend recalled that he served on the jury that acquitted Sherriff King of a murder that he had been unjustly accused. This event soured the sheriff on politics and after his term expired, he moved to Hanna for awhile. Then he moved back to Pea Ridge, Arkansas and operated a general store until he was elderly. In his declining years he moved back to Wetumka to live with his sister, Mrs. Rosa Lee Clendening. Sheriff King was an uncle to Levi Clendening.

These early events were corroborated nearly half a century later by Mrs. H. H. Holman who was living with her daughter at the time in New York City. She said her husband had helped launch the First National Bank and he had served as the second mayor of Wetumka and had been elected to the state legislature. Mr. Holman had owned the property at the corner of Main and Broadway which he sold to Turner Meadors.

H. H. Holman and his wife were teachers at The Wetumka Boarding School. Mrs. Irwin Watson, in her magisterial study of the school's history, states that the teachers got room and board and very little salary. Several of the most prominent town builders had started modestly enough at this school. They surely had not amassed much capital and this leads me to believe that much of Wetumka was financed by speculators and investors. Most of the businesses were started with very little capital. I had a chance to peruse all the records of the defunct bank at Yeager. It was started with a total capitalization of $2500 and rapidly grew past the $10,000 mark. Town building for the earliest investors was a very lucrative undertaking. The Holman's daughter was a teacher in the Wetumka schools and then an English Professor at the University of Oklahoma.

In every measure, Wetumka was the creature of the railroad which became its strongest promoter. Every brick, every pane of glass, and nearly every new resident of Wetumka, of necessity, came by rail. The railroad published its own magazine and made the most outlandish claims to lure settlers to the area. The railroad was the essential lifeline to the outside world. Wetumka citizens published articles in The Frisco Magazine. One of the more outlandish claims made was that while Wetumka already had been bought up by investors, there were stupendous opportunities to become rich by purchasing land in a new town, Lamar. One article touted Lamar as being near lands of "inexhaustible fertility that overlay vast pools of oil and and fields of coal."

At the time the railroads were the only truly big business in Oklahoma. The Frisco had its own "Development Department" which sponsored agricultural experts to advise farmers on proper farming techniques. The railroad even had its own demonstration farm near Holdenville. The demonstrators also held day long meetings at farms all over the county. Long before there was a Agricultural and Mechanical College or county farm agents, the railroads performed this function. They trained the farmers how to uniformly to pack their produce. By 1915, the "Mountain Grove Fruit Growers Association" was shipping all the fresh fruit that fifty pickers could process.

The railroad even had special lecture cars. These were passenger cars turned into classrooms on wheels. The station agent would have farmers waiting on the platforms when these lecture cars pulled in. Everyone knew to get in quickly and be seated. The time the train could wait was strictly limited. The railroad often displayed carloads of ideal dairy stock. As late as the 1940s, the railroad demonstration agents were training the farmers to prune their watermelon vines to grow more and smaller melons.

In February, 1906, the editor of THE WETUMKA NEWS-HERALD reported that the retail merchants of Wetumka, in a single day, had received enough freight to completely fill the freight room at the depot and about a hundred feet of the loading platform. And, in addition, there were still two loaded boxcars on the siding. The railroad had stockyards in Wetumka. (They were located near the city power plant and not removed until the early 1950s.) The Frisco brought 125,000 head of cattle to stations on its line in the first year after statehood.

At about this time the people of Wetumka were raising a $5,000 bonus for a second railroad. A right-of-way through the Tiger Addition had been donated by the property owners. The bonus specifically was to secure the railroad and a pledge that another townsite would not be established within nine miles of Wetumka. The proposed railroad was to be a link railroad that started in Dustin and went to Shawnee. Survey crews were seen and rumors floated. It was later believed that it would connect Muskogee and Oklahoma City. It was a phantom railroad never to make its appearance in Wetumka.

For at least half a century before there was the familiar railroad town Wetumka, there was Old Town Wetumka. It was a small Creek township that had been suddenly and completely overrun by White intruders. (In a proper sense, there never was an Indian Territory. The tribal legislature had only nominal control and the Federal Government intervened often.) These Whites were intruders who could not get "good title" to coveted farmland. They had to lease it from the Indians and thus had little incentive to conserve the soil or to make permanent improvments.

One of the earliest residents of what became Hughes County was Mr. J. C. La Porte who is still remembered today as a long time Justice of The Peace in Wetumka. He said he had several occupations but his earliest was harvesting walnut logs in the bottoms along the South Canadian River. He would lash them into rafts and float them to sawmills in Eufaula. He said the best lumber was shipped to Germany to be carved into furniture, cuckoo clocks and other items that made that nation so fearsome.

As soon as the new town was surveyed, there was no doubt that it would be the new Wetumka. Moving the wood frame buildings was not a daunting task. The distance was not great and the ground was frozen. The small shops and the few houses were dismantled or cut into pieces that could be skidded across the fields to the new town. Mr. J. C. Chowins, or as he was known "Grandpa Chowins" was as much a town mover as a town builder. He had been born in England in 1835 and immigrated to America as a young man, and finally settled in Oklahoma. He moved several buildings from Old Town Wetumka onto his lots on Main Street. He had been the first owner of the intersection lot where The American National Bank was located. He moved Mr. Dunzy's store and post office to the new Main Street. Mr. Chowins died in 1913 and is buried in Block 20 of The Wetumka Cemetery. (His grandson, Harry Glenn Chowins was my fondly remembered high school science teacher and principal.)

Mr. Lorenzo C. Gammill is one of Wetumka's founding fathers. He resided in both Wetumkas and is the patriarch of an enduring Wetumka family. He left a brief but descriptive account of how quickly the landscape of the area was transformed by the railroad. Mr. Gammill said that Wetumka, like most new towns in Oklahoma, was originally 160 acres in size. By 1904 the entire city had been built out and it was necessary to annex the Tiger Addition on the South and within another year the Bell View Addition. Then the Mingo Addition quickly followed on the north. Within these few years Wetumka stretched along both sides of the railroad and had doubled in size to 320 acres.

In 1903, the town council had acquired a plot of land that became Wetumka's Cemetery. A municipal burial place was one of the first amenities that new settlers sought when they looked for a place they could call home. The cost and fees for the acquisition of the Wetumka Cemetery came to $1044.30.

By this time the Wetumka School District had been organized. The old school buildings were purchased from the city and in 1906 a new $14,000 two story architect-designed building was put in the Tiger Addition. It was called the Central Ward School. In 1911, a second school, in the Mingo Addition, was opened to relieve some of the overcrowding. For a while there had been 85 students in Miss Leona Sharp's primary room before the Mingo School was ready and three additional teachers could be hired. (The school board's solution had been to give Miss Sharp a double session.)

In that same year, 1906, THE TULSA DAILY DEMOCRAT sent reporters to the area. They wrote that four huge saw mills were working overtime within six miles of Wetumka. The land was being rapidly cleared up. Huge fires were reducing stumps and limbs to ash.

The Irick Brothers advertised their lumber at $11 per 1,000 board feet at the mill and sawn to custom specifications. They were ready to deliver it to any lot in Wetumka for $15 in that quantity. The reporters counted 73 persons living on one square mile of cleared land and concluded that the whole area would soon become one of the most thickly settled regions in the state.

Visitors to early Wetumka were always impressed by the Wetumka Boarding School for Indian youths two miles east of town. A party from THE DALLAS MORNING NEWS gave a typically glowing news account. They said, that, almost as if on cue, the students realizing that there were visitors, immediately went to the assembly room and presented a well rehearsed program of music, short plays and long recitations they had memorized.

In those days the Mission School, or more formally The National Boarding School, was a complex of buildings on forty acres. The real purpose of the boarding school, according to its teaching staff, was to bring Indian youths into daily contact with whites. The Creek Council always disputed that stated purpose. They thought the real purpose was to turn the new generation of Indians into whites and they never supported this school or any of the three dozen or so on Creek lands.

There were other reasons for the Indians' bad feelings toward the school. The discipline was rigid and often unreasonable. The boys and girls were always segregated and none was allowed to converse in their own language at school. According to Wetumkan, Roly Canard, Principal Chief of The Creeks for twelve years, the harshest punishment was meted out to those who dared speak a native word. Mr. Canard and his half-sister, Annie Yahola, were students there and said it was a miserable existence.

Every effort was made to shelter the school from the outside world. The common cold had not been common to the Indian in the New World before the arrival of whites. Every epidemic seemed to hit the native population harder than their white neighbors. The school was often quarantined and parents were not allowed to see their children. There were many deaths at the school's hospital building. The parents were not even allowed to see their children before they were buried because it was thought that this would contribute the spread of the disease. (The sole remaining ruin at the school site is the hospital building.)

In the waning days of the Mission School, it was exclusively for boys. The girl students had been transferred to Eufaula.

At the boarding school there was as much concern about teaching Indian youth the finer points of raising livestock and of gardening as there was for their literary skills. A small bearing orchard was maintained and visitors remarked about how well the farm animals were kept.

Visitors always came away impressed with the Indians' interest in music and by how many of them had become adept at various musical instruments. The piano was by far their favorite. This part of the indoctrination seems to have had a good effect. Music would always be an integral part of the Indian church services.

One of the students, William Alligator, who by 1906 was eighteen and had gained wide acclaim as an Indian healer or medicine man. He had been mentioned in newspapers as far away as Kansas City and his mail brought desperate pleas for help. Plenty of people of the time had given up on convention doctors and patent medicine and they asked him to perform his native rituals on their behalf. They would send him a small piece of their clothing or maybe a lock of hair. William Alligator was a worthy student as well. At the close of school exercises in 1906, he stood and unwaveringly delivered a long recitation that he had carefully memorized: "The American Revolution."

Mr. Irwin A. Watson, a high school English teacher in Wetumka, is the best known authority on the history of The Wetumka Boarding School. She recorded much valuable information and many important interviews in her unpublished study. (I recently took it upon myself to put her work on a computer disc and have some copies made up for the Wetumka Library.)

Mrs. Watson did much of her research at the Gilcrease Art Museum in Tulsa. I do not believe she ever realized that Mr. Thomas Gilcrease, himself, had been a student at the school. I picked it up in a quote he made as an old man. He used words similar to these: "I had darned little formal education, and if it had not been for my time at The Wetumka Boarding School, I wouldn't had any…. I capitalized my oil company with royalty proceeds for an original Indian allotment of 160 acres in Hughes County."

In February, 1909, a fire destroyed the south dormitory at The Wetumka Boarding School. Three of the teachers and 41 students lost all of their clothing and personal effects. Colbert Turkey, a reluctant student, readily admitted that he had started the fire in the washhouse because he felt that he'd been too harshly punished by a teacher that day.

C. H. Baskin, a lawyer in Holdenville and Wetumka's City Attorney for decades, answered Mrs. Watson's inquiry about what happened to the student who started the fire. He stated that Colbert Turkey was arrested and brought to Holdenville and charged. The jury declined to convict him.

The dormitory was replaced but after the Curtis Act demolished tribal government, the United States Government was less generous in its financial support. The last Superintendent, Mr. Schengle, was elected to the first legislature after the Constitutional Convention.

Mr. Gammill had estimated the buildings and grounds as being worth about $10,000. They were actually sold for less than $2,500. The wooden buildings were torn down for their lumber.

Mr. Gammill said the pace of changes was always quickening. Land in cultivation had at least doubled in three years. But in 1906, it was his stated belief that not even twenty percent of the best land had been cleared for cultivation. While there had been a single cotton gin in Old Town, there would soon be four in operation in the new Wetumka. These gins were powered by steam boilers and during the peak periods of the harvest they operated 24-hours a day. (Ronnie Sheppard, a 1957 classmate recently showed me a photograph of the Sheppard Brothers gin which was in production at Statehood and typically it was reduced to ashes in 1911.)

The virgin soils of the area were productive and in a good year before World War I, as many as 5,000 bales of cotton would be shipped out of Wetumka. Of the cotton growing regions of Oklahoma, Hughes County usually ranked third in the State. (The Cotton King of Hughes County, farmed in the rich lands of the Pecan Grove community. His name was W. F. Samuels and he usually planted 3,000 acres of cotton and another 1,000 acres to feed his livestock and horses. He once bought a shipment of 40 walking cultivators from the A. Dolton Hardware and Furniture Store in Holdenville. It took a small army of men and horses to move them out of Holdenville after they had been assembled. In 1945, the "King" had concluded his travels and moved back to live in retirement in Holdenville.

Just five years into the history of Railroad Town Wetumka, Mr. Gammill stated that the exact location of the first Wetumka was becoming uncertain, even in the minds of those who had lived there. It was completely swallowed up by Mr. Johnson Tiger's huge cornfield

Mr. J. E. Tiger made himself prominent in both the world of the Indian and the White Intruder. He was the son of Creek Principal Chief, Motey Tiger, and was himself the last Assistant Chief before the tribal legislature was abolished. He was always a strong booster for Wetumka. He travelled to other states and distributed literature and gave newspaper interviews to publicize Wetumka's natural advantages. Later, he served on the school board with W. C. Farmer, X. X. McGee and Grant Herring during the years the Central Ward School and the new high school were built. For many years he also served as an Indian minister. He and his wife (the former Lorena Benson) were socially prominent among Wetumka's founding families. There were two residences in Wetumka known as the Tiger home. A huge two story house was located on East Broadway on the lot where Mr. Elgie Absher's house now stands. The corner where the Methodist church was built in 1951 was also known as the Tiger Corner. It's last use was as office buildings and a lawyer and his Creek interpreter had their office there. (In my recollection, this corner was an overgrown and poorly fenced cattle lot only a block off Main Street.)

In June, 2000, I visited the site of the original Wetumka with Mr. William La Porte. It is located east of Airport Drive behind the house that was traditionally known as the Hubert and Lorene Osborn home. This comports with all of the best written and oral accounts. The only remaining artifact is a well covered by a boulder.

Most towns in Oklahoma have a history of violent confrontation between the forces of law and order and the rabble element. In November of 1908, such an occurrence took place on South Main street near the T. L. Lumley Hardware store (forerunner of Herring Hardware). A person on each side of the divide between good and evil was left dead.

Ben and Jeff Smith, brothers, were under the influence of liquor at Gammill's livery barn, earlier on that November morning. There were generally being obnoxious and shooting their pistols into the air. After they started for town they met Monroe Reed in front of Fisk's Barber Shop.

There was a standing controversy over the ownership of a dog and the brothers Smith engaged Mr. Reed in a fistfight. One of them did the fighting while the other used his weapon to prevent interference.

The only lawman in town at the time was John Tabner an orphan who had been sponsored by the Williams family of The Coin Store. (They had known each other's families in Arkansas.) Mr. Tabner was asleep in his room at The Old Brick Hotel on West Broadway when the trouble started. He was sent for and as he approached the unruly scene he was fired upon by Jeff Smith. He had ordered Smith to drop his weapon but the miscreant had no intention of complying. Smith fired two shots and one of them tore away the lawman's collarbone. Tabner's shots brought him down and he died very soon on the dusty Wetumka Main Street.

Ben Smith pursued Mr. Tabner who was also out of shells. Ben was taken into custody. Jeff Smith was buried the same day. He left a wife and several children.

Mr. Tabner's injuries did not seem so life threatening at first. He was transported to Holdenville where surgeons used X-rays to see the bullet. They merely cleaned the wound and did not retrieve the bullet. While Mr. Tabner probably got better medical care than President McKinley had for a similar wound a short time earlier, he succumbed to infection.

All of the businesses closed and the town buried their night watchman as he had no close relatives. Mr. John R. Tabner lies buried in the fifth block of The Wetumka Cemetery. It is evident that his tombstone was placed some time later. The date of his death is incorrectly stated.

The Coin Store was one of the first general stores in Wetumka. It dates from 1903 when George Appling came to the new town from Mississippi. It was first located in a sheet metal building directly across from the present city hall. Very soon after the opening, Mr. Appling invited a pioneer Wetumka hotel operator, Mr C. B. Williams to be his partner. They then moved the store to south Main Street at approximately where the recreational parlors stood later. In 1912 the store was moved to its permanent site. In 1925 Mr. Williams bought Mr. Appling's share of the business. (The Coin Store lasted until 1954 when Mrs. Mary Williams sold it to the Dobson Chain.

2

Some Early Times

The Indians opened their new church on thirteen acres of land south of Wetumka in 1908. Many non-Indians attended services there and told about the rich tradition of music. In 1928, the new radio station, KVOO, made a broadcast of a special Indian music program from there.

In Oklahoma Territory, homesteads had been obtained through land rushes and lotteries. The early settlers, in Indian Territory, arguably went to even less trouble and expense to obtain land. In 1895, the lands had been surveyed and soon after that the Indian tribal rolls were permanently closed.

The original plan was to divide the land among the Indians in allotments as the government had desired before the Creek War In Alabama. An Indian's citizenship rights depended on whether they were full blood or a freed black man holding tribal citizenship. In addition to the full bloods' allotment there would be a division of "surplus" land.

Various restrictions were placed on the allotted land to prevent the Indians from losing it outright. For people intent upon obtaining land, these restrictions proved a great blessing. There was a business class of people who knew the law and how to make the most of these restrictions.

The Indians didn't usually take to market cultivation quickly and therefore were always desperate for cash. Some of the early settlers rationalized this. The land was unused (in their opinion) and the Indians cared nothing for it. Those who specialized in acquiring Indian land were especially adept at seeking out elderly Indians because restricted land could easily be willed to another. Many Indians could be induced to sign a will (something they had never dealt with) for a very small consideration. Creek Chief, Pleasant Porter, stated that at least a million acres had changed hands through these kinds of machinations by 1902.

Throughout the decades before the Second World War the Indian Service provided "Indian Farmers" or demonstration agents to model correct farming techniques. It also sponsored Tribal Fairs to encourage Indian pride in agricultural production. The results were not encouraging.

The Indians had not been well prepared for the privatization of their lands. They had vigorously opposed the alien concept of land ownership for over a century. None of the Five Civilized Tribes ever recognized private land ownership. The Indians had lived for countless centuries in their settled ways before the Europeans came. There were relatively few of them and they were widely dispersed. A cash economy had not been necessary or practical. It is said that they were happy in what anthropologists regard as an advanced way of life. It is said that the Creeks had developed over 50 distinct dishes prepared from their easily grown "Sofke" corn. The surveyor's grid made little sense to them.

They did not, by any means, willingly participate in the destruction of their new homeland. There was massive resistance in Oklahoma just as there had been when the Federal government had wanted to terminate their status and confine them as individuals to 160 acres of land apiece in Alabama. They had lost the Creek War with the United States Army and were forced to remove to Oklahoma. They were marched overland to New Orleans and put on steamboats. The men who had been taken prisoners were fitted in shackles and chains by government blacksmiths and then towed on barges behind the steamboats up the Mississippi River to the White River in Arkansas. From there they were brought by land to Fort Gibson. The lower house of the Creek legislature was known as "The House of Warriers." Indeed, they never stopped warring on the Federal Government.

The Indians knew the same sorry allotment scheme was being forced on them again. Many refused to register with the Dawes Commission. When so many of them returned their allotment deeds, unopened or with defiant messages scrawled on them, the government responded with a law that made it a crime to deface official documents.

Some of the old timers recalled Chitto Harjo or "Crazy Snake" as he is known to the history books. He and his followers had once threatened to burn down the town of Wetumka. None of the old timers could put a date to this but they swore it really happened. During the time of the seige, people from Wetumka built bonfires and guarded the entrances to town.

Rev. John Smith, whose weekly sermon in the Creek language appeared the the Wetumka newspaper for a quarter of a century, was a resister as was his father. They had refused to register for the tribal rolls and encouraged their clan, The Nighthawks, to do the same. The father was even declared an Indian terrorist. They were arrested by the Dawes Commission and detained for some time.

Rev. John Smith, half-brother of Annie Yahola, lived in a large two story frame house at the crest of the ridge just east of town. He became a fairly successful capitalist and was the owner of the hotel at Sasakawa. His sister would contest his will as she was certain he was worth more than the $75,000 he left her.

Another wealthy Indian was Thomas Long who had lived in the area before the white intrusion and had owned large herds of cattle that grazed freely on the common lands. Mr. Long, in 1920 paid $50,000 for 400 acres of land that stretched from the city limits of Wetumka to the cemetery with the railroad on one side. This was the largest land transaction in the area until the oil boom days. Mr. Long, paralyzed in his declining years, died in 1932. His widow, Jemima, lived alone in their big white house. Her life was very plain as she raised cattle, hogs and most of her food. Her concession to vanity was that she liked new Buicks and she usually had a couple of them. Their son, Noah, died a soldier in World War II. A daughter, Rachel Deer, was a fixture around Wetumka until her death in an automobile accident in the 1960s.

My parents never owned any of the land they farmed. We lived in one of the six tenant houses and worked eighty acres of Mr. Long's land. Erosion had taken a terrible toll of the land. Not only were there gullies in the fields but undermining was taking place in the pastures. It was not an unusual incident for cattle grazing on land over an underground tunnel to experience it caving in. Some of the deepest gullies I've ever seen were on that land.

Whenever Indian land came onto the market, the real estate speculators got circulars advising them of the land and its location. A person of mixed blood was authorized, under the Curtis Bill, to sell his surplus land, amounting to 120 acres, after July 1, 1906. This was one of the largest floodgates of available land to be opened during the months before Oklahoma achieved statehood.

It was reported that scores of companies were formed for the "red letter" date when land buyers could go out after all the farmland in sight. Large amounts of speculator funds were pouring in from other states for this purpose.

This is part of a account published in The NEWS HERALD at Wetumka, I. T., on March 23, 1906: "Between now and that date (July 1) thousands of deeds will be made out and the transactions will be completed between the land speculators and the allottee up to the point of the final transfer. On July 1, when the restrictions shall be removed, runners will be ready to go to the homes of these allottees, if necessary, and bring them to town or finish the transaction at their homes."

On July 27, 1906, it was estimated at the time that another 25% of all the land "contingent to Wetumka" would come on the market when a ruling came down regarding "Dead Claims." This was thought to be one of the worst abuses. Inherited land could be more easily disposed of.

At this point I'd like to add, at least parenthetically, what Mary Pace Andrews told me a few weeks before her death this summer at the age of 89. She said that you could be 100% certain that if you see a really nice brick home in Wetumka or in the county, it was originally built by a court appointed guardian of an Indian. This is the case for all of the brick homes on Wetumka's Main Street starting with the Eastep-Stout home, the Julian and Nellie Peixotto home, that of Cecil Kilgore's, Travis Watson and many others. The Creeks had occupied log cabins before the arrival of the Whites and they were not accustomed to maintenance procedures to keep them in good repair. Brick houses needed less upkeep and were more durable. There were a number of spectacular frame houses built in Wetumka for Indians. None of them survive.

3

Political Rivalry

I n the early years of the history of Hughes County there was one political issue that nearly overshadowed the disposal of Indian land and other scandals. That was the location of the County Seat.

Before the Constitutional Convention, the people of Wetumka felt assured that Wetumka would be the county seat of the proposed Scott County. When Holdenville gained that prize, they were certain they had been double-crossed. They were not the only Oklahoma town left dissatisfied. The first legislature passed a bill that enabled a town to petition the governor for a special election. A county seat could moved this way but it required a 60% vote.

In 1908, Wetumka surely did petition for a special election. The law required that a county seat be located reasonably close to the center of the county. Wetumka could not be relocated again. The proposed solution was to make the county smaller and this would re-position Wetumka to satisfy the law. Wetumkans embarked on a loud campaign to convince voters that the South Canadian River was a natural boundary and should be so recognized. They contended that it would bankrupt the county to bridge the river there.

In the general election nearly every town in Hughes county put its name in contention to be the county seat but it would be a war between Wetumka and Holdenville in the runoff. The only ally that Wetumka had was Wewoka, the county seat of Seminole county, which found it undesirable to have another county seat just six miles from its own corporate limits.

It really was not much of a contest and the misguided arguments about bankrupting the county to bridge the South Canadian did not sway very many voters. The people of Holdenville, understandably and almost unanimously, voted to retain the county seat. Wetumka simply did not have a large enough electorate to win. Shrinking the area of the county to move Wetumka closer to the center was not broadly persuasive in the county and it had no appeal in Holdenville where the majority of the electorate lived.

The election settled an issue but did nothing to quell the lingering bitter feelings between the two towns. In the 1950s there were still people alive who often remembered and bitterly resented what they thought had been a dirty deal. (It was said, at the time, that a number of prominent Wetumkans were so ill because of the issue that they could not immediately receive the bad news. Wetumka charged fraud and tried to get a new election.)

After the election, THE WETUMKA GAZETTE groused about the county seat affair: "Yes, the county seat has been located at Holdenville, and the pententiary should be also; it would be a great saving in the transporting of convicts, for thus far in her history, Holdenville has furnished more convicted felons, than any other town of its age and size in Oklahoma......Holdenville famous as the town of empty store-buildings, broken-defunct banks, bankrupt businessmen, the home of the Tribune, and a large colony of ex-convicts, "the Botany Bay" of Oklahoma, and the county seat of Hughes County."

The fact that Wetumka would not be a county seat had an impact on its ability to attract new settlers and new businesses. Being a government center has always been an asset to a town. The drawing power of the county seat was demonstrated which an execution was carried out near Holdenville on April 22, 1910. There was no courthouse or even a courthouse square designated at the time. A gallows had been set up just outside of Holdenville. It was estimated at the time that two thousand people had arrived to get a glimpse of the condemned man. A small enclosure hid the proceedings from the general public. The only

witnesses were the jury which had convicted him and other public officials and newsmen. John P. Black, a colored man had been convicted
of killing a Holdenville farmer. According to press reports, he maintained "an attitude of nerve" and even told the crowd in a somber voice
that he was sorry for what he had done. Then he was obliged to listen
to a letter from the widow of the man he had murdered which ended
in "and now it is your doom to pay the penalty." Sheriff James King,
formerly a Wetumka lawman, sprung the trap at 1:20; "the scaffold
and all the arrangements for the execution, and everything pertaining
thereto, was carried out without accident or interruption, and the officers carried out the law and attended to their unpleasant duties with
credit and are deserving of commendation." A short time after this
Oklahoma adopted electrocution and the function was transferred to
the State. According to records kept by the Department of Correc-
tions, none of the 99 persons since executed at McAlester, had a
Hughes county address.

The issue of the placement of a courthouse was bitterly fought in
other places. Perhaps the worst was the rivalry between Checotah and
Eufaula. A Sunday morning confrontation between armed citizens
from Checotah left one person in Eufaula dead. The final election had
to be held twice there because the ballots had been mutilated before
they could be officially reviewed. Eufaula retained the county seat.
Shawnee was eventually able to take the county seat away from Tecum-
seh.

There was a $200,000 county bond election in 1920 to build the
courthouse and the bridge across the South Canadian river. Not many
people in Wetumka had gotten over their hard feelings enough to
openly give their support to the issue.

Many of the people who settled around Wetumka had good reason
to feel at home. The biggest migration of Arkansas residents to Oklahoma started shortly after the state was fully opened to settlement in
1907. From then until about 1915, the removal was said to be at its
peak. Several localities were selected and populated almost entirely by

"Arkansawyers" in the early years. This was true of Wetumka but also of Holdenville, Duncan, Lawton, Clinton, and Oklahoma City and to a lesser extent around Norman. Starting in 1937, Holdenville staged an annual "Arkansas Day" which was as much a reunion as a celebration. Delegations from several of the western counties of Arkansas would be cordially received every year.

H. H. Darks is very well remembered in Wetumka. He was a real estate broker, lawyer, county judge and producer of nationally renowned quarter horses on his 1,000 acre spread west of Wetumka. He was often the grand marshal of the Arkansas Day parade. He was the first of his family to move from Magazine, Arkansas in 1915. His home is the two story building on the corner of the 500 block of East Broadway. C. B. Williams, founder of The Coin Store came to Wetumka from Etna, Arkansas. The Williams homeplace is also on East Broadway. (The family's hitching post is still very much in evidence.) Another business in early Wetumka (next to The Coin) was a family operated business for most of the century.

This is the Herring Hardware Company which was acquired in 1910 from T. L. Lumley. "Captain Jack" Herring was listed as the president and his son, Grant, was manager. Captain Jack was born in England and his wife was a native of Switzerland. They raised their family in Billings, Montana. Mr. Herring was a globetrotting sales representative for The International Harvestor Company. When he finished this career, he settled down in Wetumka. He was active in civic affairs and headed the cornet band that gave concerts at the flagpole. Captain Jack's home is located on East Broadway, a block from the Baptist Church. It is one of the best preserved and possibly the oldest continuously occupied house in Wetumka. The first newspaper ads for Herring Hardware emphasized that they carried a complete line of general hardware and farm implements. They also sold caskets and burial robes. Every business in Wetumka had formidable competition. The Mackay Hardware store sold all of these things and in addition they had an undertaking department.

After a disasterous Main Street fire in 1930, the Mackay family moved to Holdenville where Kate Mackay opened a funeral parlor that persisted for decades. Her husband had died mysteriously during the revelry that followed the end of the First World War. Some people think he was deliberately shot and others think he was a victim of the rain of lead after the celebratory shots had been fired. Their son, Castle Mackay, served as mayor of Holdenville after World War II. The whole family was buried in their plot at the Wetumka Cemetery.

4

Between Black and White

On February 23, 1906, J. R. Rasor, a Wetumka Colored Man, went by passenger train to Holdenville to watch a balloon ascension. On his way home, he stopped at the office of THE WETUMKA GAZETTE to renew his subscription which was $1 a year. He also paid $1.50 for another subscription for J. R. Rasor of Cross Hill, South Carolina. The other man of the same name was not his father. He was his former owner.

Mr. Rasor was 60 old, and his former master was 83. He explained to the inquiring man at the newspaper office that he and his old owner of "the slave days" had kept up a lively correspondence through the years. He explained about their names. Freedmen despised their slave names and since they had never had a family name (and usually not even a family), it was a common practice for them to adopt the name of their former owner who usually didn't object.

Like Mr. Rasor, former slaves wanted to move as far away from the former owners as they could. They wanted to move just to prove to themselves that they really were free.

Historians often repeat the contention that Oklahoma had more all-black towns than all the other states combined. Even the Federal census for Negroes was taken separately and published in a segregated volume. Within a few years the number of Coloreds around Wetumka actually exceeded the number of people who identified themselves as Indian

The author recognizes that these terms, Coloreds, Negroes, are not often used in polite circles today. It would be an *anachronism* or a term used out of historical context to say "African-American" because this term was devised only a few years ago. The rude "N-word" which was bandied about so freely earlier will not be used in this essay. There are those, of every race, who feel that any discussion of past racial tension is offensive. Their viewpoint has not been completely disregarded. These chapters are "stand-alone" essays and can be read in any sequence or disregarded. It is a more realistic course to confront the past and deal with it. Any history book dealing only with pleasant aspects of the past only would be a very slender volume.

The Five Civilized Tribes had been slaveholders in the Southern tradition. After 1869, the U. S. government stopped making treaties with the Indians as sovereign nations. After that point they entered "agreements" with them. One of the agreements which the Indians found particularly disagreeable was the obligation to adopt their former slaves as citizens and place them on the tribal rolls.

There were farmers around Wetumka that the newspaper referred to as "Creek Freedmen" and if they was any thing that former slaves or the descendants of slaves coveted, it was land. The largest rural settlement of Negro farmers was east of town in an area known as Wisener. The first farmer in the area was Napps Wisener and a separate school was established in that area. It was sometimes called Wisener Chapel because there was also a church there.

Oklahoma seemed a promising mecca for Colored People. They thought they would achieve a position of at least an equal footing with the Indians. Until the Oklahoma legislature had its first session, there were no public laws to enshrine bigotry. The Coloreds were ably represented at the Constitutional Convention and no one recognized that more quickly than William "Alfalfa Bill" Murray the Convention President. He knew he was making a shrewd political move when he forced all the Colored delegates to sit together and then had them screened off with a curtain.

The Convention openly discussed "Jim Crow" laws. They did not engage in euphemisms; they used the actual term. Some delegates wanted to embed discrimination in the fundamental law. Others were more politically adept and recognized that this issue would get them elected to public office. One political pro of the time stated that if an aspiring office seeker went to a rally and hollered the "N-word" louder than any of his opponents, he would be the one elected. And he should end all of his speeches with the ringing words: "furthermore, if I am elected, they shall not have social equality!"

The railroads lobbied against the separate accomodation laws on the grounds that the costs would be prohibitive. It may have been a compromise that they didn't have to put on special coaches. But they did build separate waiting rooms at the depot. There were separate water fountains, rest rooms, etc.

At the depot in Wetumka there were two lines at the ticket cage; the races could not freely mingle. On the Frisco passenger trains there were Negro porters and occasionally one of them also act as the conductor and was allowed to punch tickets without much incident. The Wide-A-Wake café which in later years was known as the Wetumka Steak House was the only place north of the railroad tracks which had a Colored entrance. There were a couple of booths set up behind the kitchen and it seemed to have been well patronized. There was no other place where Colored People passing through town could be served.

The problems of Colored People and those who might in some way befriend a person of color were chronicled in the press on a regular basis. Negro jokes in dialect were a newspaper staple.

In 1913, THE WETUMKA GAZETTE, front paged the story of a white farmer who seemed to be suffering a string of unfortunate incidents. His barn had burned on the previous Saturday night and the sheriff's office had not come to investigate. They said his place was hard to get to.

He lodged a complaint and the sheriff did pay him a visit but found no evidence as to who the perpetrators might have been. It was suggested that his problems started when he had allowed a Negro tenant to work some of his land.

The sheriff thought his problems may have been affected by the fact that the farmer, Mr. Gus Whitfield, was a democrat while his neighbors were heavily socialist. The Oklahoma Socialists had even held their annual encampment nearby. Anyhow, it was finally determined that his property was just over the Seminole county line and out of the jurisdiction of the local sheriff.

No other type of news story got as much printer's ink in THE WETUMKA GAZETTE as did the stories of the lynching of Negroes. Local lynching were not reported the same way but they did happen. Mr. Johnson E. Tiger told a newspaper Dallas newspaper about such an occurrence in Holdenville in 1911. It was not covered by the local press.

The Wetumka paper reproduced a dramatically written account of a lynching at Anadarko in 1913. The ostensible purpose of these regularly occuring news articles was to amuse whites, but also to intimidate and terrorize local Negro citizens. This is an excerpt from that article of June 20, 1913:

While the mob laughed at his prayers and pleas for mercy as the flames leaped up to his body, Bennie Simmons, an 18-year-old negro boy, charged with the murder of Susie Church, 16 years old, near Cogar, was lynched here between 3 and 4 o'clock Friday morning by a mob which was estimated to include probably 1,000 people.

All of the residents of the Cogar neighborhood, where the crime occurred, seemed to be in the mob and sympathy here was with them to such an extent that there was little effort to hinder the mob in its course. The crime was so brutal in character and feeling in the neighborhood was so high that Simmons was rushed to the county jail here immediately after his arrest to avoid the vengeance which had been threatened if the murderer could be found. All day Thursday the mob was forming at Cogar and the more conservative citizens of the community, who were at first inclined to let the law take its course were swept away by the tide of popular feeling and the impassioned arguments of the mob leaders that such a brute should not be allowed to live even another day and by the time the start was made for Anadarko there was no division of sentiment and all alike were crying for blood.

The sheriff's office here had been notified that the mob was form- ing and when assurances had been received that it had actually started for this city, the negro was removed to the old federal prison in "old town." Little difficulty was experienced by the mob leaders, however, in locating him, and the guards who had been placed over him there made only a perfunctory resistance when the mob reached the old jail and demanded the prisoner.

He was taken out to a wagon bridge northwest of the city and hanged to a big cottonwood tree growing alongside the stream. The coal oil (kerosene) was poured over his body and lighted. The negro prayed and shrieked in agony as the flames reached his flesh but his cries were drowned by the yells and jeers of the mob.

As his cries grew fainter and it became evident that he was losing consciousness a volley of shots came from the mob, every member of which, heavily armed, emptied his weapon into the swinging body, which was literally cut to pieces by bullets.

The members of the mob then departed for their homes, leaving the body still swinging. When news of the affair spread throughout the city great crowds thronged out to view the gruesome spectacle. The body was still hanging until after 8 o'clock when it was cut down by the sheriff, who is preserving in his office the rope with which the hanging was done.

In 1917 there was a lynching at Wewoka that was reported fully in the Wetumka paper. It seemed that the traditional excuse of "giving offense to a white woman" was reason enough for a lynching. This article, in full, is from the June 22, 1917, THE WETUMKA GAZETTE:

Within the shadow of the home he invaded and in the presence of his victim, Henry Conley, the negro who attacked Mrs. Jess Burford, wife of a Seminole county farmer, a week ago last Saturday morning, was hanged to a tree in the Burford yard last Saturday afternoon. A mob of 800 citizens looked on while a dozen determined men performed their self-appointed task of execution.

The body continued to hang from the limb to which it was attached late tonight, when officers from Wewoka went and out and cut it down.

Conley was captured at Randolph, Johnson county, early Saturday morning, after a running gun fight in which he was wounded in the hand.

After five days' search through the hill districts of Seminole and Hughes counties, made by officers and possemen, word was received from Mill Creek Thursday that Conley's wife had been arrested there and that Conley who was in that county, had escaped pursuring officers.

A special train carrying fifty-two Wewoka citizens was immediately rushed to the scene and the posse from here, aided by Johnson and Marshall county officers, spread a complete net around the country in which the negro was said to be hiding.

At daylight Saturday morning Conley was driven into a jungle where the Frisco railroad crosses the Washita river, and there run down and caught by bloodhounds from the state penitentiary.

The hounds were in charge of Bill Nutt, a life-term Oklahoma convict, who was the first man to seize the negro.

In June of 1921, the largest race riot in United States history occurred at Tulsa. The National Guard at Wetumka was in the first phases of becoming an organized unit. A message came to the commanders to get together about 25 men and send them by train to Tulsa. This was probably the first ever deployment of Wetumka's National Guard.

The early 1920s was the high water mark for Ku Klux Klan activity around Wetumka. Not all of the activities of the "Invisible Empire" were hidden. They allowed themselves to be seen when they wanted to be. In early 1922 there was a KKK automobile parade through Wetumka. The cars bore banners warning lawbreakers. The townspeople speculated about whether there was a local Klan organization. This was visible proof that there was. About twenty people were robed in the cars and they came in rather suddenly and left the same way. Wisely, no one attempted to follow them.

For the newspaper editor their appearance on such a cold night was enough to convince him that the organization is made up of men with nerve and will do what they say they will do. He had found an envelope under his door a few days earlier that contained $50 to be used by charity.

They tried to present the public image of being do-gooders. A group of them, in their Klan regalia, visited W. J. Mabrey, a farmer with a sick wife. The next day he came to town with the news that the Klansmen had driven up to his door and invited him outside. He said he was handed a letter in silence and they departed. The letter was attached to a twenty dollar bill. He said that as soon as his wife saw the money, she immediately took a turn for the better and was now on the road to recovery. The editor's account of what the woman said was: "The good lady vows that the Lord was working through the Ku Klux Klan in sending relief and a word of cheer." It was signed Knights of the Ku Klux Klan, Wetumka Klan Nr. 25, Realm of Oklahoma.

It seemed that the Klan was gaining mainstream respectability that year. Back in February of 1922, Dr. Franklin Moore, pastor of a Methodist church in Shawnee, delivered a message to an overflow crowd at the Methodist Church in Wetumka. His topic, which kept the crowd utterly spellbound was "The Knights of the Ku Klux Klan vs. The Knights of Columbus." The Knights of Columbus are a Catholic layman's group.

According to THE WETUMKA GAZETTE, February 24, 1922, the good Doctor had given much study in the preparation of his address and he had been able to glean that the Klan stands for what every good citizen and true American stands for, and that he is for them, and it was evident that the crowd was with him.

The KKK was not just an anti-Negro group. They didn't like Catholics or Jews or any of the foreign born that were "polluting" our shores. Dr. Moore reminded his audiences that Catholics could not be trusted. They were directed from Rome and they were intent on dominating America. The KKK always made the same claim about Negroes wanting to dominate all the rest of society. Their preposterous claim was that the African race would outbreed whites and some time in the not-so-distant future all good white Americans would come under their heel.

Later in 1922 a group of about 75 robed men paraded through a reception at the Baptist church. They gave the pastor a letter expressing their "thanks for the work he was doing in our midst." It was said that the jolly crowd was sombered by their quick appearance and disappearance.

David Baird and Danney Goble, in a textbook intended for senior high and junior college students, state their belief that perhaps a majority of the Oklahoma legislature in the 1920s were members of the KKK.

It was a time of great disillusionment. The American people only found out World War I after it was all over. They wondered what they had gained from such an enormous sacrifice. Then the wartime boom ended in a sharp economic downturn that took several months to abate. By then there were plenty of prophets of doom and gloom who paved the way for the KKK.

In 1923, the Nusho ran the long picture, "Birth of A Nation," which is considered a great technical achievement, but also portrayed the KKK in a very favorable light.

By the mid-1920s there was a judge from Duncan who was unintimidated and began to speak out. He said that the KKK was a mob like any other mob.

The influence of the KKK dropped off very rapidly as the decade wore on. They seemed to lose out in Oklahoma soon than in other states. Before the end of the decade Oklahoma had passed a law specifically outlawing groups of people going around with concealed identity.

Lynching would be a part of the history of Oklahoma and the rest of the country for another thirty years although the number of incidents lessened. It was not just Negro males who were lynched. There was no hesitancy to lynch Negro women and there are many instances of this. Not all of the victims were of the African race.

The activities of the KKK had only served to further legitimate the discrimination meted out to the Negro population of Wetumka. Most people of the time thought they were less deserving than the rest of the people. Few people would ever advance the claim that the "equal protection of the law" clause of the Fourteenth Amendment to the United States Constitution was ever extended to them even though it was written in their behalf.

In 1903, Wetumka had secured, at tax payer expense, a burial ground for its white citizens. Negroes were not welcome and they had to purchase their own cemetery east of Wetumka. They had bought a small parcel from a farmer who was leaving the country. He neglected to tell them about a lien against the land. In the mid-1930s the lender tried to collect from the new owners.

It was not until 1936 that any provision was been made for any high school subjects at the Douglass separate school. They had never had a music teacher and their opportunities to participate in organized sports were severely limited. Holdenville had long provided for a modest high school program although they had a smaller population to serve in their separate school

None of this would ever be at the expense of the schools in Wetumka. The separate schools were operated with county funds.

In August of 1935 it was announced that Douglas, in the next term, would offer an accredited two year high school program.

Not much can be said for the school buildings provided for Negro children. The classroom building was a classic "doghouse" school. It looked like a house with a door cut in the side. (The new brick building did not open until the very eve of court ordered school integration).

The largest racial disturbance in Wetumka occurred in April 1926 and circumstances quickly ripened for a lynching. Two policemen in Wetumka, Deputy Sheriff Mitchell Compler and Weldon Wilson of the Wetumka police department were shot and killed after they had arrested a Negro man named Roswell Hamilton for selling illicit whiskey.

The facts are not clear and newspaper accounts of the time are so overblown as to be unreliable. The indications are that the lawmen failed to thoroughly search the man they arrested and he was able to shoot the man at the steering wheel of the Ford as well as the one who was riding on the running board near the Frisco depot.

A more probable scenario was that the lawmen terrorized the Negro with talk about a public lynching. He fired his second gun in self-defense because selling illicit whiskey was not such a grave offense. Every bootlegger considered it an occupational hazard and he had stashed money for the fine which he regarded as part of his normal overhead.

It was an unpleasant time because the bootlegger was at large for over a day and because the weather was so bad. During these hours there were armed mobs of people (from Wetumka and other other towns) parading through the streets in that section and making vicious threats. Most of the Colored population wisely fled to other places.

Hamilton was summarily tried and sentenced to death seemingly in response to the clamorous demands of the people of Wetumka. According to extant records his sentence was commuted by Governor Trapp. This was an area in which the governor's constitutional authority was unambiguous. This clear prerogative was jealously guarded. It was hardly uncommon for a governor to take this action when he was convinced that the condemned man hadn't got much of a trial.

Governor Johnston Murray once drove himself to the prison at McAlester, unannounced, and interviewed a man on death row because he could make so little sense of the trial transcripts. It was reported that they "had a good smoke and drank coffee together for over two hours in the prison cafeteria." In the end he did not spare the man's life.

World War II was again the great watershed event in race relations as in so many other areas in the nation and in Wetumka. Long before the U. S. Supreme Court handed down its desegregation decision in 1954, there were nearly 100 Negroes attending colleges in Oklahoma because the state had miserably failed to provide "separate but equal facilities" in many occupational areas.

Wetumka and Hughes County seemed to moving backward when finally a bond election was held to build new public schools for Negro students. The Lincoln School in Holdenville had burned down and the Douglass School in Wetumka hardly even resembled a public school. It looked like a couple of houses that had been shoved together.

Very little interest was shown in the election and the issue would not have passed without the participation of the Negro population. The actual balloting in June of 1947 was 115-53. Stona Fitch had been elected County Commissioner for the first time in 1946 and building the new school in his district became his responsibility. A Henryetta construction firm got the contract for $61,250. The entire building was constructed from salvaged materials that the county commissioners had purchased from the War Assets Administration at Camp Gruber, near Muskogee.

No matter how many cost-cutting measures were taken, the building of separate schools was not economic. The cost of the Douglass School in Wetumka, taken on a per student seat basis, was at least five times as expensive as had been the construction of the Wetumka High School seven years earlier. (There were only 112 students.) The Douglass School operated only one school bus but it necessarily had a very scattered route and often resulted in losses of instructional time. (The new athletic grounds at the Cemtral grade school and Wetumka high school (and repairs to the junior high wing) authorized in early 1955 were capped at a cost of $75,000.) Separate schools were thus wasteful from every perspective. The new Douglass school was abandoned in less than seven years because the state would not continue to provide financing for a separate school. Integration seemed to happen peacefully in Hughes County. The first school to be fully integrated was Fairview in 1955 and this happened since they were on a harvest schedule. According to Raymond Willingham, Superintendent, Principal and teacher, there was "not one problem."

Robert E. Ferguson, Ada architect, drew up the blueprints for the separate school which provided for a combination gymnasium-auditorium, a study-hall library, and five classrooms. The building was attractive with its large windows in front which provided ample light and ventilation. The contract specified that all interior walls were to be plastered.

As far as I know, this was the only school building project that Stona Fitch ever had to preside over. He'd been easily elected two years earlier with the simple claim: "I think all county roads should be maintained year-round." He certainly did avail himself of the political wisdom of the time. The State wanted to consolidate as many rural schools as possible but the biggest obstacle was the poor roads which kept schools isolated. Lawnwood School remained open long after its enrollment dropped below thirteen because impassable roads actually kept it open as it was an "isolated school."

Mr. Stona Fitch was one of the firmest pillers of County society of Hughes County. My first awareness of him is at his cattle holding pens in back of the city hall near Hershel Wilson's Welding shop. He long traded in cattle and in the early 1930s, he, like so many other prominent Wetumkans, ran a gas station. His establishment was on West Broadway and he invited his friends in to see "Stony and Tony." Tony was Tony Lucas. During these years he also assisted Colonel Keifer in his auctions or "cry sales" as a clerk. He gradually picked up the auctioneer's chant and became the busiest auctioneer in the area. He had a brother who worked in Brazil and another brother, Rolla, who remained in Arkansas. Rolla Fitch became Govenor (of Arkansas) Orval Faubus's Chief of Staff after serving as his successful campaign chairman. Mr. Faubus, himself, was remembered as a teacher by several people around Wetumka who had migrated from Madison and Marion counties in Arkansas. My earliest recollection of Stona Fitch is from the night of March 16, 1946 when I was only eight years old. My father took me to a fund raising event at the Wetumka High School Auditorium. I was completely bewildered by The Womanless Wedding and it took considerable explaining to make me understand. Nearly all of the prominent businessmen of Wetumka were dressed in women's clothing and that was scary enough. But at 8:00 "vows" were exchanged by Joe Meyers, "bride," and Kirk Meadors, "groom." James Robertson gave the bride away. Bridesmaids were Jeff Biffle and Charles Klein. Mervin Nicks served as flower girl. Marvin Weast was the ring bearer. Elmer Brooks served as best man. Others participating in this mock nuptial were O. L. McNutt, Stix Manney, Travis Watson, Cecil Fair, Armand Gibson, Jack McGee, Jr., Stona Fitch, Argie Taylor and Herbert Darks.

A outstanding leader of the Colored community during and after World War II was Dr. F. E. Wesley, a veterinarian. Dr. Wesley had a thirty year association with Wetumka starting in the 1930s when he was in town once a month at a mule barn where farmers and others could bring their animals to be doctored. In the early days he lived in the community of Vernon, near Hannah. Then he took up residence near Wetumka and was the president of the Colored People's Chamber of Commerce.

Dr. Wesley was much resented as an educated Colored person who provided a vital service. Scurrilous things were said about him: such things as he must have had some White blood. He was aware of this and was careful when visiting farms in his late model Chevrolet. His home and dispensary still stand on Highway 75 about half a mile from the underpass. There was no driveway. Access by a winding road through a neighbor's field.

Earlier, in this essay, I stated that none of the persons executed at McAlester had an address in Hughes County. This is true. But in 1945 there was a Colored man executed for the murder of Arley Keck of Keck's Grocery on the outskirts of Weleetka. He did not have a Hughes County address but was not unknown to the law eforcement people in that county. He had already done time for stealing a cow from Ray Meadors and was considered a shiftless sort but few thought he was a violent man.

Mr. Keck's murder was mysterious and the investigation methods primitive. Much of the popular wisdom surrounding this matter is utterly untrustworthy. It seems that Mr. Keck had had his store broken into several times and he'd taken to sleeping on the premises to safeguard his stock. It also seems very likely that the murder occurred when a burglary was foiled. Mr. Keck was killed with a meat cleaver from the store. The law enforcement men involved bragged about how they obtained a confession by utilizing an old Negro superstition called the "Dead Man's Eye." Some Negroes, as well as some Whites, believed in this phenomenon. Supposedly, the image of the last person the deceased had seen was seared into his eye. The lawmen claimed they had seen the Negro's face in the dead man's eye and when confronted with this he paniced and confessed.

5

Wetumka and Its Great War

The people of Wetumka were hyper-patriotic during World War I. The government had done an excellent job of selling the war to the people. All of the news was very good news. Private Webb Fulks wrote long and sentimental letters to his parents in Wetumka. He was shrewd enough not to be specific about anything and his intact letters were gratefully received and published locally. Most newspaper headlines blared about the rapid mobilization of the country and how well the economy was working. *"Jerusalem Falls to The British, Christians Hold Their Shrine, for the first time in 673 Years,"* was the type of feel-good headline permitted by the Wilson administration's "Committee for Public Information."

In 1917 the selective draft process had gone smoothly at first. The country was divided into sixteen zones as that was the number of divisions the Wilson administration proposed. Oklahoma and Texas were in the fifteenth region and the sparsely settled western states constituted the sixteenth.

The local people had blamed outside agitators for the "draft riots" that were quickly put down. Supposedly there were about 250 persons arrested in the area of Seminole, Hughes and Pontotoc counties. Only one ringleader, Roy Crane, from the Oak Grove community was arrested in Hughes county. There was much talk about seeking the death penalty for these treasonous individuals. The organizers were thought to be from the Working Class Union or from the ranks of the Socialists.

On the first Saturday in May, 1917, a Patriotic Day celebration was held in Wetumka which drew a large and enthusiastic crowd which has no rival to this day. The Wetumka band provided patriotic music from the early morning. There were speeches at noon and at 2:00 in the afternoon a parade assembled near the city hall. The parade was led by an Uncle Sam in uniform and closely following were fifteen hundred school children from Wetumka and the surrounding towns and districts. Each one carried a tiny American flag. Next came a large number of men from the lodges. Then came the "cavalry" or local men on horseback. This was followed by at least 75 "trimmed" automobiles. The parade was a mile long and marched down Main street a couple of times and reassembled at the flag pole.

The hushed crowd stood in awe as two Civil War veterans, W. B.Mannors, a confederate and M. B. Parker, a unionist, hoisted Old Glory up the flagpole. Then W. C. Farmer, one of the earliest Wetumkans, gave a rousing speech. This was followed by a special reading by Mrs. H. H. Holman, another Wetumka pioneer. Everyone commented on the appearance of Miss Rose Galloway who played the role of Betsy Ross stitching the flag and Miss Atha Meadors who was Miss Columbia. One of the greatest hits of the day was two-year-old Thomas Mackay who was "Uncle Sam Jr." (He would reach maturity and lay down his life in the next World War. Major Thomas W. Mackay, WHS 1932, died in a California plane crash in November of 1944 just three days after returning from the Pacific Theatre where he had served 29 months.)

Col. Blankenberry (an early Wetumka auctioneer) and Charley Darks (brother of H. H.) were dressed as mounted policemen. The picture show was free all day thanks to the merchants who gave out over 1,000 tickets.

With the collective spirit running this high, everyone was watchful for any sign of disloyalty. It was learned by the "counsel of defense" in the Greasy Creek community that a certain person had bought a huge quantity of flour and was hoarding it. His neighbors ordered him to return the flour but he refused. He stated he was allowed to keep 150 pounds for his own use. His home was searched and 900 pounds of flour were located.

His flour was loaded into his wagon and he was forced to return it to Wetumka. He was "arrainged" before a group of patriots. At the "trial" he evaded all questions about his political affiliations and information about war measures. He claimed he did not take a newspaper and knew nothing of the war provisions. It was further determined that he had never attended a patriotic meeting or purchased a Liberty Bond or contributed to the International Red Cross or the Y. M. C. A.

The patriots did not want to be unfair. The agreed to let him go if he would purchase a $100 bond, contribute $10 to the Red Cross and $5 to the Y. M. C. A. He was required to attend all patriotic meetings in the future and most important of all he was to ride out of Wetumka waving an American flag and to display it at his residence.

Then a group of Wetumkans crowded into cars and caught up with him. Just as they suspected, he had discarded the flag. This incensed the crowd and they sent the team of horses on the man's home with a young boy. They then dragged Mr. Woodrome to the side of the road and gave him a sound thrashing.

World War I was a short war for the Americans. It really only lasted about thirteen months and the Allied Expeditionary Forces were subject to combat for only 150 days. Yet, it was the deadliest war Wetumkans ever fought. Ten Wetumka soldiers are known to have died during the war. Most of them did not die from direct hostile action.

Such training as the boys received was in France at an American base not far from the front. Charlie Sheppard died in an explosion in the American training camp in France on November 28, 1918. The war had ended almost two weeks earlier.

The first combat death of a Wetumka lad is believed to be Clarence Kitchens. It is for him that the local post of the American Legion is named.

There were no funerals for those Wetumkans killed in France until after the war. The bodies were first interred in American cemeteries in France. They were slowly returned one-by-one after the war.

In 1920, the first remains, those of Private Willie Beaver, were brought home for burial at Wetumka. His death had come early in the period of American involvement and he was said to have died from pneumonia. It may have been influenza. Large concentrations of men confined to small areas in fairly unsanitary conditions promote epidemics. The influenza outbreak of this time was believed to have originated at Fort Riley, Kansas.

It would be the worst epidemic ever to hit the earth. Some estimates were that 100 million people, all over the world, died before it ran its course. Some of the people moving to Wetumka during this time said their move was influenced by this fearful epidemic. They thought Wetumka might be a safer place than the one they had fled.

Local people could not even begin to realistically grasp the great distance they were from the battlefields of France. They behaved as if they thought the Germans were looking down on them from the nearby hills. At any rate they were going to guard Wetumka from its enemies, domestic and foreign. Very early in the war, in May of 1918, there was an urgent meeting the men of the town, regardless of age or physical condition, at the Commercial Club. That evening they organized the Home Guard of Wetumka. The county attorney and Captain Homes of The Holdenville Home Guard were there to act as advisors. Sixty-two men signed up immediately.

Within a few days they had organized themselves into a military company with a strength of 125. They agreed to meet three times a week and to drill on the streets of Wetumka for an hour and half each time. Even Dr. Hemphill, the pioneer Wetumka physician, signed on as a private. As a military organization, the Wetumka Home Guard was an absurdity. They had neither military weapons or uniforms and none of them had had any war time experience. (Only one person buried in the Cemetery at Wetumka served in the Spanish-American War of 1898; he is not believed to have been a casualty of that war.[1])

This is how the members of the Wetumka Home Guard organized themselves:

Captain—J. P. Freshour

1st Lieutenant—H. H. Darks

2nd Lieutenant—J. C. Puryear

Chaplain—Rev. A. J. Cook

Company Clerk—X. X. McGee

Sergeants—G. L. Herring, W. S. Robinson, W. B. Kirkpatrick, Charlie Jones, F. C. Misner, W. C. Farmer

Corporals—H. L. Jones, J. A. Grotts, Raymond Saxon, C. S. Darks, H. E. Brown, C. B. Williams, J. B. Nicks, C. E. Jarrett, P. E. Mitchell, W. A. Geren, C. N. Hamilton, Kenneth Lucas.

Privates—G. D. Foster, Charles Bachus, J. M. Allred, Neal Parsley, Carl Haubold, P. H. Foster, R. W. Stanfill, Charles Nichols, W. H. Lett, Ed Rosebaum, M. M. Brotherton, R. W. Eakin, Elmer Jones, B. B. Stephens, J. C. Hansford, Virgil Murphy, Ova Webb, G. T. Gibson, C. S. Darks, W. M. Allred, Martin Moore, J. F. Lucas, Foster Lynn, W. L. Hawks, J. B. Nicks, Don Wilbanks, C. C. Darks, Thaddeus Lynn, Roy Gammill, James Clanton, Buford Arnold, Professor Mockel, Lem Richardson, Jack Murphy, Odie Vaughn, John Ledbetter, H. H. Johnson, L. M. Ross, Roy Letter, Roger Chaney, Frank Meadors, Rev. T. J. Townsend, Earl Poole, W. A. Ferguson, Ernest Martin, Bertie Wolfe, Charlie Webb, Oscar Burrow, J. E. Chowins, C. I. Clanton, J. M. Watkins, W. A. McCoy, Ray Meadors, Don Darks, T. W. Mackay, Birch Walker, Terrell Baugh, O. V. Arnold, Famous

---

1.   My research brought me to the conclusion that another Wetumkan was a veteran who was with General Pershing in the Mexican Border skirmishes with Pancho Villa. This was Roley Buck, who in the 1950s, would be elected principal Chief of The Creeks. The Indians were not obligated to serve in the armed forces as they were not granted full citizenship until 1924. They did volunteer and as in all our wars they were vastly over represented in the armed services.

Lucas, H. J. Hays, Willie Rice, D. J. Chancey, Clifford Hays, Dewey Jones, G. L. Woford, Ed Morrison, H. L. Rogers, Nathan Lee, C. E. Shaber, J. A. Hemphill, Glen Wheat, Clarence Collins, Walker Jackson, H. M. Brazil, Kermit Smith, Paul Nichols, Frank Sheppard, W. R. Mastin, Tom Moore, Harlie Gibson, Frank Thompson, J. K. McKinzie, A. M. Martin, E. T. Mayfield, Claude Rice, O. B. Hayden, J. J. Jones, A. J. Healey, Otto Moses, Charles Burrow, Leman Collins, George Knierim, W. H. Burkes, Jesse Boles, Joseph Dunzy, B. Parker, R. S. Poole, Virgil Fulks.

Already, there had been seventeen men recruited from Wetumka for the regular army.

These are the "Wetumka Seventeen."

George Cook, Charles Rice, John Klein, Chas. Bradbury, Harve Woford, Murvin Nicks, Bill Mullins, Bob Sheppard, Bliss Bignell, Earnest Woford, Chas. Appling, Jim Harjo, Chas. Burrow, Carl Clark, Tulman Flutey enlisted May 31 at Okemah, in Troop A, Oklahoma Cavalry, left Okemah for Forth Worth Texas; transferred to 111th Am. Tn., 736th Division.

Charles Burrow was discharged on account of bad eyesight, Bob Sheppard was sent to the base hospital, Bliss Bignell went to the 111th Sanitary Train, Charles Appling, officers training school, Earnest Woford went to the Quartermaster Corps at Camp Bowie, Texas.

The remaining men left for Camp Mills in July. They were in camp there for eight days and sailed on the liner Orizaba. They landed in Brest, France on August 12th and moved to Fregreas September 5th. They were in Maxent until September 27th and moved to Camp De Coetgaidan. They returned by way of St. Nazarre, France and sailed for the United States on March 1, 1919. They landed in Newport News, Virginia on March 18th. All of them were discharged at Fort Worth, Texas, March 31, 1919. They had not seen a lot of action nor had they even seen any decent scenery.

This is an effort to identify some these men who would play an important part in the life of Wetumka in decades to come:

Men of the Wetumka Home Guard

Professor Freshour-principal of Mingo School, Boy Scout Troop Leader, Future Superintend of Wetumka Schools.

H. H. Darks—Lawyer, judge, mainly a real estate broker.

X. X. McGee—Bank employee, insurance agent, patriarch of a Wetumka family.

G. L. Herring—Manager of Herring Hardwardware, also, agent for Dodge Brothers Automobiles.

W. B. Kirkpatrick—Owner of early hotel in Wetumka at the site of the present City Hall, also owned a grocery story and was grocery department manager at The Coin Store for 28 years.

W. C. Farmer—Bank Director and Wetumka Mayor.

Raymond Saxon—Also known as J. R. Saxon, father of Raymond and Jimmy Saxon.

C. B. Williams—Father of George and Dr. Roper Williams, founder of The Coin Store (with partner George Appling)

Neal Parsley—Partner for many years in the Tomberlin and Parsley (T&P) Mercantile Company.

J. C. Hansford—Long term barber in Wetumka.

J. F. Lucas—Early rancher and one of the earliest Wetumkans.

Roy Gammill—Established gasoline station, was farm implement dealer.

James Clanton—Was known around town as the "radio man" as he ran a repair shop.

C. I. Clanton—Owned photography shop in Wetumka before statehood. Became radio dealer and electrician; was Wetumka's first light plant superintendent.

Jack Murphy—The town tailor and owner of Murphy Cleaners.

J. M. Watkins—Editor and Publisher of THE WETUMKA GAZETTE.

Frank Meadors, Ray Meaders, brothers; sons of Turner Meaders of Meadors Brothers and Busey.

Dewey Jones—A Carpenter in Wetumka for many years.

Nathan Lee—Russian immigrant who rose to own Dry Goods Store, and be the Ford Dealer and a substantial businessman.

B. Parker—Built the brick "B. Parker Building" across from the town hall in 1925.

Webb Fulks—Became county surveyor.

World War I "Wetumka Seventeen"

Charles Rice—The Founding Captain of one of the National Guard Companies at Wetumka in 1921.

Harvey Wofford—Member of the first high school graduating class, for over 50 years manager of McIntosh Lumber Yard.

Bill Mullins—Head Custodian at Central Elementary School.

It is also known that several Colored soldiers from Wetumka also served in the segregated units of World War I.

In 1921 the American Legion sponsored a free showing of "Flashes of Action" which was a movie that had was pieced together from action scenes by the US Army Signal Corps. Enthusiasm for the war was still running high. The Legion even adopted a resolution condemning President Harding for pardoning Eugene V. Debs, the famous socialist who had been imprisoned for opposing the war.

Long before the disillusionment of the people toward what eventually became an unpopular war, the practical effect in Wetumka was a severe economic recession for its largest group, the farmers. Farm commodity prices had been artificially high during the war because American farmers had also been feeding European countries as well as the American Armies.

It is a sad commentary that the benchmarks for what farmers should be paid for their commodities are based the prices the could get during wartime.

This was the beginning of The Great Depression for farmers around Wetumka. The bad times of the 1920's only went from bad to critically bad during the next ten years. Farmers were not able to pull themselves out of these difficulties until the next World War which forever transformed Wetumka and the world.

6

Recreation in Early Wetumka

O ne of the most common events to placate the crowds in the early days in Wetumka was the community barbecue. The tradition is as old as the town itself and predates the State. On July 20, 1906, there was a huge "Statehood-Harvest" picnic and barbecue at Plateau Park. The familiar agenda included racing, music, ball games and of course political speaking.

Oklahoma's first governor, the Honorable C. N. Haskell of Muskogee, was there and spoke on many political subjects of interest to the people of Wetumka. Senator T. P. Gore, the blind orator, of national reputation, most favored democrat aspirant to the United States Senate following statehood was on hand. (He was the grandfather of the novelist, Gore Vidal.) There were a great many other speakers to enlighten and entertain the crowds. None of them were Republicans although several had been invited.

The people of the Wetumka township were so proud of their steel bridge which crossed the Wewoka Creek a mile east of the old Wetumka Indian Boarding School that they often held picnics there. It was the first steel bridge in Hughes county and came before there was anything more than a low-water wagon bridge across the North Canadian. The Fourth of July was celebrated there for several years with fireworks and patriotic music. (This was a well maintained 80 acre complex with picnic tables and plenty of shade trees to accommodate large crowds on an outing.) In 1927 the Fourth of July picnic celebration lasted for four days. A good many people from Dustin, Weleetka, and other towns came and camped out. There was a spring in the area that provided good water. There was fishing and swimming in the nearby North Canadian river. (In my own recollection the most important form of recreation was simply the mingling of the crowds.)

In Early Wetumka, as in cities across America, there was a speaker's bureau known as the Chautauqua. There is no doubt that people yearned to listened to accomplished speakers and a ticket for one night's program could cost as little as fifteen cents and a season pass could usually be had for a dollar. The Chautauqua was a secular organization without religious affiliation and had to provide its own space. It was usually held during the summer months in an outdoor setting under a magnificent tent. A typical program, in 1913, featured speakers who tried to combat the lure of the city. It was an effort to make the farmer and especially the farmer's son content to live on the land and not be corrupted by the rough, hurly-burly excitement of town living.

The crowds were very receptive to these lectures. One that was repeated often was "The Psychology of the Boy." Presumably, girls did not have a recognized psychology.

In 1915, the Chautauqua featured as its opening act "those jolly Chautauqua singers." It was said to be the only such program on the Frisco line from Sapulpa and Dennison, Texas. Congressman James B. Aswell was the featured speaker.

There would be a play supervisor at the grounds for children to young to be part of the audience. The opening day saw a concert by the "playsingers" and there was usually a male quartette, a piano, harp and cello. There was often a "reading in costume." Madam Butterfly was a favorite. The Chautauqua usually lasted five days and was much anticipated in Wetumka.

The Chutauqua implied high brow entertainment. The Old Fiddlers' Contest on Trades Day stood for just the opposite. It was explicitly stated that no "violin" players were needed. There was another contest called Fiddlers' Duet and there were usually prizes for the best jig dancers over 50.

In 1917 Wetumka started holding Trades Day, Seed Corn Day and Auto Day on the same Saturday. All of the auto agents throughout the county were encouraged to bring the latest model from their manufacturer. There was an agent for the King automobile line at Hanna and he always brought the latest model and gave rides and demonstration drives.

Drawings for wagons were important events. In December, 1917, George Brown (Colored) drew a new Springfield wagon. Then Dewey Kimbrel, living a mile and a half north of town, took the Leudinghaus wagon. Eli Grace, living three miles west and one mile north took the Milburn wagon.

No school district had a stronger tradition of a community Christmas Tree than Fairview. They usually had a pie supper around Thanksgiving and used the proceeds to purchase large quantities of candy and fruit in bulk. A committee would divide this mountain of Christmas treats into individual sacks. On the particular Trades Day, just mentioned, a large number of people were holding tickets for Fairview School. Lumus Achtley took the fourth wagon which was a Columbus. (The drawing was halted while Colonel Blankenbaker auctioned off the wagon for $110. The "colonel" was the pioneer auctioneer who was so much in demand because people were always coming to Wetumka and plenty were always leaving. Colonel Blankenbaker's business card said that he would conduct "Cry Sales" of any kind.)

The fifth wagon was a Winon and it went to R. G. Wolfe who lived five miles east of town.

The November Trades Day was a really big show. Professor McNutt, one of the best known balloon riders of the time, ascended thousands of feet into the air and made a parachute leap.

The world's first motion picture was shown in Paris in 1899. In much less than a decade a whole new industry had developed. Motion pictures were relatively cheaper than circuses and street shows and of course everyone was fascinated with the medium.

During the summer of 1917 a motion picture was made in Wetumka to be shown in Wetumka. The Majestic Theatre contracted with the Syndicate Film Company to make a full length movie featuring townspeople. There was the inevitable parade with trimmed cars. Everyone who came to town on the big day had a part in the show. There was a Queen of The Wetumka Motion Picture and two runners-up. But every girl who entered the contest was featured in every scene made on the streets of Wetumka.

The Wetumka Motion Picture was the first example of home movies ever shot in Wetumka. Everyone wanted to see it again and again. And it was played time after time throughout the years. It was probably the most commercially successful movie ever shown in Wetumka.

While the first talking picture was not shown in Wetumka until 1930, the movie business was growing by leaps and bounds. In 1927 the manager of the Nu-Show (an ordinary store front building) had an air conditioning system installed that was the wonder of the whole community. He installed huge blower fans that pushed a large volume of air over vats of ice water in the back of the theatre. He said that he bought a ton of ice each week to keep the system going. And he bragged that gentlemen could wear their coats regardless of how hot it was outside. (The Nu-Show manager never took credit for inventing this device, he said it was in general use in his other theatres in Oklahoma and throughout the country.)

On Columbus Day, 1928, the people of Wetumka thronged the streets to see the The U. S. Navy's big dirigible, "Los Angeles," on its way from the American Legion Convention at San Antonio, Texas, to its base at Lakehurst, New Jersey. The huge 654 foot craft floated so leisurely over town that the markings were clearly visible. (This was the type and size of dirigible that would soon be regularly plying the Atlantic to Europe.)

The merchants and business class of Wetumkans conducted good will tours throughout the 1920s to nearby communities. The purpose of the trippers was to foster good relations with all of the communities in the Wetumka trade area. A typical tour in 1929 took four days. Stops were made at Moss, Lamar, Carson, Dustin, Big Prarie and Lone Star on the first day. On the second day the parade of automobiles visited Gopher Hill, Hobson, Hickory Ridge, Tiger Flats, Prairie View and Phillips Plant. On the third day they left from Wetumka again and visited Pleasant Ridge, Texas Banner, Yeager, and Fairview. The final day was devoted to stops at Wisner's Chapel (a Colored community) Lawnwood, Lone Oak, Hune's Store and Friendship.

The support of the outlying communities was vital to the economic health of Wetumka. When a customer entered a store in Wetumka he was treated like royalty. The most successful merchants had highly refined personalities attuned to catering to the every wish of the customer. Every transaction was extremely important and if it took all of the clerks in a store to help a customer that was how it was done. A customer was never left unattended in a store. Every thing was behind the counter and every pain was taken to insure the customer a pleasant experience.

The merchants were actors and entertainers. They would regale their customers with appropriate short stories and go through amazing antics. People like Henry Bowles and George Williams would take the customer in hand and practically waltz them around the store and assign them to an amiable clerk. Henry Bowles clowned for his customers in a manner seldom imitated. He made such a big production out of snapping open a paper sack with a loud bang that it would have made The Three Stooges jealous.

George Williams, proprietor of The Coin Store was not to be outdone in getting publicity for his business. In 1918, on one occasion, The Coin paid out $800 for 100 cases of eggs. This was 3,000 dozen that were shipped out by train. He always paid a premium on Trades Day for the largest number of people coming to town in one wagon or to the family that rode a split log drag the farthest to town. Another publicity stunt was to freeze work shoes and other merchandise in large blocks of ice at the ice plant. The person who guessed how long it would take to melt completely would claim the prize from the ice.

Mr. Williams allowed three weddings to take place in his store on Saturday during the 1930s. It was quite a festive draw and the store would be trimmed a week in advance.

The Coin was entertaining in other ways. The office was at the back of the store and elevated so that everything could be seen from that perch. There were no cash registers on the floor. The clerks filled out a sales slip and took the customer's cash and put it into a wooden cup and sent it flying on a conveyor system that radiated out from the office to the various departments of the store. The clerk gave the cord a jerk (like starting a lawn mower) and this is what propelled it to the office where the arithmetic was checked and change was made.

Sacks were unknown in the dry goods stores of the time. The clerk would make a huge production out of tearing off a colorful strip of butcher paper. Then he or she would wind up the package with twine string in a rapid flourish of movements that reminded me of calf roper tying up his quarry.

Before the streets of Wetumka were paved there were many interesting events involving automobiles. With every model change there would be an Automobile Day in Wetumka. There were agents for many types of cars in the county and on that day they would giving demonstration drives to everyone remotely interested in buying. (They especially liked to give the ladies a ride as they were the ones who determined whether or not a sale would ultimately take place.)

One of the best contests, held on a regular basis, was just the opposite of an automobile race down Main Street. A 600 foot course had been marked off and the object of the event was to take off in high gear and drive the 600 feet at the slowest pace without stalling. The winner was determined by a stop watch. The driver who took the longest to finish was obviously the winner. The streets were lined with judges and cheating was hardly ever attempted. This was a beneficial way of slowing traffic. Motorists were constantly practicing for the event whether they acknowledged it or not. (A car that could pull the Mission Bottom hill in high gear also conferred special bragging rights on its owner.)

The automobile was as much for entertainment as it was for transportation. The people of Wetumka always enjoyed sitting their cars on the busy streets. Parking was a difficult matter on the weekends. And until—motorists parked in the center of Main and Broadway for several blocks in each direction. Even on week days and evenings favorite parking spots were taken. It was not uncommon for Wetumkans and people from the countryside to come to town and sit in their cars for hours.

The last full time blacksmith in Wetumka was James Bridges and his last shop was at the eastern city limits on Highway 75. (His first shop was next to the Chevrolet Building on Main Street.) He loafed in the evening at Walter Smith's gas station and grocery store across the street. He was a long winded story teller and often his stories were of early Wetumka.

Mr. Bridges once said that he'd managed to save $6,000 from putting shoes on horses and and beating out plow shares on the anvil at ten cents a copy. Then his first wife had a lingering illness and when she passed away he found himself penniless. The only object of pleasure that he owned was a Model T Ford which he kept close to him in the shop. It was from the early years without a starter or side curtains.

On a select few fair weekends of the year Mr. Bridges would get the Model T out and make several trips through the town and country. I would see him filling the radiator and pumping up the tires and know that he was planning to drive his car. He never drove it to town or on an errand. He always walked to town to pay his bills and get what ever he needed in his business.

Mr. Bridges customarily sported a stubble face. But on the weekends when he drove the Ford he'd be clean-shaven and wearing freshly pressed khakis. He usually invited passengers along. He would take people from the neighborhood or family members with him on his jaunts. In a weekend he'd make several trips. He'd visit the cemetery and sometimes drive through the Mission Bottom. Before it was late on Sunday he'd have the old car back in his shop sitting high up on blocks with the radiator drained. He'd probably owned that same car his whole adult life and his simple pride of ownership was a joy to behold

The town's last blacksmith died in 1954 and his family members sold the Model T Ford to Carlos Garrett for the Wetumka Ford Showroom floor. The story that went around was that Mr. Garrett paid Mr. Bridges' family the original purchase price which was a quite modest amount.

The rodeo was an institution in Wetumka for many a season. Sam and Josephine (Bessie) Proctor owned and operated a "mom-and-pop" gas station on East Grand throughout the years of World War II and into the 1950s. Very few people remember how involved they had been in the rodeo circuit. They staged a rodeo at their own arena, eight miles from Wetumka, nearly every year throughout the 1930s. Sam Proctor was an excellent calf roper and most amazingly, his wife was also. Bessie was hailed by all of the newspapers of the time as the women's World Champion Calf Roper. In 1941 they performed in Wetumka at the football field which was hastily converted into rodeo grounds with chutes and pens. The inevitable parade featured the round-up clubs from Okemah, Henryetta, Holdenville as well as Wetumka's. Jess Goodspeed had already performed at Madison Square Garden in New York City. Buck Goodspeed was the recent winner of the Forth Worth Rodeo. (Sam and Bessie are so worthy of remembering because they were deservingly famous for their accomplishments in their own time. Afterward, they settled down in Wetumka to a very sedentary style of life and their customers got used to them as members of the older set. They were both slow talkers and they moved about at an agonizingly slow pace. This made it easy to forget that they had once been so fast at rodeo, the only American sport based on an occupation.)

7

The Oil Boom in Wetumka

Wetumka's oil boom days began on the Saturday afternoon of October 12, 1922, when word of a strike on the Martha Gregory farm reached town in the middle of the afternoon. The editor-publisher of THE WETUMKA GAZETTE were out of town. An apprentice printer, recognizing the extreme frenzy of the moment and the magnitude of the event, took it upon himself to gather the news and rush out a special edition.

He wrote: "Businessmen, women and all, went wild with excitement. "Many of them closed their business houses and hurried over to see the well." Within a few hours the streets of Wetumka were lined with strangers and the two and a half-mile-road to the well was "a seething mass of traffic."

That first well was brought in as something of an accident. The driller had nearly reached a depth of 3320 feet and was told to shut down at that depth. But, as it happened, he was called away for a few minutes and his assistant continued to drill another ninety feet.

At 3330 feet the drill penetrated the oil sand and oil gushed wildly over the wooden derrick. Earthen tanks were hastily dug to contain the flow which would amount to a respectable 1,000 barrels a day. Oil industry publications of that time agreed that this was one of the strongest wildcat wells drilled in the state in some time.

In less than two months there were fifteen new drilling rigs in construction or operation near Wetumka. The timber was soon on the ground for two more rigs near the discovery well which was holding up very well.

A new radio station, operating in Bristow, began a special broadcast each evening to inform the state about the happenings in the Wetumka Oil Field.

Skelley, Gilcrease, Phillips, Slick, and most of the big names in the oil industry were rapidly involved. Lease rates were jumping just as rapidly. Charles Casey realized a windfall in a lease of 40 acres for $40,000. Transcontinental Pipeline and a host of pipeline companies arrived on the scene very quickly. Pipelines were constructed to connect with those at Wewoka and Henryetta and points beyond.

This pipeline construction marks the beginning of an industry that for generations has employed more Wetumkans than the oil business ever did. Oil storage tanks were hastily assembled in the field as nothing that large could be hauled to the site.

It was said, at the time, that more than half of the people in Wetumka were strangers to each other. Wetumka's boosters were always busy sending out bulletins and posters that convinced plenty more people that Wetumka was still one of the most promising cities in Oklahoma.

The economic prospects for Oklahoma had never seemed so positive. Just weeks before the Wetumka oil field was opened, the newspapers announced that Oklahoma's crude oil production had surpassed not only that of Texas and Louisiana but California's as well. With 13 million barrels produced, Oklahoma was becoming the undisputed leader of the oil producing states. Even the federal government was issuing reports at this time indicating that Oklahoma's mineral wealth might be greater than that of any state.

Wetumka's petroleum discovery came a littler later than most producing areas in Oklahoma. There had been the huge Seminole pool and even Weleetka had 75 producing wells before Wetumka had one. Wetumka's wells had been "gassers" and during World War I the gas mains had been installed to heat and to light the homes of Wetumka.

The mid-twenties were the second large building boom in Wetumka and the growing pains were very severe. The 1920 census had pegged Wetumka's population at 1421 and by 1925 it was being estimated at 3500 to 4,000. The city clerk's office canvassed all the residences and rooming houses within the town boundaries and their figures showed 3512.

Wetumka had completed its first separate high school building in 1921 in the Hall-Williams addition "east of town." In 1925 there were 25 teachers in Wetumka for an average class size of 60. Some of the classes were even larger than this. This was especially the case in the elementary grades. (The teacher count includes the Superintendent and principals.)

While there were not enough instructors, the most acute problem was that there simply was not enough instructional space. Elementary classes were also held at the high school, in the former coal bins at Mingo school and for a while in the loft over the Ford Service station. By 1925 there were more students enrolled in Wetumka schools than there had been people in the general population when the Federal Census was taken in 1920.

The editor of THE WETUMKA GAZETTE estimated that there were at least 28 new residences, a number of new rooming houses and small hotels under construction with an estimated value of $500,000. Dr. Gille, Nathan Lee and J. C. Laporte were building new rooming houses. (Each evening a committee of citizens scoured the city for rooms to accommodate the new influx of people. It was said that people were sleeping in garages, attics and tents.

The year, 1925, can be recognized as another high-water mark in the building of Wetumka. It is different from 1911 because things were moving at a faster pace. Construction materials and methods were very different. Practically all of the buildings were of brick with very little use of native rock.

It was faster to haul bricks from the train station than it was to gather rock from the hillsides and cut them into regular sizes. Native stone had been very difficult to lift into place as buildings rose in height. Skilled brick layers could put in a wall faster than stone masons could and it was even becoming cost effective.

Mr. B. Parker built a new brick building on Main Street across from the City Hall. On the other side of the street a new "Art Decco" brick filling station was completed that year. Gas stations were springing up all over town and oil companies were trying to differentiate their brands with their distinctive gas station architecture.

It had been recognized that Wetumka could benefit from a substantial hotel so that oil men and other important visitors would have a headquarters . The city dads set about getting private subscriptions for a planned $45,000 structure. This project never got beyond the planning stage.

In April of 1925 it was announced that the dreams of the citizens of Wetumka to have a first class hotel would surely be realized. Work had already started when the announcement was made. The hotel would be the Meadors Hotel and was contracted by Richard E. Richter and would take about five months. It was to be three stories high with a basement, comprising sixty rooms. The hotel would be built up around the Meadors store at Main and Broadway.

The new Meadors Hotel held a grand opening in October, 1925. Fifteen hundred people attended the gala opening. There was an orchestra from Shawnee to inaugurate the new ballroom and hotel. Then speakers commended Meadors & Meadors for the interest they had shown in building up Wetumka. The Mayor, Charles N. Hamilton, stated that this firm had probably built more new residences in Wetumka than any other.

The public was unable to inspect the rooms that night because they were all occupied. But there were cigars for the men and flowers for the ladies. The appearance of Wetumka was changing. Main Street and Broadway had been paved with bricks less than a year earlier. Both bank buildings were building office annexes.

The most significant construction was in the developing oil industry. Several huge lumber yards sprung up to stock the huge timbers used in building drilling rigs. These were the McIntosh, Billington, Producers, Tulsa Rig and Reel, The Weleetka Lumber Yard and The Ozark Lumber Yard and all of them had acres of derrick size lumber piled around them. In two months in 1925 there were over 1,000 train carloads of oil field supplies unloaded at the Wetumka depot.

While the new $70,000 high school had been completed in 1922 by Chowins & Jarrett in the Hall Williams Addition, the area began to develop with the oil boom. Local people had always customarily spoken of the high school as being located somewhat inconveniently "east of town." Lots were selling and this was becoming a residential area. (This was a swampy area of town that drained poorly. In the 1930s, one WPA project was to bring in 550 yards of soil to "level the playing field" at the high school.)

The real economic activity was happening outside the city limits of Wetumka. Several of the drilling sites were taking on all of the attributes of city. Within a year of the discovery well, the Prairie Oil Company had put up a huge warehouse of five acres just outside of Wetumka at the Crawford well. They had their own lumber yard, pipe storage racks, and several worker houses. The foremen lived, with their families, in modern cottages and shared a four car garage. There was a modern water system and a self-contained electric light system.

James Slick, the legendary wildcatter, was one of the first operators on the scene after the discovery well was brought in. His drilling efforts, just to the west of Wetumka, were amply rewarded and in short order there were homes, stores, a picture show and even a 75 member Chamber of Commerce. The area was known as "Slick City" for a time. (This was a thoroughly lawless little town and Saturday night killings were not infrequent.)

Developing the field was not Slick's specialty. He quickly sold out to the Papoose Oil Company and the town gave notice that its would henceforth be known as Papoose.

The largest investment in Hughes County by any oil company was what was known as "Phillips Plant." It came closer than any oil settlement to being a city. There were dozens of company houses for workers and the streets were well maintained. There was a community church. The Wetumka Chamber of Commerce was constantly improving the roads to Phillips Plant. This community lasted until well into the World War II era. Ultimately, they were allowed to run their own water lines to the back side of the Wetumka Lake.

Phillips Plant was only two miles north of the Lawnwood School but it nevertheless had its own school with grades through high school. This was a just another county school operating in company buildings with some company subsidies. Not all of the students were children of the oil workers; anyone in the area could send their children to this school.

This was the largest and most lucrative investment in the Wetumka oil boom. Phillips spent millions developing what they acknowledged was the largest gasoline plant in the world. Hundreds of rail cars of materials for this plant was off loaded in Wetumka.

The Wetumka Chamber of Commerce had been a forceful booster of this kind of activity. They had raised $5,000 that went to building roads and installing telephone lines that connected Wetumka with these oil fields and the one at Cromwell.

Getting roads to the drilling sites was of prime importance. In August of 1924, there were 327 carloads of oil field supplies received and it was not uncommon for 30 or 40 cars to be unloaded in a single day. There were over a hundred trucks and at least that many teams employed in moving the material out to the fields.

By the end of 1924 there were 400 men employed in building a 25-unit absorption gasoline plant. This gasoline would be shipped out of Wetumka. It was piped to loading racks near the depot. (The Phillips Company had secured the patents to the absorption process of obtaining natural gasoline from natural gas in 1923. This company also pioneered the development of high test aviation fuels and many petroleum derivatives.)

By the summer of 1925, ninety-thousand gallons of gasoline was being pumped to Wetumka daily and loaded into rail tank cars. This amounted to more than ten carloads a day. In July, 1925, more than four hundred cars of gasoline were shipped out of Wetumka. This amounted to about 3.6 million gallons. One train, that month, comprised 856 ton weight and required one of the largest Frisco engines to pull it. It was cleared to roll, as one unit, all the way to Bayonne, New Jersey.

Just before Thanksgiving, 1925, members of the Wetumka Chamber of Commerce and their wives were invited to a fellowship meeting in the spacious company dining hall at Phillips Plant.

Grant Herring, the Chamber of Commerce president, reported that the party left Wetumka, and although the roads were not good, they covered that distance of nine miles in less than an hour.

They were treated to a tour of the entire facility and then they retired to the dining hall where they were sumptuously fed. The menu consisted of fried chicken, mashed potatoes, fresh beans, peas, brown gravy, fresh tomatoes, lettuce and salad dressing and four deserts. He said that "the boys made hogs of themselves but were quick to apologize." After the cigars were well lit there were speeches which were followed by an address by Guy Barrett, who represented Phillips Petroleum Company.

That year the Holdenville and Wetumka Chamber of Commerce hosted a special train load of financiers on an inspection tour of the oil fields. The train manifest showed that the three Phillips brothers were present along with dozens of Eastern financiers from the most prestigious investment houses of Wall Street and Chicago. One of the guests came and went almost unnoticed. He was the latest in a long line of men to bear the name of Hamilton Fish and he was currently serving as the governor of New York.

There were three companies, in addition to Phillips, shipping out of Wetumka which for a while was actually the second busiest freight shipping point in Oklahoma. The depot handled a considerable volume of freight and an engine was kept on the sidetracks day and night to switch cars and make up trains.

The net effect on the economy of Wetumka and surrounding area was definitely positive but short term. According to Census data most of the houses occupied in Wetumka today were constructed during these generally optimistic times. (Geologists had long believed that Wetumka was actually sitting over a huge pool of oil. The city leased land for drilling near the light plant and at the edge of the cemetery. The results were dismal.)

Had it not been for optimism generated by the oil boom, the city's downtown might not have been paved in 1924. When it was proposed that downtown should be paved in 1921, the cost to the individuals was prohibitive. Nearly every commercial and residential property owner filed a protest. The law at the time required that the entire cost be borne by the property owner whose property abutted the paved street. The city had vastly improved its revenue stream by 1924, and was pressing ahead with the new light and water plant.

Paving were no less prohibitive in 1924 but with the oil boom on merchants were more likely to accept such a liability. The city was now collecting a cent for every gallon of gasoline sold within the city limits. Yet it was the sheer optimism of boom times that allowed the business district to have paved streets. The total amount for the job was never announced. It was done piecemeal and after the two downtown blocks were finished, neighborhoods were petitioning to have their streets paved. The bids for various types of brick construction were not modest. (They amounted to what would be $60 to $80 per square yard in today's dollars.) Broadway was "boulevarded" to save on the cost as was a good portion of south Main Street.

The present Baptist and Christian churches were built in 1928 amid the good feelings of the oil boom. The Christian church was rebuilt at the old site. The Baptist church cost about $45,000 to build while the Christian church cost about half that. It was only one story over a basement. But its congregation was smaller. The Baptist Church was built by a large congregation. The architect selected the highest place in town for its location. It looked like a Greek Temple and could be seen for miles outside the town. The Christian Church was less spectacular only because it was considerably smaller. It's stained glass windows were its distinguishing feature. In the same year, 1928, the Assembly of God church on Canard Street also was extensively remodeled.

Not many months after these buildings were first occupied, The Great Depression was affecting nearly every person in America. In 1935 a bank foreclosed upon the Christian church and the congregation was locked out. Everyone saw this as a deplorable and pathetic symbol of their own personal economic desperation. H. H. Darks led a vigorous city-wide drive to raise funds and help the people of that church repurchase their building. (They met for over a year in the old armory building.)

Every decade in Wetumka's historical development, Wetumka, has coincided with a distinctive historical period. If the 1920's had been something of a binge, the awful 1930's can only be remembered as ten years of unprecedented suffering.

8

Education in Wetumka Before World War II

School life in Wetumka can be remembered with pride and satisfaction by the many thousands of students who have scattered themselves over the globe to find their own place in the world. Schools in Wetumka were gradually opened under conditions of great adversity and the struggle to keep them open and functioning never lessened. Many capable and energetic people have performed their school duties in a manner that can only be thought of as "good soldiering."

The original school was operated by the town of Wetumka in the Central Ward in the Tiger Addition. It was a collection of unsightly frame buildings pieced together from what could be salvaged from Old Town Wetumka.

During the summer of 1906 the school board engaged G. R. Parsons and Sons of Fort Smith to draw up the plans and specifications of a new building and it was agreed that it would be erected upon the old site just one block off mainstreet.

A fourteen thousand dollar building would enhance property values all over town and especially in that tract. All students would be housed at this site until the Mingo School Building was completed to relieve crowding during Wetumka's first great growth spurt. The Mingo school was completed in 1911 at the end of North Main Street in the tract known by that name.

By 1908 there was an enrollment in 269, of which 19 were high school students in grades 9 and 10. The first graduating class would not happen until the high school had been extended to a full four years in 1916 and there were nine students in that first class: five girls and four boys.

Overcrowding was the overriding issue from the very beginning. The system simply could not afford or even find enough teachers to have reasonable class sizes.

Miss Leona Sharp was in charge of the primary room in 1908 and she had 59 students. Miss Jessie Wheat of the second and third grades had 52 students; Miss Zephie Hayes had 45 students in her third and fourth grades. Professor Payne and Mr. Welday taught the seventh, eighth, ninth, and tenth grades with 54 enrolled.

Even at this rudimentary stage there was the beginnings of a library. Great emphasis was placed on giving every student to learn the finer points of public speaking and parliamentary procedure.

On January 1, 1914, Oklahoma beefed up its teacher certificate requirements. A simple examination, as in the case of lawyers, was insufficient.

A teacher candidate had to have done some work in a college or normal school (commonly called a teacher's college). To be a third grade teacher it was necessary to have taken courses from this group: Arithmetic, algebra, agriculture, civics, domestic science, English grammar, geography, Oklahoma history and government, U. S. history, orthography (penmanship), physiology and hygiene, reading, writing, theory and practice. They had to maintain an average grade of 75 and be at least eighteen years old.

Prospective second grade teachers had to meet these requirements and to complete course work in American literature and elementary psychology. A higher average grade was required.

First grade teachers usually had to work up to this position from another grade or meet these course requirements with a higher grade and in addition they had to be at least twenty years old. It was thought that the most competent teachers and should be the ones that started students in their school careers.

It was also thought, at the time, that first grade teachers should be accorded the most prestige because they were usually the senior teachers. They not only gave students an effective start but they represented the school system in initial contacts with parents.

Teachers enjoyed considerable social standing in the community. They were regarded as the best educated members of society. The newspaper followed their social lives with great interest and always published essays about what all the teachers did on their vacations.

In theory it was possible for a member of the public to be fined $5 "for giving offense" to a teacher. Oklahoma casually adopted, in copy-cat fashion, many laws from other states.

The observer is struck by the fact that elementary teachers were invariably single women or if infrequently one of them married or had been married they rarely had children of them own at home. It was though that women could not adequately care for children of their own and everyone else's. Some school boards openly announced that they would not hire married women and they would not rehire those who did marry.

By 1916 there were two buildings at the Central Ward site. The enrollment there and at Mingo Elementary School had reached 511.

Enrollment by Classes in 1916:

Seniors-9
Juniors-15
Sophomores-19
Freshmen-37
Eighth Grade-24
Seventh Grade-30
Sixth Grade-42
Fifth Grade-47
Fourth Grade-52
Third Grade-58
Second Grade-61
First Grade 107

There were only nine members of this first graduating group of seniors. This pattern would hold until the Second Word War. Throughout the 1920s and 30s the Sophomore class would be half that of the Freshman class.

In a typical year if there were 63 Freshman students, the Senior Class would have no more than 21. Of this number several students would have asterisks after their names in the newspaper to indicate they had not completed every requirement for graduation.

Wetumka schools did not adopt letter grades until 1935 and many people objected then because they saw this as a deliberate blurring of the lines. (College students usually got percentage grades at this time.)

The first high school building was constructed in 1922 in the Hall-Williams addition. Wetumkans spoke of its location as being "just east" of town. The school board acquired two full blocks which constituted 6 and 3/4 acres of poorly drained land.

The building and grounds cost $70,000 and was a significant financial undertaking at the time. The Contractors were Chowins and Jarrett. The Chowins portion was Harry Glenn (father of the future high school principal) and the man who had first installed concrete sidewalks and would do all of the concrete work on the new Wetumka lake in the winter of 1931. Mr. Jarrett was the proprietor of the Ford Filling Station.

Building lots near the new high school would be heavily promoted for several years. They were usually available for $100 to $150 and terms were usually available. A building site could be acquired for a third down and $10 a month.

By 1924 it was reported that all nine of the graduating boys in the class would report to college in the fall. Of course, four girls were planning to attend college as well. More attention was paid to the attention of males although girls usually outnumbered boys in the senior classes two to one.

Just getting through high school was a middle class thing. Most boys found jobs or other ways to validate their passage into adulthood.

This did not change until the depression years closed off alternatives and the classes began to show a gender balance.

Overcrowding in the schools was the greatest problem for the schools from the very beginning. The oil boom brought on a great expansion in population. By 1925 there were as many students enrolled in the schools as they had been inhabitants of the town at the Federal Census of 1920.

In 1921 the school district first acquired five "trucks" as the early buses were known. There was little to distinguish them from regular trucks. They had been fitted with wooden bodies, had a flat tar paper roof and windows that fell out easily.

Much of the enrollment growth can be attributed to the consolidation of country schools into the Wetumka district. It was thought the country schools could not have as much impact on the life of the student as the larger city schools. Just getting the kids to town was considered an accomplishment.

These buses did not provide comfortable or reliable transportation. They had splintery floors, their roofs often leaked and none of them ever had a heater. They were regarded as unsafe.

In all the years that Wetumka operated school buses on routes there was only one serious accident. In 1928, on a frosty morning in February thirty-four students were injured in a bus roll over.

The "truck driver" Mr. J. F. Reed, had completed all of his stops and was proceeding up the Mission Bottom Hill. When he downshifted the transmission locked up. His brakes failed and he attempted to guide the bus backwards down the hill. At the bottom his luck ran out and he rolled the bus over into the ditch. It was demonstrated rather conclusively that the bus design was unsound. It did not support the weight of the chassis. The sides were reduced to splinters and there was broken glass all about.

And most of the children were unable get out. One girl ran to a farm house. In a short time townspeople had descended upon the scene and rolled the bus onto its side.

All of the children and the driver required medical treatment. Five Wetumka doctors worked feverishly and determined that fourteen children were seriously injured. One boy had a dislocated rib and was said to have been unconscious for an hour.

X-ray examinations were made of several students. The ususal injury was cuts which had to be stitched and bandaged. None of the skull concussions proved serious.

Until the mid-1930s the Wetumka athletic teams were known as *The Eagles.* The Eagles played football and other sports whenever and where ever they could get a game. They once traveled by train to Tulsa and played Tulsa High School. The Tulsa team considered that a practice game but the Wetumka boys took it in good spirit.

When the name change was made there was little fanfare about it. At first they simply called themselves The Chiefs. Much later they adopted the more familiar *Chieftains.*

The decade of the 1930s is the era of The Great Depression. It brought the greatest stress to economic and social life that the people of Wetumka ever experienced. All of this shared hardship focused on the schools. And, yet, this was the period that saw more building, renovation and expansion than any other comparable ten years in the history of Wetumka schools.

The makeup of the school population had changed drastically since the oil boom of five years past. Many of the transient oil workers' families had left Wetumka for other work. In 1930, fully half of all the students attending Wetumka schools were from the rural areas. The school district was running seven school buses a day. Some of the buses picked up two and sometimes three different routes of students. This meant that some students had to wait after school for up to two hours for their turn. School didn't begin in the morning until around 9:00 a. m. to give the bus drivers two hours or more to complete their rounds.

In 1932 the Wetumka School District had a total operating budget of $29,569.76.[1] This was conservatively estimated to be $8,000 less than the minimum required for a full nine-month term. It would hardly last seven months. It was anticipated that state aid to weak schools and transfer fees might keep the doors open for one month.[2]

One of the less visible effects of the depression was the overall lowering of property values. The valuation of the district in 1932 was only $1,489,050 which had recently been lowered a full one-third from $1,921,645.[3] As recently as 1930 the property valuation in the school district had been $2,421,110 and the tax rate was 23.4 mills.

The pain was widely shared. Salaries for teachers were cut across the board a full ten percent and some school employees were asked to take a 50 percent cut. The district employed 31 teachers, 8 truck drivers and 3 janitors. (The superintendent, R. B. Knight, declared the district needed four more teachers and two more trucks as a bare minimum.)

The average monthly grade school teacher's salary sank to $66.90 while the average at the high school was $87.35. The amount spent per pupil had become just $28.01 annually. It was widely known that the equivalent of two teacher salaries were being paid by private donations and help from the merchants through the Chamber of Commerce.

As bad as this sounds it is really a rosy picture compared to the private remarks of teachers and others who lived through the times. Teachers had always been a little more prosperous than most citizens and were likely to have a few dollars in a bank account somewhere and they were not likely to be supporting large families. They were asked to make great sacrifices.

---

1.   The Wetumka school budget had been $43,364.41 for the term 1928-29. (It is somewhat ironic that between 1929 and 1934 nearly $700,000 had been expended in Hughes County on US Highway 75 and US 270. While it could be stated that US 75 was not an all weather route, the pavement became gravel a short distance south of Calvin.)

2.   In August the State Board of Equalization ordered a reduction of 30 per cent in assessments all over the state. This action further reduced the budget by $2500.

3.   There were many Sheriff's sales of property for delinquent taxes as the terrible decade wore on. Outside investors reaped great windfalls on the courthouse steps. At one point prime building lots in Holdenville were selling for fifty cents (and there were few takers.)

Teachers were paid by warrants which are collection items convertible into cash only when sufficient funds are deposited. Clarence Hastings, the County Treasurer, handled these accounts and he gave notification of when the warrants could be honored.[4]

The "truck drivers" were supporting families on their meager salaries and they informally organized and walked out. They promised not to transport another student if they were not paid. They were promptly provided some relief. But for teachers things did not improve. Late in the 1930s, if the Wetumka schools finished their nine year terms it was usually due to the teachers forgoing pay during the final weeks.

The situation couldn't worsen, it seemed, but in the evening of October 11, 1933 it certainly did. The Central School Building was badly damaged by a fire that left it uninhabitable. It was thought that the fire originated in a closet under the stairway near the main entrance.

The Board of Education tentatively made plans to house the student population at the "Old Brick Hotel" which had most recently been home to The Neely-Penn Hospital. Other shop buildings on Broadway were to be utilized. But it was quickly realized that the students were in greater hazard than they had been at the Central School.

The grades were distributed between the Baptist, Methodist, and Christian churches while efforts were underway to repair their school.

During the winter recess of 1933-34 there was another fire at the school which was undergoing repairs. It was another fire of unknown origin that destroyed the building and contents and left only the bare walls. It started shortly after midnight on January 1, 1934. Carl Clark,

---

4.   Mr. Hastings is poignantly remembered by many Wetumkans because of the sad way he and his wife died in 1942. The South Canadian River was in flood stage when they drove across the bridge near Atwood. They could not see the floor of the bridge and could not know part of the bridge had washed away. The car and four bodies were recovered within days. Mrs. Hastings' remains were located on a sand bar 75 miles away near Eufaula nearly two months later. She was identified by her wedding band.

himself a volunteer fireman, was doing some oil field rush work late in his home workshop a block away.

When he removed his welder's helmet the night sky was all lit up. He ran to the fire station, gave the alarm and drove the fire truck back to the scene. He realized the futility of fighting the fire and the fire hose was not even trained on the blaze.

The new building was constructed with a thirty percent grant from the state, an increase in the mill tax and ultimately with relief labor. It was not quite ready for the opening of the term in September 1934.

The new building consisted of just one wing which faced east. The architect was a likeable man from Ada (Mr. Albert S. Ross) and he designed a building the community could be proud of. It was constructed of a buff brick and trimmed with white limestone. It was 205 feet long and 72 feet wide. A space was left on the west side for an auditorium. (This structure would not be built until the mid-1950s.)

That portion of Central Elementary School that has been known as the Primary Wing was a New Deal relief program (WPA) project. Work began on this building of four additional classrooms on September 16, 1936. When this project was completed the primary students who had been meeting for so long in the former coal bins at Mingo School could be transferred to a healthier learning space. This was a thirteen thousand dollar project and while the district paid for the materials and skilled labor it could not have been built at the time without relief workers.

The Federal government was really getting underway in its expenditures for relief work in Wetumka by this time. Mingo school and grounds had been given a good going over and the roof was repaired. Badly needed sidewalks had been laid. And finally indoor bathroom facilities were installed. Wetumkans had long grumbled about students having to trudge through the wind, rain and snow to "those old outhouses." They had often been pronounced "the shame of our town." Complaints had been voiced that the students who attended "Old

Mingo" came from disadvantaged families who unlikely to have very much clout.

The rural schools in the Wetumka district, if anything, fared even more poorly than those in town. There seemed to be an inexorable movement afoot to close as many of them as soon as possible. After 1932 the County Superintendent was Jim Ragland who remained in office until he was appointed Superintendent in Maud. Then he returned to Wetumka and served longer than any other superintendent.

Mr. Ragland would visit a school and spend a good portion of the day there and actually take part in daily instructional activities. He evaluated the school and its program. He was always on a quest for a few more dollars from the county or the state but it was often necessary to close a rural school before the end of the term. Those schools with the fewest students and the poorest attendance were the most vulnerable.

The teachers in the rural schools were even more poorly compensated than most. Only a few schools, Fairview and Lawnwood are examples, had a teacherage or lodging for the teacher on the grounds. In 1929-30 Hughes county had 55 men and 84 women teachers in its rural schools.

The average salary for men was $1,132 for men, while the average salary for women was $831. By the Depression year of 1933, the teacher force in rural schools had been reduced to 36 men and 36 women. The rural school budget had been reduced by two-thirds. It had been $131,153 in 1929. By 1933 it was a mere $46,000. Men's salaries had slid to $672 and that of women teachers to $606.[5]

Many newspaper editorialists thundered about the way teachers were being asked to bear the brunt of government cutbacks. The *Wetumka Gazette* stated on December 15, 1933, that "schools have

---

5.   It was not until the 1940s that Oklahoma teachers organized themselves into an association to provide a meager retirement. Many of the teachers in Wetumka spent forty years or more in the classroom with very modest retirement credit.

borne more reductions than all other governmental units combined." They went on "teachers are expect to draw cuts while politicians draw fat paychecks."

The casual observer could conclude that the in the 1930s there was an epidemic of school house fires. Actually it had long been that way. In the early 1920s schools were destroyed by fire in Dustin and Hanna while they were in the course of construction.

On January 10, 1930, Holdenville's high school which was only five years old, was totally destroyed by a blaze that threatened the junior high school building as well.

The people of Wetumka were mindful of fires because they had experienced some spectacular blazes in the downtown area. They really took fire drills seriously. The town officials would pull a surprise visit and fire alarm at the schools. Central School had, on one occasion, been completely evacuated in an amazing 24 seconds. Apparently they were less concerned about kids being trampled than having someone left behind.

On October 28, 1938, shortly after midnight the alarm was given by Jack Morris to Night Officer Joe Bement that the Wetumka High School was ablaze.

Soon after the fire department arrived on the scene the flames had leaped through the roof. Within two hours the whole building had been reduced to rubble. It was thought the blaze started from a smoldering fire in the hallway.

The firemen concentrated on saving the band equipment, football suits and science equipment. Fortunately, the records kept the the principal and superintendent's office were rescued.

Despite all the painful educational contractions that had taken place during the Depression, the School Board had seen fit to maintain adequate insurance coverage.

The citizens of Wetumka lamented their loss of such a handsome building which had been in use for less than fifteen years. It had been built under the guidance of the school board of pioneer Wetumkans: G. L. Herring, W. C. Farmer, J. E. Tiger and X. X. McGee.

Before the end of 1938 a new high school was well past the planning stage. On December 9, Congressman Lyle H. Boren notified the Wetumka School Board that their application for WPA assistance was approved.

The new building would cost $108,000. About seventy-thousand of that would come from insurance proceeds on building and contents. This type of work was ideal for WPA work. It was low skill and vastly labor absorbing. In keeping with that point, it was decided that the red brick from the old building would be salvaged one-by-one. This was done and the mortar was removed and the bricks cleaned with wire brushes.

The only new bricks that would have to be bought would be the buff colored facing bricks.

9

Public Utilities

For over forty years, every kilowatt of electricity consumed in Wetumka was also generated locally. Motion picture theatres thrived in Wetumka long before any current was supplied by the city. The Lyric Theatre opened in 1908 and three years later, the Electric Theatre and then the Princess Theatre. These businesses produced their own electricity from steam boiler-generators.

The city accepted a new light and water plant from a Dallas contractor in January of 1911. Wetumka really pulled ahead of some of the nearby towns when it became an "electric light" town. The source of the electricity was a steam generator of the type employed in the oil fields of the time. (The equipment was supplied by the Westinghouse Corporation) Until 1915 it was in operation for only four hours each evening. The town had installed fifteen arc lights to illuminate the streets and only gradually were homes wired for the new electric lights.

The lighting of the town was a very dramatic development. Most people, in those days, customarily went to bed early. Kerosene lamps gave off a poor light and they would smoke up a room. With the coming of electric lights the night-time glow of Wetumka was visible for miles around on a dark night. Going to town "to see the bright lights" was not a mere idle phrase. It was well worth the trip to town to enjoy the lights. All of the lights were bright because there was only one bulb size.

At first the light plant was just that. It supplied electric current for lighting only. There were no other appliances available. Hardly anyone had even seen a radio and the telephone exchange was operated by a local battery system. (Radio came to town in 1921 when it was demonstrated to a grateful crowd at the Red Cross Drug Store.)

The hours for power generation were extended after the city acquired an additional generator in 1915 and the merchants began demanding power for fans in their stores. The electric fan was the first household appliance that most Wetumkans would own.

Electrical service was soon extended to all of the classrooms of the schools and people began to wonder how they had managed without artificial light even in the daytime. (Wetumka generated its own electricity until the Spring of 1951 when a contract was negotiated with the Southwest Power Administration for 400 Kilowatts monthly.)

Running water was a much more difficult issue and, for over a decade, almost an intractable problem. There was never enough water and this shortage would be the most daunting problem facing a rapidly growing town. It would remain the most urgent emergency until the winter of 1930-31 when the Wetumka Lake was completed.

According to some of the old timers the first municipal water supply had been a well that was situated at the intersection of Main and Broadway. The fire bell and a bandstand were also located there and people were free to bring their buckets and draw all they could carry.

Wetumka had acquired a light and water plant from the same contractor in early 1911 at a cost of about $41,000. This was the largest city expenditure so far and it included a 60,000 gallon tank at the top of a 125 foot water tower. Originally water was pumped from five big wells in the city to a concrete settling basin.

The gravity pressure was adequate to deliver water all over town. The pressure could be increased, in an emergency, to 180 pounds by pumps. It took a tremendous amount of water just to fill the four miles of water mains.

The city was adequately furnished with fireplugs and the town council had arranged to buy 1,000 feet of fire hose long before a fire truck was acquired.

The amount of water available for city use proved inadequate very soon after the system was installed. There were only 50 houses connected at first. The newspaper stated the common belief that the capacity of the wells was nearly inexhaustible. Civilization in the early Twentieth Century, in Wetumka, advanced to the point that more water was needed, per person, than ever before.

Two more wells were added before 1913. The brothers, A. E. and Ben Preston, dug the wells which were ten feet in diameter. Ben had to finish the second one alone. His brother had been seriously injured in a cave-in of the first one. Each of these wells was expected to supply an additional 30,000 gallons a day.

Before the year was out the city had already run a pipeline to the North Canadian River and installed a pumping plant there. The water was not drawn directly from the stream. A four inch pipe and three two inch pipes were driven into fourteen feet of riverbed sand 25 feet back from the river. It was believed that this would assure a supply of pure sand-filtered water. There would still be almost daily shortages and the city could not supply any water to the four gins. This is understandable as the city population tripled between 1920 and 1925.

Water was being used on a ever larger scale. Pumping capacity was always being increased and in 1916 the Town Council spent $16,000 on the beginning of "public sanitation sewers." This vastly increased the need for good water.

Nearly all of the city water came from the river during the era of World War I and its immediate aftermath. The amount furnished by the city wells had become negligible.

The water usually had a disquieting odor throughout most of the year and by early 1922 Dr. Fred B. Hicks, the City Health Officer, declared the water unsafe. He was merely public stating the obvious. The state chemist had tested the water and found it very high in bacterial contamination. The city had been drawing so much water from the river that even large stagnant pools were emptied.

Dr. Fred B. Hicks and his brother Dr. C. A. Hicks were for many years in a medical co-practice in Wetumka. Dr. C. A. Hicks married the daughter of the town's wealthiest citizen, Turner Meadors.) Another brother, Ed Hicks, along with their father, established the largest produce house in Wetumka in 1915. This was to be one of the largest businesses in town. They purchased everything from pecans to live chickens from the farmers. Ed Hicks would expand into the scrap metal and rubber business in World War II. His ads said they were located a block west and a block north of the flagpole and that they would pay top dollar for skunk hides in good condition.

No greater crisis could have faced Wetumka than to have its meager water supply condemned. The city was growing by leaps and bounds and would soon have 3500 residents. The ice plant (founded in 1915) helped by distributing water along with ice from its big yellow wagons. Townspeople transported water from farm wells nearby.

The solution was to build a permanent light and power plant in a palatial building that was erected alongside the railroad at the northeast edge of town. In 1925 the city completed this "state-of-the art" system. The water would be sand filtered and purified in a huge settling pond. This solution seemed the permanent answer to providing a plentiful amount of water to serve a city that might soon reach a population of 10,000.

The electrical generating capacity was also modernized. The switch was made from steam to diesel. THE OKMULGEE DAILY TIMES sent their most capable reporter to tour the facilities. To him the operation of the plant was a glimpse of the future and he described it in almost poetic terms.

It was stated that Wetumka had no general tax and required its citizens to pay nothing toward the support of municipal government because the city was in the business of generating electricity at wholesale and retailing it to a grateful population. The reporter concluded that this new equipment would pay for itself in four years and soon after that would begin to pay for the water treatment plant as.

The equipment was truly impressive. The electricity was generated by twin DeLaVerne Diesel engines that generated 2,000 kilowatt hours. The genius behind this local generation project was Ben McFall who was ably assisted by his chief engineer, Ed Mayfield.

Only one diesel ran at a time. They were rotated in 72 hour shifts. Compressed air was used to start an engine and momentarily both of them would be running. The people of Wetumka never sensed a flicker when the switch-over was made and there were never any general power outages as the plant was not affected by lightning or by the weather.

A huge traveling overhead crane was built into the walls and ceiling of the building and enabled one man to handle any piece of the big three cylinder engines alone. The water that cooled these engines was circulated into a holding pond where it could be aerated and the oil in the huge crankcases was constantly being cleaned or changed.

Ed Mayfield would preside over the operation of the light plant for over forty years and his acquaintances said he never missed a day. He wanted to be consulted for any necessary trouble shooting, even on his infrequent day off.

The Okmulgee reporter stated that Wetumka was the best lighted city in the entire Southwest. There were then 144 lights on the streets and they were not shut off at midnight as in most towns. They burned until daybreak because it was no extra expense to the city. (The city merchants usually had two meters. They were afforded a special rate to light their windows and to keep a few night lights on after closing hours.)

Wetumkans could be justly proud of the way the business district was lighted. Early in 1924, before Main and Broadway were finally paved, the city began installing underground cables and putting up steel posts for what was to become proudly known as "The Great White Way."

It was a more uniform way of lighting the streets. These were still streetlights, not floodlights. They looked like they were in perfect alignment in a shining row that seemed to reach to infinity. The effect was stunningly dramatic and made the night town scene very pleasant.

The completion of Wetumka's Great White Way rekindled the rivalry with Holdenville. That city would not complete its whiteway until the Christmas season of 1927. They had to outdo their little sister city. Holdenville's whiteway extended 32 blocks. They had a celebration that attracted people from all over the county and region. The merchants of Holdenville had blocked out their store windows and prepared artistically decorated displays with Christmas themes that were unveiled before the crowds just as the whiteway was turned on for the first time. They even had arranged to have three out-of-town orchestras to play for street dancing.

With the building of the power plant, new ways of regulating the current delivered to stores and homes in Wetumka, were employed. One of the greatest improvements was transformers attached to power poles. This enabled the city crews to install high tension cables and do away with the dozens and dozens of separate wires that had characterized the early electrical grid. Wetumkans, with a long memory, said that the benches at city hall were always in the shade from the lattice of overhead wires.

With the building of the new water and power plant the people of Wetumka thought they would never again be plagued by water shortages. It was just not to be. A reliable precursor of the problem to come was when in the late 1920's sportsmen reported that fish and other water life had completely disappeared from the North Canadian river.

The city had invested heavily in reaching the capacity to draw a half-million gallons from the river daily. Wetumkans who were paying $1 a month for the first 2500 gallons of water knew the water was becoming more salty each month. By January, 1930, it was agreed that the water was undrinkable and practically unusable.

While Wetumka had one of the best filtering plants in the state it was simply impossible to take the salt of the water. The culprits could not be more obvious. Oil companies carelessly discharged salt water

and other contaminants with reckless abandon. (On the road to Okemah there was nearly a section of land that appeared to have been
ruined permanently. There was absolutely no plant or animal life of
any kind all the way to the horizon. With nothing to hold the soil in
place, the entire topsoil layers had washed away. Vast deposits of salt
were visible to the passerby.)

At the same time that Wetumka civic leaders were courting the oil
companies, during the astounding oil boom, they were preparing to
sue them for ruining their municipal water system.

Ben McFall, the Superintendent of the Water and Power Plant, is
given credit for assembling the evidence against the oil companies. In
May 1930 the city council of Wetumka filed lawsuits against oil companies operating in the Slick, Seminole, Earlsboro and Oklahoma City
oil fields. The amount sought was $225,000.

By September the Oil Companies were offering seriously to negoti-
ate a settlement. They saw no advantage of going into court where
important precedents could be set.

Judge C. H. Baskin, Wetumka city attorney, reported that oil companies involved were offering $60,000 through the Seminole Oil Asso-
ciation, their trade organization. This was the most satisfactory offer
made and the one that would ultimately be accepted by the city council although hope was still held for action from other independents
who had been included in the lawsuit.

At any rate this devastatingly real emergency had to be dealt with.
On December 1, 1930, the city council solicited bids for the construction of a lake. There was a clause in the instructions stating that the
preponderance of the laborers had to be local citizens who had regis-
tered with the City Clerk. Over 500 men had signed up and more than
that number would work on the project at one phase or another.

The city council met in a long session on December 10th, and the
bids were reviewed and contracts offered. Work began at the proposed
lake site literally within hours.

There had been a good deal of discussion about the best site for the lake. A number of proposals had been discussed to located it near the new US Highway 75 which had finally been paved to Wetumka from the north and continued on for a mile to the South where the pavement ended at the edge of Elam Osborn's farm.

The council selected a site on the Charles N. Casey farm less than three miles from Wetumka on the Weleetka-Okemah road. The projected lake would actually lap into Okfuskee county.

It appears to have been one of the best sites available. It was recognizably a huge natural drainage basin. Several seasonal streams emptied into the area and flowed through a deep ravine. The dam was to span this ravine and be 600 feet long. The maximum height was to be 60 feet and the lake would have a shoreline of about six miles. The amount of water to be ultimately impounded would be about 600 million gallons or enough to sustain the town through two years of continuous drought.

There were three prime contractors on the lake project; two of them were local men. Harry Chowins was awarded the contract for the intake tower, pump house and spillway. The total of this contract was $16,753. C. I. Clanton, a local electrical contractor, was given the contract to construct necessary power lines. The amount was $2,188. Clearing the area of timber and constructing the dam was the other contract and it was awarded to Pharaoh and Company of Henryetta in the amount of $23,905. (When Mr. O. J. "Bunk" Pharaoh, died at his lavish home in Henryetta in February, 1947, the newspapers hailed him as a self-made millionaire who started as a tenant farmer before statehood. He had pulled himself up by branching out into cattle and construction. The unincorporated town between Weleetka and Henryetta was named for him.)

Mr. C. I. Clanton was an early resident of Wetumka. His photography studio was on Main Street and he did photography for individuals, the newspapers and the railroad. By 1906, he had disposed of this business. His next venture was in electrical contracting. He and his son,

James, wired most of the early homes and businesses of Wetumka. He was Wetumka's first light plant superintendent. Later he operated a radio and battery repair shop. He sold radios and would build one to the specifications of his customer. Mr. Clanton also repaired batteries of all types.

The construction of the Wetumka Lake is one of the most glorious chapters in the history of the town. Work was started two weeks before Christmas in 1930. The weather was bitterly cold but the rains held off for the most part. Practically all of the work was done by the muscle of men and their horses. The dirt contractor had a steam shovel and two trucks but this equipment was awkward to use and inefficient.

On a single day there were as many as 98 teams of horses with their drivers at work on the dam. Relatively few townsmen were employed because it was farmers who owned draft horses and the essential piece of equipment which they called a slip.

The slip was a giant scoop that farmers used in farm tasks like terrace building. It could hold over a thousand pounds of dirt and was skidded to its destination. The draft or pressure on the teams of horses was not unreasonable. The chief advantage was its simplicity which translated into safety. It was not like pulling a heavily loaded wagon where the driver often had to brake with all his might to prevent the load from running over his horses.

Mr. Ed Adkins, 91-year-old resident of Wetumka told me in February, 2001, that he had been employed building the lake. He worked for "old man Pharoah" and operated a land scraper known as a "Fresno." It took four mules to pull it and the operator could dump his load in a pattern as smooth as "your living room floor." (The "Fresno" was a land leveler developed to prepare land in California's central valley for irrigation and was named for the valley's largest town. It found other applications, such as road building and dam construction. Mr. Atkins also told me that this road had recently been the designated route of U. S. Highway 75 and that he'd helped maintain it and it had been the only way to Weleetka at the time.)

The scene of 98 teams of draft horses depositing fill on the rising dam was nothing less than the largest horse parade ever staged in the area. They moved a tremendous amount of fill and in a single day they could, if things went well, raise the dam two feet or more.

The most remarkable aspect of the lake construction is the haste in which the work was done. The men work very long days and paused only long enough to water their horses and eat their simple lunches brought from home wrapped in newspaper or carried in lard buckets.

There was always a genuine sense of comradship and plenty of hot coffee. The farmers of that time had not mastered the finer points of recreation and relaxation. The work ethic was very strong and many a man stated that his mind was more at ease and he was happiest when he was engaged in a hard day's work. The men on this project were mighty grateful because they could not work in their fields at this time and the economic depression was only getting worse by the day.

There were crews of men removing the timber groves that ringed the work area. Two men were kept busy dynamiting boulders which, after they were broken up, provided excellent rip-rap for the face of the dam. A full time blacksmith kept the horses shod and the equipment repaired.

There were no cost overruns and the project was completed far ahead of schedule. In little more than six weeks after the first excavation had started, water was being impounded. Before March of 1931, lake water was being pumped through the water mains to a grateful citizenry. It would be the middle of April before every detail had been wrapped up. Fences had to be built and cable guards strung on each side of the road across the dam.

The hill on the south end of the dam had been graded down and much of this material went into the dam. This was surely one of the deepest road cuts that had been made anywhere in the county until that time.

Most of the fill that went into the dam was clay which compacted well. A span of mules pulled a huge roller across the rising dam, constantly, to compact the newest layer. No leaks were ever reported in the dam and the lake was never jeopardized by flooding conditions. The spillway was very well designed and a concrete channel directed water over the Casey property below the dam and back into the creek. (The good fortune of Wetumka's well constructed dam stands in stark contrast to other projects in the area. During the floods of the Winter of 1945, amid the greatest manpower shortages ever, the Wewoka Dam was breeched twice and the city's water supply was lost. Water was pumped from deep wells as citizen committees tried to cope with emergency repairs. Acquiring pipe during the war was nearly impossible.)

The Indian church located on the northern shore of the Wetumka Lake has always been referred to as Salt Creek. This is the name of the small creek that became a "permanent flood" when the lake's dam was finished. Mr. Casey had allowed about two dozen Indian graves to be placed on his property. These graves were recent and of necessity they were removed to another part of the Casey farm. To the credit of Wetumka, carpenters were employed to build traditional Creek Indian grave coverings.

These were miniature houses that were complete down to the smallest Victorian detail. These burials were in a common plot in a perfectly straight row about 100 yards south of the Casey residence and visible from the road. The Indians who held to the old ways believed the spirits of the deceased would come back from time-to-time and take up residence in these shelters. The Indians did not maintain these highly painted structures because they believed that after a few years, gradually the spirits would stop returning. During this time there were Indian burial centers scattered all over the county. They looked like small-scale cities.

Harry Chowins had long been a concrete contractor and had been involved in building Wetumka's first city hall, sidewalks and the first high school. In 1928 he'd built the Chowins Building to be an automobile showroom. It is the long narrow building across the alley from the Meadors Hotel. He was also a prosperous farmer and the same year he built a new home on his farm which was east of town between the new Highway 75 and the North Canadian River. In 1930, he and his son Glenn, reported harvesting 450 bushels of high grade potatoes. (Mr. Glen Chowins, everyone's high school principal, helped his dad on the lake project. He alluded to it in his unsuccessful campaign for County Commissioner in 1932.) Mr. O. J. "Bunk" Pharoah had been in the area since statehood and had worked himself up from being a tenant farmer to a position of prominence as a farmer, stockman and contractor. It is for him that the community of Pharoah between Weleetka and Henryetta are named. When he died in 1947, the Henryetta newspaper proclaimed him a self-made millionaire. I communicated with his daughter Ethel, in her nineties, through the Henryetta librarian who also supplied me with a good deal of written material. Mr. Pharoah's earliest ambition was to own land of his own. This goal was well accomplished and he cleared much of the land himself. From 1912 to 1920 he operated a general store at the place which became known as Pharoah when a post office opened there. The first oil well drilled in Okfuskee County was on his land. For the rest of his life he realized a staggering income from oil royalties but thought the depressed oil business was a flash in the pan. He never became an oil man but expanded his contracting business to build roads, bridges and dams. He was very proud of what he'd accomplished with just one year's formal education.

The Wetumka lake did not immediately live up to expectations as a sportsman's paradise. There was considerable farming going on in the area and silting was a problem. The ground around the lake had been disturbed considerably and it was necessary to build a number of small check dams to stem the shore side erosion. Roads to the water's edge did not exist for about ten years. (The first access had been near the "fireboys' hut." Upon it completion, it had been adequately stocked with fish but most of them seemed to have disappeared. At one point a trench was dug around the spillway and the lake level was lowered three or four feet. The prevailing opinion was that this would help settle the lake. By the time fish were regularly being taken from the lake it was reported that native fish had returned to the river.

In 1932 Weleetka entered negotiations with Wetumka to provide them electricity at rates more favorable than they were obtaining from the Public Service Company. Plans were even drawn up to add a third generating unit to the light plant. Weleetka could not get out of its contract and the talks fell through

Throughout the thirties and forties the power plant was entirely adequate for the city's needs. About fifteen percent of the power generated was used to light the streets of Wetumka. Nearly fifty percent was used to pump water and only about thirty-five percent of the available power was actually sold to merchants and to the townspeople. About 14% was expended in line-loss before these calculations could be made. (At the time it was estimated that on an average day at least 100,000 gallons of water was pumped into the water mains.)

Dalton Fuller was the mayor of Wetumka in 1951 when the next public utilities crisis hit. Ed Mayfield was finding it ever more difficult to find repair parts for the light plant because this type of system was being abandoned. An outside engineer was hired to evaluate condition of the plant. His conclusion was that the machinery was being used to the breaking point and that if it went out an expenditure of $10,000 might be necessary to get it back into operation.

The city council frantically made arrangements with the Rural Electrification Administration (REA) to provide emergency power in case their was an interruption. Tom Steed, by then the Congressman representing Wetumka, went into action. The solution was power from the Southwest Power Association.

In the third week of March in 1951, there was a city election and Herman Darks, then a councilman, defeated Dalton Fuller (450-340) in one of the "heaviest" city elections ever. It was really a mayoral race simply because Haskell Brock and David W. Peixotto, city clerk and treasurer were unopposed. None of the councilmen had opposition. They were D. F. Burns, Bill Tankersley, and Logan Walker.

The new power agreement was for Wetumka to purchase 350 kilowatts at the rate of $820 a month. The powerlines were strung and the electricity was turned on almost the same day the new Methodist Church was declared completed (April 18, 1951). Construction had begun September 1, the previous year.

In actuality the power used in Wetumka came from the Public Service Company and was merely replaced by the SPA. As I've already said the constant unbroken theme in the history of electricity has been the steady increase in demand. In those days most of the people of Wetumka were able to purchase television sets and refrigerators for the first time. (The Ice Plant was entering its last days and soon Paul McBride was able to make all the deliveries in their trade territory by himself.)

On the national scene the Korean war was cranking up. President Truman had just fired General Douglas MacArthur for insubordination. And by then Robert S. Kerr, former governor, now U. S. Senator Kerr emerged as Truman's most energetic defender. He jumped at the opportunity to come to Wetumka, again. He'd been there many times for political reasons and that was the precise reason he'd return.

Senator Kerr brought his own press correspondents on the plane to Tulsa. They came to Wetumka in a motorcade and the purpose was ostensibly to congratulate Wetumkans on their wonderful power lines. But not really! As if on cue, a reporter asked him a hostile question about his unstinting support of the Truman administration. Senator Kerr, the consummate actor, threw down his notes and took off his hat. In a loud voice he began to blast MacArthur while building up

Truman. His remarks began with these words: "That kind of remark gets me hotter than a depot stove!"

In effect, Senator Kerr brought his own power to Wetumka. The reporters dutifully scribbled down everything he said and rushed off to file their reports. Senator Kerr had clarified where he stood and thereafter when he was asked about MacArthur or Truman, he replied, "My Wetumka statement! And I'm sticking with it!" Everything Senator Kerr had said about MacArthur and Korea resonated with the hometown crowd which had just experienced the terrible anxiety of having its National Guard company mobilized and loaded aboard ships in New Orleans enroute to a training camp in Japan. The Senator promised to do all that he could to keep them from being committed to a war with China.

Everyone in Wetumka was not happy with Senator Kerr's performance. Ray Meadors said that he was a "MacArthur man" and he would have preferred Congressman Steed "to this Kerr." C. A. Ticer said: "I thought this was going to be a celebration but the show was hogged by a politician tooting his own horn." Most were of the opinion expressed by Darvin Osborn, a farmer and pumper living south of Wetumka, who told THE HOLDENVILLE DAILY NEWS reporter that he thought the SPA thing would work out and that he really enjoyed Senator Kerr's stunt.

10

Good Roads and Bad

When an early Wetumkan spoke of the good road into Wetumka, they were surely talking about the railroad. No other intercity route was ever surveyed and engineered even close to railroad specifications in Hughes County. This is the road that brought Wetumka to life. Its right-of-way also brought the telephone lines and within a short time, even before there was electricity in town, Wetumkans could make voice connections with St. Louis and Kansas City and the rest of the world. (The Wetumka telephone exchange was a "local battery" type and would be in private hands for over thirty years.)

It was just about thirty years after Wetumka was established before there was a hard surfaced road into town. Highway 75 was paved in patches by 1930. These were "seedling miles" built with matching funds from the Federal Government. Contracts were let when there was money available. The North Canadian bridge was built in 1929 and for about a year it was a bridge to nowhere. The state could not get Federal assistance in building bridges due to complex formulas that ensured that states (with or without lots of rivers to cross) would be treated in a reasonably equitable way.

There was not a less favorable location for a bridge on the North Canadian river. It was just down stream from a major bend in the river that caused formidable swirling currents. The bridge was an obstacle in the path of these currents. It had been known for several years, from an earlier survey, that the streambed gradient of the river drops more than sixty feet within ten miles downstream from the bridge. Gravity did a might job on this portion of the river which was the swiftest known. In the 1941 flood, the approach to the bridge was washed away, along with about forty feet of pavement. The state sent a caravan of trucks to transport fill from the south side of the highway at the crest of the hill. The telephone poles look like they were stuck in small islands; this was once a continuous bank that hid passing trains. A rock quarry was opened halfway between the bridge and Weleetka to obtain material to "rip-rap" the crumbling riverbank.

This is not to imply that there were no roads into Wetumka. There was a far greater total mileage of roads in the area then than now. These were, for the most part, section line roads. The law required that property owners not interfere with the passage of traffic alongside their property. There was actually an immense grid of roads in the county early in the Century.

One of the biggest problems was that these roads really didn't go anywhere. A traveler had to know the countryside or follow the tracks of other traffic just to get to Weleetka or Okemah. Only gradually did these country roads become main traveled roads and this meant that a great number of others fell into disuse.

US Highway 75 and State Route 9 are essentially section line roads themselves. US Highway 75 hugs the terrain all the way through the county. The deepest road cut in the county is where the hill, approaching the Wewoka Creek, was graded down.

For over forty years, nearly every ton of freight arriving at Wetumka or being shipped to the rest of the world was handled by the railroad. The Frisco Depot agents said that Wetumka was one of the most important shipping points on the entire line and during the oil boom years that was pre-eminently the case.

When the new two unit National Guard armory was built as a WPA project in 1935, nearly all of the bricks and other materials were off-loaded at the Wetumka depot. The cement for that project amounted to twenty-two rail cars. The bricks, nearly all 600,000, were shipped by rail from the state penitentiary at McAlester.

Improved roads were not such a pressing concern before the arrival of wheeled traction. People drove their wagons or buggies or rode horseback along lanes that were always muddy or dusty but were rarely impassable. They could usually detour around the worst spots.

The first road builders were the farmers who only wanted to get to town. The common practice, in Hughes County and every county in America, was to make a split log drag. A heavy log would be split into two halves and held about three or four feet apart with scrap boards. The bottom edges of the logs bladed the road, filling in ruts and moving rock to the side. For several years Wetumka merchants had "Trades Days" on Saturday and awarded prizes to the farmers who had pulled a log drag to town over the greatest distances. (The farmers were very good at maintaining these simple wagon roads. They knew when the moisture content was just right in the ground. They could drag a road and make it very smooth. It would dry in a short time with a uniform crust that other travelers would really appreciate.)

With a 21st Century perspective it is easy to discern that the automobile was a firmly established fixture of life long before there were roads to accommodate it. Everyone who had ever ridden a bicycle was highly receptive to the possibilities of the car.

The arrival of the first auto in town, in the summer of 1909, was one of the most anticipated events ever to take place in Wetumka. There were only 680 automobiles in the state of Oklahoma that year: one for every 1,380 people.

One of Wetumka's most respected citizens, Mr. B. F. Scott, had to go all the way to Michigan to acquire the first car that ever entered Wetumka. It was one of the most highly publicized events of the summer of 1909. The local newspaper plotted his painfully slow progress during the long month that he and his hardy passengers spent trying to drive his automobile back to Wetumka.

There was a lively and impatient crowd in town on the appointed day of his arrival. The editor of THE WETUMKA GAZETTE did not know what kind of car it would be. He could only promise that it would be "a fat, juicy one, with a leather top on it, and it would come rolling into town puffing defiance at us...."

He wrote that "wonder gave way to agitation" when the traveling party arrived in Wetumka late in the day on the train. They had reluctantly left the automobile in Okmulgee for repairs.

The disappointment of the townspeople was profound. The prominent men of the city were waiting as patiently as they could. They had their names on a list for a first ride in one of those mechanical contraptions. The rest of the crowd was excited but they would have been supremely content with the mere chance to stare at one of those things in the first motorized parade ever through town. (The first automobile in Wetumka was an Auburn.)

Newspaper advertisements of the time pictured store-bought wagons in the same way automobiles would be advertised in a few years. The Herring Hardware store sold "The Bain Wagons, The Best on the Market." Meadors Brothers & Busey, competed with the Moline wagon and John Deer horse drawn implements. The largest wagon factory in Oklahoma was already in production in Dustin.

Drawings had been held for years in Wetumka and factory built wagons given away. It would be 1933 before the first new Ford automobile would be given away in a drawing.

By the summer of 1913, there were ten automobiles plying the unpaved streets of Wetumka and Clarence Pool enterprisingly started the first garage and service station by opening up the front of part of the "Wiggins Building" on Broadway.

Mr. Pool invited his customers to drive right into his building and he would happily fill their tanks from a gasoline drum. He stated: "I intend to make this a first class establishment in every respect. "I will be happy to check your oil and see to every mechanical detail of your automobile. "I will even put *wind* in your tires."

He was quick to realize that very soon in Wetumka, as in every other American town, the automobile would not only be regarded as a first class status symbol but quickly be a cornerstone in the local economy. The newspaper on March 31, 1916, published a survey of locally prominent men and their choice of transportation:

FORD—B. H. Harrison, Willie Buck, L. A. Woford, J. E. Tiger, J. F. Lucas, Walter Brooks, G. W. Turner, Dr. G. W. Patterson (2), Dr. Mitchell, Ed Mayfield, Jeff Jarrett, Ed Jarrett, H. H. Holman, J. M. Duncan, Rev. J. A. Kenny, J. H. Williams, Bert Sharp, Ed Browning, Frank Meadors, Charles Darks, Wm. Ryan, Dr. O. S. Burrows, Dr. Hemphill, H. M. Brazil, Geo. Appling, Dr. Gillie, B. B. Brownlee, Frank Stewart, and Jarrett Brothers, Ford Agency.

CHEVROLET—Dr. Vanderpool, Louis Dunzy, C. L. Brown, Dr. Hicks, and I. G. Berry, Chevrolet Agent.

DODGE BROTHERS—Carl Haubold and Captain Jack Herring, Dodge Agents.

STUDEBAKER—W. A. McCoy.

BUICK—Morris Bloom.

KRIT—Walker Jackson.

DORT—J. C. Richardson.

CADILLAC—Jess Poole.

GRANT—J. Ray Brown.

AUBURN—B. F. Scott.

OVERLAND—W. Farmer and Turner Meadors.

It is easy to see that doctors were among the most enthusiastic of the early car owners. The first two-car family in Wetumka was that of a doctor. Even the early cars were less temperamental than a horse. Horses, after all, didn't live many years. They had to be stabled as far as possible from the house because they dropped large amounts of excrement that had to be shoveled. A man could crank a car and be about his business in less time that it took to harness an unwilling horse to a buggy. And the car could be kept really close to the house.

Getting out of town in an automobile would remain a sporting proposition for several years. Getting people into town was absolutely vital and these doctors, lawyers and merchants were well aware of that.

Improving the outlying roads was a very high priority from the beginning.

Early bridges were timber brides and were restricted to streams that flowed most of the year. For decades the county could not afford very many culverts. The roads were simply graded through small creeks (at places called crossings). Farmers forded the streams or waited for the water to run off. The South Canadian River was not bridged until 1920. There had been a ferry there but every summer it was possible to ford the river. In 1909, James Shores, the aptly named operator of the ferry, was arrested for felling a tree to obstruct passage through the shallow part of the river.

In 1915 the businesses of town started closing on Tuesdays and at least a hundred men would go out to work the roads. In June that year a huge crew of men went out to work on Mountain Grove Hill (or Betts Hill) three miles north of town. This is the highest elevation in Hughes county (according to county surveyor Webb Fulks). The type of roadwork done by storekeepers and clerks was primitive but necessary. Drainage ditches had to be dug on both sides of the road. This dirt was piled up to elevate the roadbed. Sandstone and rocks were broken up to ease the way through deep puddles.

Rock outcroppings had to be blasted and chiseled down in order for the mail to get through. The first wagon bridge across the North Canadian River costs $500 and was borne by the Wetumka Commercial Club. Throughout the 1920's the Chamber of Commerce or the Commercial Club paid to have plank bridges maintained over some of the creeks.

What started out as a "semi-voluntary" roads day soon became a matter of law. In 1921 town council passed ordinance 162 that required that every able bodied male in town work on the roads for four eight-hour-days each year or be subject to a fine of $2.50 for each day he missed. The only exception was for those who had not lived in the county for thirty days or could prove they had worked in another county that year. (A person with a team of horses could fulfill his obligation in half the time.) The amount that a dirt road could be improved was limited because improvements washed away. The county commissioners did hot heartily appreciate the amateurish road work. One of them groused: "Now, let them pay their school tax by running the schools a few days each year."

The first steel bridge in the county was across the Wewoka Creek a mile east of The National Boarding School. This was in 1910 and the county provided the bridge and the Wetumka township agreed to construct the approaches. This was worked out informally. Public law limited how much the county could spend on one particular bridge. This would have limited construction to a "tinware bridge." With the city and county sharing the costs, a substantial and modern factory built steel bridge could be used to span the creek.

At the time this was an important route to Wetumka. It led to communities like Lone Star, Wisener, and Dustin. And the people were very proud of this public possession. For years civic groups, church organizations and others had outings, picnics and dances "at The Steel Bridge."

"Road Days" continued throughout most of the 1920s. Merchants closed up one day a week and a different approach road was worked on each week. The County Commissioner usually showed up and "made a hand."

On a typical day in 1921 businessmen "laid aside all business and gave a full day's hard work for the good roads cause." The roster of those who worked were always published. The merchants who were not up to the rigors of this kind of work were compelled to contribute a few dollars to the cause.

The list of those "making roads" was a virtual "who's who" in Wetumka. Ray Meadors, who customarily spent most of his time looking after the extensive Meadors land holdings, was always among the laborers. He was also a volunteer fireman and was very well respected by all. To this day you hear Wetumkans say: "I really liked "Ole Ray."

This was the era of the road boosters as well. Every town of conse-
quence, in the United States, had its own good-roads club. In late
1921, a half dozen men from Wetumka even participated in a booster
trip to Dallas.

They said some of the worst roads they encountered were in Hughes
county. They went through Calvin but the first car to join them was in
Allen. They felt they had made good time when they made it to Ada
before nightfall. In Ada they were well entertained and given rooms as
the Harris Hotel. The Ada Secretary of the Chamber of Commerce
and several others joined them. They said they had very good dirt roads
all the way into Madill. Once they got across the Red River they were
on an excellent Pike all the way into Dallas.

As long as the counties were trying to coordinate the best routes for
highways, the result was sheer chaos. Hughes county would mark its
portion of the Lincoln Highway (that really went nowhere) or later the
Cotton Belt Highway that was projected to reach all the way to Dallas.
This is why early development was uneven and largely determined by
the strength of the local good roads boosters.

The early good roads boosters had their counterparts in nearly every
other city and town in America. Even the railroads were strong supporters of the good roads movement as it would benefit their service
areas. The first roads were "opened" or authorized by the government.
It was usually up to the boosters to mark them. This was typically done
by painting boards or pieces of sheet metal with broad bands of paint
and nailing them to trees or fence posts.

This is a lesson soon taken to heart by the Federal Government. US
Highway 75 would transform Wetumka but it was painfully slow in
coming. Every town lobbied to get it through their town. Holdenville's
boosters were notably vigorous in their failing efforts to get Highway
75 routed through their town. Federal authority reigned supreme
because this is where most of the money came from.

Long before Highway 75 was paved it, was opened and gradually drained and then, little by little, graded. It was declared an "all weather road" several years before it was paved through Wetumka. Enthusiastic speakers visited Wetumka and proclaimed that the highway would be a Master Highway, the longest north-south highway in the United States: from Galveston, Texas, to Winnipeg, Canada. It was envisioned as a "three-track" road in railroad parlance. The two outside tracks would be restricted to cars because drivers could legally go thirty-five miles an hour throughout the 1930s. Loaded trucks would use the middle track and the top speed allowed would be eighteen miles per hour. (No one had ever really seen a functioning highway. And hadn't trains always had to stop for one another?)

Other than for its wars, the U. S. Government had never been involved in anything as expensive as paving roads. Every five miles could cost the equivalent of a new school building or a courthouse.

The techniques of road building were said to be improving with every mile of paving. When the highway came through Wetumka the procedures were still painfully primitive.

One five mile stretch of road in Hughes County, over a fairly unchallenging terrain, cost $66,272. The slabs were probably thicker than necessary and roadbed preparation was hardly an exact science.

While there were motorized concrete mixers, most of the work was still done at the site and the concrete was laboriously poured into long tracked wooden forms. (The cement was still delivered from the railroad in barrels.) Construction techniques required much steel reinforcement and the chemical make-up of the cement was still relatively primitive. It was necessary, according to the prevailing wisdom, to cover a finished segment of road with dirt to allow the concrete to cure slowly or it might soon crack or be brittle. (The engineering triumph during the time US 75 was being built was that the highways were crowned. This means the middle is higher to permit drainage.)

After the overburden of earth was scooped up or swept off, it was necessary to grout the huge cracks between the slabs with hot tar. US Highway 75 out of Wetumka was never a smooth ride.

While the new federal highway was under construction, travelers took the back road to Weleetka. To drive to Holdenville, it was necessary to detour through the Yeager oil fields.

Everyone has seen how highways are built today and there is a tendency to think it was always done in a similar way. Actually Highway 75 was paved in fitfully short segments.. In August, 1929, Highway 75 was completed from the Hughes-Okfuskee county line into Weleetka. The road out of Weleetka was a gravel road all the way to the "Y" which connected with the Henryetta-Okemah highway. (Dr. Robert Allen Rutland, Chairman of the History Department at the University of Virginia and author of many important works, spent his boyhood at Okemah. In his autobiography he joked: "Henryetta was not so far away, just a tank of gas and two flats.")

With the pavement ending just south of town and the many other unanticipated gaps that would confront a traveling party, the roads were still a great boon to Wetumka's economy. There were eight major gas stations inside Wetumka. The Chamber of Commerce had determined that the traffic was getting heavier and that on a typical day 400 out-of-town cars went through Wetumka.

While there had been only ten cars in Wetumka in 1909, within another ten years there were literally hundreds. Parking space was always scarce and drivers were allowed to park in long lines in the center of Main and Broadway. When the state decided to bring Highway 75 through Wetumka down Grand Avenue, the center of that street was also being used for as a parking lot. The State obliging built the highway a couple of feet wider on each side to accommodate this practice.

In 1936 a small tourist court of detached "cabins" was opened north of town just beyond the railroad overpass. There were about a half dozen units which were usually filled by nightfall, and also there was the inevitable gas station and tiny grocery store on the premises.

US Highway 66 was a well traveled road and as such it got priority treatment. Yet, there were many unpaved gaps within Oklahoma. In 1932, the Oklahoma highway system had a total of 6,971 miles. Only about a third (1,952 miles) had any pavement. Only about three hundred miles was of asphalt and there were even forty miles of brick highway.

The great problem in road building was that the economy was not performing well. It might have done better if good roads had been in place. A suitable system of financing had not been formulated. Federal Aid was the backbone of road funding but the state had to come up with matching funds. Most of this came from bond sales.

The genius of the post-World War II Interstate Highway System was that, while it was the most massive construction project ever undertaken by any government, it was a pay-as-you go proposition. The users of the system paid at the pump. No interest was ever paid on this system.

This was just not practical in the 1920's and 1930's. The national automobile fleet was still rather modest. And road construction was slow and prohibitively expensive. S. O. Maxey, who paved several segments of Highway 75 close to Wetumka stated that if the roadbed had been properly prepared, the weather held and all other factors were positive, his crews could complete a mile of pavement in six or seven working days. (This was absolutely astounding because paving at the time was like building a basement floor over the uneven landscape.)

State Highway 9 is a vast different story altogether. Although it was a much needed road, it would be worked on for over thirty years (sometimes by very large crews) before all of the gaps would finally be paved from Eufaula to Norman.

Highway 9 was intended to follow what was known as the "air line" road. In 1921 markers, visible from the air to aviators of the time, were placed in a line from Oklahoma City to Fort Smith to guide airmail pilots and others. Wetumka, itself, was a marker on this route. A huge name sign had been painted on the roof of the Billington Lumber Yard with arrows pointed to the landing site west of town.

In 1928, Senator Tom Anglin, who represented the area for a generation, persuaded the state highway commission to "open" the airline road. This road, "the University Highway" was first projected to run the entire distance across the state. Construction actually started in April of 1934. That month a large number of men and horses and one county road grader started work on the road from Wetumka to Dustin. The right-of-way engineers were designating the route. No one was paid for the right of way and the highway was originally planned to come through Wetumka on Tiger Street. But it was shifted a block south because that street was less built up.

If Highway 9 to Dustin was difficult, the part to the Seminole county line was nearly out of the question. People who tried to get through said it was like trying to drive a car through a muddy field.

It was toward the middle of 1938 before the road was made passable to the Seminole County line. The state had constructed two bridges in the area and the road was finally elevated to provide necessary drainage. On April 8, 1938, the newspaper editor visited the construction site. He reported there were approximately 100 WPA relief workers employed with "half a hundred" teams of horses and mules, and graders and tractors.

Actually the hills west of Wetumka were not graded down until well after World War II. In the early days of Highway 9, it was very difficult for motorists to ascend these steep grades in bad weather. The clouds of dust, thrown up by cars in the summer, reduced visibility to mere feet and nearly stifled people in their cars.

Hughes County was as hard hit by the Great Depression as any county in the United States. Hundreds (perhaps thousands) of men who had never experienced long term unemployment were thrown onto the relief rolls and were thereby eligible to perform public work 112 hours a month for their $32.

The New Deal's Works Projects Administration undertook the most widespread market roads improvement ever in Hughes County. Grants totaling several hundred thousand dollars enabled the county to extensively grade the roads taken by school buses and mail carriers. There were projects that were for "Indians Only" like the grading and gravelling of the roads throughout the Mission Bottom. This was thought to be an area of concern to the Indians because they still maintained a small chapel at the site of the former boarding school.

The Dustin to Weleetka market road was purely a WPA project. Work was carried on in all kinds of weather and when this road was ready for gravel the weather was in one of its worst phases. Trucks actually had to travel through Wetumka to Weleetka to gravel that end of the road. The route of that road was very different from what it is today. It crossed the railroad and connected with US 75 a mile north of the Hughes-Okfuskee county line.

In the summer of 1938 nearly $100,000 in Federal funds were made available for WPA road projects which were called "Farm to Market" road projects. In actuality, these were more like Market to Farm roads and each started from Wetumka.

At the time huge crews of WPA workers were assigned to improve the roads leading our of town. A project began at the northwest corner of town and went north to the Wetumka Lake and onto the county line.

From the same point northwest of the city the road which led to the Phillips Plant gasoline refinery was improved and graveled. A better route to Fairview was a priority. This road from Highway 75 three miles south of Wetumka was realigned and much improved to the Fairview schoolhouse.

The road leading to the Wetumka Cemetery was improved (with culverts for the first time) and some of the streets within the Cemetery were graded and graveled for the first time. The ten-mile long dirt road that ran in front of the cemetery was a major route between Wetumka and a community known as Big Prairie. It was much improved by the WPA.

Another crew was assigned to improve a four mile segment of the Horntown-Lamar road to Highway 75.

At the time the new two unit Armory was under construction the Roosevelt Administration approved the expenditure of $38,000 for the improvement of about 150 blocks of unpaved road within Wetumka and all of the alleys in the business district were finally graveled. This work on the residential streets of Wetumka cost more than the whole armory project which came in at $37,000.

Until after World War II, Hughes County could not afford the culverts and bridges that were needed. The Chamber of Commerce tried to occasionally re-floor some of the bridges across creeks to see that mail was delivered. The Chamber paid to move and rebuild a wagon bridge across the North Canadian River at about the time the State was building the highway bridge. It was important to keep the road open to the Gopher Hill community. In March of 1938, Herman Darks (state representative, post master, baker, etc. and future Mayor of Wetumka) was serving as a Deputy Sheriff of Hughes County. He and his partner were called out to see about a domestic disturbance in back of the Wewoka Creek. The water was rising at the "crossing" which was just a place built up with rocks and concrete. They got to the middle of the stream and the car drowned out. Mr. Darks went to call a wrecker and when he came back the car was nearly submerged. It was a couple of days before they could retrieve their water logged car.

11

The National Guard in Wetumka

The Oklahoma National Guard established two companies in Wetumka right after World War I. Their first deployment was in 1921 when a message came in to get 25 men together and proceed by train to Tulsa to assist the police in what is remembered as the largest race riot in American history.

The founding commanders were Charles C. Rice (a veteran of The Great War) who commanded Company "I" of the 179th Infantry Regiment and Captain D. J. Walther of Company "A" of the 120th Engineers. Wetumka was indeed fortunate to get two companies as the payroll would be a vital stimulus to the local economy during the Depression. (There was only one Engineers company in the state at this time.)

Within two years the two National Guard companies had enlisted about 175 men. In the early days the men trained with over 100 horses which were stabled locally. The men drilled on the streets of Wetumka and for ten years they did not have an adequate drill hall. The first armory was in rented space. It was a native rock building that stood across from the McIntosh Lumber yard and the Old Brick Hotel on West Broadway. The only permanent home the Wetumka companies ever had was the two unit armory that was constructed as a Works Projects Administration (WPA) project in 1935, next to the Central Ward School.

Starting in 1923 the annual encampment was at Fort Sill. The men were transported in a special train.

On June 3, 1924, Wetumka was devastated by a tornado. Seven people were killed outright and at least fifteen were seriously injured. Within twenty-five minutes, the men of the two National Guard companies were performing duties related to rescue and medical assistance. They remained on guard around the clock for two days.

The United States retreated into isolationism soon after The Great War Ended. Political leaders felt that a standing army was an open invitation to get involved in Europe's interminable quarrels. Yet, it was recognized that the country had to have some semblance of a military profession. From 1924 about 30,000 young people from all around the country trained at 28 "citizens' military training camps." The government paid the transportation costs and other expense for those selected. Each training session lasted a month in the summer. Those who were selected four years in a row could apply for an officer's commission in the Reserve Officers' Corps.

In early 1930 there was a shakeup in the command of the two companies. Thomas J. Davis, a former high school principal and the first Agriculture Teacher in Wetumka, was made captain of the Engineers. Lieutenant Robert D. Sheppard took command of the Infantry company. Sergeant Glenn Chowins (the future football coach and Wetumka High School principal) was commissioned second lieutenant.

Thomas J. Davis was a very prominent citizen of Wetumka and his advice was sought on practically every matter. He lived just a mile and a half south of Wetumka near the end of the Highway 75 pavement. As the Depression sank in, chicken thievery became more of a problem. Many of the people of Wetumka kept chickens in their yard and practically every farmer had a flock. There was a city ordinance passed to warn would-be thieves. Everyone bringing chickens to sell in town had to be personally known or had to have a proper bill of sale. Mr.

Davis raised Blue Ribbon Chickens. His neighbor, Elam Osborn, lost 45 pullets one night to thieves. Mr. Davis rigged up a lethal trap for anyone who might try to enter his chicken house. On January 2, 1929, a young Okmulgee man was killed by the discharge of a rifle when he attempted to enter the chicken house at the Davis residence. By 10 O'clock the next morning an inquest was held before Judge J. C. Laporte and a jury rendered the following findings: "That said John Doe came to his death on the night of January 2nd from effects of gunshot wounds inflicted in the chest of the deceased in a manner unknown and by a person or persons unknown to the jury, and unknown as to whether said wound was inflicted by accident or otherwise." Most Wetumkans could not sympathize with a chicken thief, yet, many of them did condemn the prevailing double standard which put a person of substance above the reach of the law. If the police had been interested, the full details of the matter were published in THE WETUMKA GAZETTE.

By 1935 the Engineer company making its summer camps at Camp Luna, near Las Vegas, New Mexico. Army transports arrived in Wetumka on Sunday. On the first day they reached a camping point near Oklahoma City. On the second night they camped at Amarillo, Texas and arrived at Camp Luna by the end of the third day.

The personnel of the Engineers were: Officers: Captain Thomas J. Davis, 1st Lieutenant Glenn Chowins, 2nd Lieutenant Edward W. George.Sergeants: Glenn Nichols, Monroe Landeth, Bill George, Clinton L. McCallie, Herbert Osborn, Willie Russell and Clarence Wilson.

Corporals-Lloyd E. Harmon, J. B. Paschal, Jack Rice, Earl Stuckey and John Ozment.

Privates First Class: Muriel Biggs, Baskin Bowman, Clifford Chastain, Hallie C. Clark, Coad Dilday, Thomas P. Dilbect, Armond Gibson, Robert Harmon, Hayes Heath, Frank McCoy, Irvin, Morrison, Wilburn Neese, Davis Roberts, Everette Sims, John Smith, Leldon L. Williams.

Privates: Bruce Barnes, Hubert Brochman, Harold Bolin, Roy A. Blankenbaker, Lewis Barnes, Dale Burris, Aubrey Carlton, Ora Clayton, Lewis J. Clark, Clarence Darnell, Harold Darks, Oliver Earl Elzy, Harry J. Gotts, Roy Halliburton, Harvey Hughes, Ira Lee, Leland Lelgerwood, Valas Mayhan, Raymond Marshal, Delbert H. Martin, Mike McCallie, Clyde N. Meadors, Jack P. Morris, Norman Ogletree, Castle Riley, Hiram T. Roberts, Morris Stanley, Glen White, Elzie White.

The Infantry Company was commanded by Bryan Nicks who was also, for several years, Postmaster in Wetumka. He and Captain Davis would command the local companies until they were mobilized for World War II.

The Infantry Company continued to train at Fort Sill. Captain Nicks was designated train commander as he was the senior officer aboard.

In 1936, these were the personnel of the Headquarters Company:

Officers: Bryan Nicks, Captain, Dixie G. Hall, 1st Lieutenant, Leroy Lambeth, 2nd Lieutenant.

Sergeants: Omer C. Bowman, Rufus J. Lucas, Roy R. Martin, Logan B. Walker, Wiley W. Woolverton.

Corporals: Louis W. England, Harold G. Flaughter, William W. Jackson and Woodrow W. Osborn.

Privates: William A. Brady, Charles A. Canard, Ethred L. Carlton, Arthur C. Clingman, Lee R. Cook, Ronald C. Duan, Everett B. Fuller, Mancho R. Herrera, Carl E. Hughes, James L. Pippen, Martin McLemore, Bert Shaber, Jr., Pete R. White, Wendell S. Wiggins, Charles E. Bowman.

Elzie A. Absher, Maurice D. Absher, Dean A. Baker, Rex T. Barrett, James K. Bennett, John B. Breedlove, Alva O. Books, Arthur J. Brown, Odell A. Burkes, Chester C. Carlton, Matthew J. Cherry, Lewis J. Clark, Jay G. Coachman, Lessel F. Crittendon, Halin J. Curry, Robert E. Ellison.

Donald B. Fisk, Edward M. Fuller, Roger L. Herndon, Olium R. Hollingsworth, Cloyce R. Hubbs, Quinton Hulstine, Ted Kelley, William F. Leake, Scottie J. London, Jake Marshall, Millard McElvany, Robert W. Meadors, John W. Smith, Elza Stuckey, Conivor R. Ward, Edward O. Webb, Calen C. Williams, Wm. F. Johnson.

The 45th Infantry Division was mobilized for a period of one year beginning in March of 1941. Wetumkans were among 10,500 Infantrymen who left Fort Sill on March 7 for Camp Barkley, near Abilene, Texas. It took a caravan of trucks sixty-six miles long to transport them. More than 19,000 Oklahomans would be in the mobilization. Congress had authorized the mobilization of four National Guard Divisions.(The newly selected Superintendent of Schools in Dustin was ordered into military service with the Guard.)

Soon after their arrival at Camp Barkley, The 45th Infantry Division received three train loads of new trucks. These are the vehicles they would take to the War in Europe.

On August 11, 1941, Wetumkans witnessed a military parade of the Second Cavalry Regiment from Fort Riley as trucks passed through Wetumka for three hours. The parade included rolling kitchens, supply trucks, trucks carrying horses, and squads of motorcycles. The most interesting vehicles were the new "little jeeps."

The deserted armory was turned into a peanut warehouse.

Following World War II, the National Guard was reorganized in Wetumka but there was only one understrength company: Company A, 180th Infantry Regiment. At about the time Wetumka was celebrating its first Sucker Day, the 45th Infantry Division was being mobilized as replacement troops in Korea.

By August of 1950, the men of "Able-Company" were drilling three times a week and a significant portion of them were performing guard duty and bivoacing at the armory. There were four officers and 55 enlisted members. (Actually, there were 26 sixteen-year-olds or men even younger who could be mobilized into service only with the written consent of their parents.)

Captain Paul Marshall had three lieutenants: Howard Nicks, Russel Ticer and Eddie Hodges. The roster of enlisted men was a veritable cross-section of Wetumka's manhood. The enlisted men were: Calvin Howarth, Forrest Poole, John G. Nicks, Glen Nichols, Tommy Kiser, Armand Gibson, Bill Rash, Bob Murray, Eugene Smith, Dale Wheat, Wiley Tate, Burkes Paul Sparks, George Bryant, Bennie Gooden, L. D. Dearman, Clarence McDowell, Bobby Meadors, Jack Smith, Amos King, Charles R. Smith, John Ed Hansford, Lyle Redding, Monroe L. Ray, Robert Montgomery, Carrol White, Charles Bryant, Evert Chastain, Donald W. Dyer, Denver Goswick, Joe Tom Bement, A. B. Clements, Jr., Elmer Shropshire, Jessie Basquez, Dick Ladlee, Dale Nolen, Thirl Hardcastle, Arlus Dyer, Richard Crowels, Leland Hensley, Eugene Tiger, Walter Bray, Glen D. Conley, Julie O. Gammill, Bert Hampton, Kenny L. Martin, Jack Spear, George Banta, Bobby Marsh, Robert Dilbeck, James Rogers, Clifford Carrigan, Kenneth May, Billy Watson, Kenneth Kelley, Jack Allen, Loyal Dyer and Houston Hill.

In a few weeks they had finished crating their supplies and equipment. Then, late one September evening, a special troop train stopped in Wetumka and the bulk of the company boarded. There are many people who still remember the mournful sound of the train's whistle as it traversed the crossings where silent groups of Wetumkans stood in awe and waved like it was World War I all over again. Most of them were convinced that some of the men would not return. But, according to my research, all of them did return. Several were hospitalized in Japan. Armand Gibson and some of his buddies told me about their Rest and Relaxation (R&R) leaves in Japan. The Wetumka company went into combat right at the end of the year and within about thirteen months, all of them had been rotated back home. (The American involvement in the Korean fighting actually did prove longer than than of the First World War.)

Lieutenant Howard Nicks became the Company Commander at a training camp on the Japanese island of Hokkaido and would lead his men in Korea. He was my first Company Commander of a reorganized National Guard in 1956. He had just been promoted to Captain. (Captain Nicks completed college and then opted to complete his career in the Regular Army. He retired as a Lieutenant Colonel. I am advised that he died at the age of 67.)

There was a very sad incident aboard the ships going from the Japan training base to Korea. The executive officer of the Headquarters Company from Holdenville, Lieutenant J. B. Loftis was killed in a gun accident aboard the ship enroute to Korea.

12

The Great Depression

The onset of The Great Depression, the sharpest and long lasting economic collapse in American history, can be pinpointed in Wetumka. There was a brief but severe recession in the national economy right after the first World War. American farmers had been feeding armies, our own and those of our Allies. The government had increased the money supply to expand the economy during the war. At the conclusion of the war, the United States went back to the "sacred gold standard." Farmers could not find markets for their produce.

This happened at the time the population was increasing rapidly. In the 1920s, farmers around Wetumka experienced really hard times. The next ten years, thought of as the depression, were an extension of the hard times of the twenties which seemed to worsen every year.

In places like Wetumka the problem was "structural" or built into the economic system. Farm tenancy is a cruel and brutal system. Tenant farmers worked over 70% of the land in Hughes County and every county in eastern Oklahoma. There were too many farmers and not enough farms. It was the tenant farmer who pledged everything he owned to get a bank loan of $80 or $100 to purchase the essential seed and fertilizer. (The interest rate was usually 10% for ten months) The bank took a listing of all he had acquired, from the team of horses he worked every day, their harness, to every cow and every rusty farming implement he possessed.

As the depression deepened it became a family crisis in every farming household. Because of the overproduction, the poor prices paid at the cotton gins, the bowl weevil, hail storms, droughts and floods, it became difficult to stay in farming. It was almost impossible to get out. Farm sales did take place but there would be a bank representative to see that an outstanding loan was taken care of before any mortgaged property changed hands.

This was a severe problem for a town like Wetumka that prided itself on being a farming community. The pain and suffering was quickly passed up the economic ladder. There was a consensus that farmers had to "get out of cotton." The only thing wrong with fifteen cent cotton was that in the 1920s, prices for all the essentials the farmer needed for a bare existence continued to rise.

In a larger sense, the first World War had only interrupted a downward spiral in the farmer's purchasing power. A government report stated that in 1909, an acre of corn would buy 79 pounds of coffee, but only 59 in 1913. Just one acre of cotton would afford a farmer twenty-seven pairs of 98-cent overalls. By 1913, the purchasing power of the farmer had dropped to 24 pairs. The price parity index for farmers just got a lot worse.

Farmers could market their corn in the 1920s. Within a few years there were no buyers for corn although the Wetumka Chamber of Commerce scouted far and wide. The "ginning fee" or the difference in what the farmer got and the gin owners got was never less than two to one. The Oklahoma Corporation Commission sued the ginning associations, repeated, with poor results. Lawyers for the gin associations contended that they were in a capital intensive industry and the wholesale markets in Memphis and Galveston fluctuated wildly.

The farmers did experiment with other cash crops. They shipped carloads of cantaloupes to Omaha, Nebraska and hundreds of bushels of graded potatoes to eastern markets. The experiments did not yield much income because these shipments were consignments to a faraway produce marketer. Freight rates were on the rise throughout the Depression years.

The strain reached everyone in Wetumka. Both the American and the First National Banks showed strong balance sheets, but in a business sense, they were not profitable in their market. The American National Bank eventually moved its operation to Wewoka. The First National consolidated with the Bank of Commerce. (A Tulsa Bank actually came to the rescue and bought a large block of the bank's stock) The empty bank buildings were not vacant for very long. A lot of new businesses were started in the Depression; self-employment seemed the only alternative to unemployment. The former bank buildings became cafes in short order. There were already at least a dozen cafes in or near Wetumka.

Business optimism never completely failed. January 1930, was typically a cold and rainy month. In that month the WETUMKA CHEESE factory went into operation. It occupied a well situated two story stucco building, a hundred yards from the railroad. Mr. H. N. Bancroft moved to Wetumka to manage the new plant. He was said to be experienced and successful in his line. He installed all new equipment in the Wetumka facility. At the beginning, over a thousand pounds of fresh milk was being brought daily. The plant had been designed to handle a capacity twenty times that. It was reported that very soon the cheese factory would reach the production level that would enable the new firm to establish routes and pick up milk daily from the outlying farms.

Everyone was encouraged to buy WETUMKA CHEESE. The plant's appearance in Wetumka had taken most people by surprise. Its sudden closing within a few weeks was just as mysterious and unexplained. Within a few months the operation was up and running again with new management. This time the product was labeled OKLAHOMA CHEESE. The second venture was also very brief. Within a short time the plant was stripped of its equipment to satisfy creditors.

The Jarrett Ford filling station had been in business at Main and St. Louis for over fifteen years when there was a disastrous daytime fire. Carlos Garrett was tuning an engine when it backfired and caught the gasoline and oil saturated floor afire. The loss was total.

Mr. Jarrett had already acquired another Ford franchise in Tulsa at 809 South Main Street. He sold the ruins of his Wetumka business to Nathan Lee. Mr. Lee then transferred his dry goods store to a fellow immigrant, Sam Kolodny. Mr. Lee had plenty of business backing because no one locally doubted his business acumen. The personal biography of Nathan Lee is an inspirational "rags to riches" story. As a young man, he immigrated from a part of Russia where Jews had been persecuted and massacred for centuries. He spent three weeks in transit and wound up alone in Wetumka tattered and penniless. In the early years he earned a business stake by peddling bananas and other tropical fruits on the streets of Wetumka. By the 1920s, his social prominence had risen and he married Rosa Bloom, the widow of a dry goods store owner. He remodeled the store into one of the most attractive in town with huge glass windows (a novelty for the time). He rebuilt the Ford garage in 1930 when conditions looked the darkest. Within a few years he could claim in his newspaper advertisements that he'd been in business longer than any dealer in Hughes County. Mr. Lee also owned other property in Wetumka, had interests in oil leases and was a major investor in a hotel in Shawnee. His shop foreman, Carlos Garret who had burned down the original building, succeeded him as the Wetumka Ford Dealer in the early 1950s.

The Lee Motor Company was extensively remodeled and expanded before May of 1931. No Wetumka business ever had a "grand opening" amid such publicity. The Ford Zone manager and other officials were present. The entire building had been emptied out and several hundred folding chairs grouped around a small movie screen. Talking pictures had reached Wetumka earlier that year and everyone thought the sound quality and synchronization was very poor. The Ford promotional films and the portable equipment was of a much higher quality.

Talking motion pictures were shown for the first time in Wetumka in 1930. The first "talkie" was Will Rogers starring in "They Had To See Paris." One observer attended this movie and said it was very unsatisfactory. The "horn" or speaker was too loud and the sound was out of synchronization with the picture. It was very difficult to follow. The first sound tracks had been records and the projectionist could never keep them aligned with the action on the screen.

Enthusiastic crowds waited in line for hours for their turn to see what the Ford factories looked like and how a Ford got to be a Ford. But it was the newness of the motion pictures that amazed them. The most devoutly religious Wetumkans would not taint themselves by entering a motion picture theatre. This was an opportunity savor the miracle of motion pictures in a neutral setting.

In two days, it was estimated at the time, 2,000 people were treated to the show and given small gifts. The finale came on Saturday night when an orchestra from Shawnee played for a dance.

In January, 1932 Henry Bowles opened his store and it became a local legend: Bowles Cash Grocery.

It was a prime example of an integrated business. He operated his own farm and raised cattle and hogs that he and his helper butchered for their own meat counter. His helper, on the farm and at the store was known only as "Jimmie." He was a handicapped man who seemed to do the work of two men just to drag himself around.

The Chamber of Commerce tried to cope with the continuing disaster by distributing garden seeds so the most needy families could grow vegetables for their own table. The merchants of Wetumka even experimented with issuing their own currency to men whose families were thought to be suffering the most. Mayor Ben Harrison hatched this idea of issuing script to pay men to work on the city streets. Each merchant who handled the script would add his stamp until it had been stamped fifty times and then it was taken out of circulation. At one time there was over over $900 in these "Wetumka Half-Dollars" in circulation.

Also, in January 1932, another hardware and furniture store was opened by a man Wetumkans remember well, Mr. G. Laswell. He leased space in the Meadors building on North Main.

Before Roosevelt was sworn in the situation in Wetumka and Hughes county was recognized to be as dire as the aftermath of the tornado that hit Wetumka in 1924. The pain, danger and panic reached into nearly every household. In March 1933, just five days after Roosevelt became president, an emergency shipment of flour arrived at Holdenville. It was four rail cars or 172,800 pounds and was distributed to the neediest.

It should be emphasized here that the people of Wetumka recognized that the national and local emergency was not a crisis of production. It was simply a crisis of distribution. The economy had failed. Farmers were frantically growing more than they ever had and there were enormous surpluses in practically every farm commodity.

The flour that was given away in Hughes county was shipped directly from Chicago. A year earlier the US government had purchased huge stocks of wheat in a dismal effort to stabilize that market. There was no recourse to milling these bulging warehouses into flour and consigning it to the American Red Cross.

The Depression did not bottom out in 1932. The economy, for most people in Hughes county who were farmers, just continued to collapse.

There was other events that year. The Lee Motor Company received the first Ford V-8 in Hughes county and it was quickly sold by their salesman who was a well known man by the name of Jack Bloom.

In July, Jim Ragland, a teacher at Gerty, defeated the incumbent County Superintendent of Schools by over a thousand votes. The

Wetumka Junior College was doing very well with new courses in Spanish, French and Science. (Miss Mary Dickinson, of Norman, was the foreign language instructor. She married George Williams and they were the last generation of operators of The Coin Store.) The City of Wetumka even bought a new Chevrolet fire truck that year.

No greater contrast between wealth and poverty was ever demonstrated in Hughes County than in the palace which was under construction in 1932 at the Northeast entrance of Wetumka. It was located just beyond the city limits in an area opened up by the new Highway 75.

It took nearly three years to complete this palatial estate on fourteen acres that were mowed and landscaped with rare trees and shrubs. The owners were a reclusive couple, Mr. and Mrs. Terry Walker, and were known to the people of Wetumka as simply "wealthy Indians."

The home consisted of twelve rooms in the Old Spanish style of architecture and was built of rough clincher brick which had been specially formulated for that job. It had a huge reception hall and every room was decorated in a special theme. The master bedroom was "draped with gold and purple Sicilian satin with Tuscan netglass curtains with a Mohawk Wilton rug floor covering, furnished with a six-piece modernistic bed room suite."

The house had its own huge tiled swimming pool and there was a large sunken garden nearby. The architectural theme was carried over into the double car garage and servants quarters. The generous driveway was winding and nearly as wide as Highway 75. The entire property was ringed by a high security fence. It was of a chain-link design and of very heavy materials and had highly ornamented posts.

The house was built over a full basement the housed a furnace for a new type of steam heating. The rest of the basement was a recreational room with expensive pool tables.

No one in Wetumka could realistically speculate about the happiness of the reclusive couple who lived so quietly in their mansion. Some time before 1937 they were divorced and Mrs. Walker married Frank Autry.

In the early hours of January 15, 1937, the house caught fire. The loss was total because it took a few minutes for the volunteer fire department to assemble. They were handicapped by the location of the house which was just outside the city limits and far from a fire hydrant.

The loss of the house was total but Mr. and Mrs. Autrey, their two boys and six high school students who were house guests that night managed to get out safely. The house and its elaborate furnishings were lost along with a valuable collection of Indian artifacts. (The house alone cost $35,000. With the grounds it would cost over $1 million to duplicate in contemporary terms.)

Everyone agreed that it had been a grand house even if it looked grossly out of scale for Wetumka. It was never stated if there was adequate insurance. The brick walls were hastily cleared away but the Autrys seem to have closed the massive gates and forever abandoned the property. Far many years passing motorists stared at the ghostly site and wondered what had stood there. The servants' quarters and garage were neglected until the early 1950s. Leonard Bryan, the barber, moved his family in for a few years. The site did eventually become one of the most desirable building locations in the area when Mr. Bill Love, the Rexall Druggist built his home (the first of several) at the edge of the former palatial estate.

School enrollment held steady. By the end of the thirties Wetumka was graduating more than forty seniors each year and there was the beginning of a gender balance. Until the depression it had been difficult to persuade a boy that education was relevant to his presumed occupation of farmer or tradesman. The feeling was that the sooner he got started raising livestock and working his own little piece of ground or apprenticing in a trade, the sooner he could validate himself as a man. It is worth noting that the term "teenager" was not even used until the era of World War II. Until that time a young man could be defined as any who had not reached middle age.

In the years before World War I the merchants of Wetumka had held trades day on Saturday and awarded premiums. One merchant would give a set of dishes to the largest family. There was always a special prize for the shortest married woman. Barbershops would offer a free haircut to the man who had the longest hair. The Coin Store would reward the man who had pulled a split-log road drag the longest distance to town. Another merchant would have a premium for the most people who came to town in one wagon. They had even had drawings to give away new factory made wagons.

This practices was revived in 1933 as a community morale booster. On January 5, 1933, a new Ford automobile was given away in a drawing at Main and Broadway. It was a standing-room-only crowd that stretched to the edge of the business district.

Nathan Lee was chairman of the committee of the Chamber of Commerce which took responsibility in this matter. (His dealership had provided the car.) At the appointed hour he selected Elam Osborn, a farmer and dairyman who lived two miles south of town when Highway 75 ended. Mr. Osborn selected a group of advisers and among them they those chose a young girl to be blindfolded and to reach into the hopper, which had been turned and churned so many times. They chose Miss Geneva to the honors. She drew the name of Sulkey Bird. This turned out to be a very needy person who had never owned a car.

This event is memorable. Miss Geneva would always be Miss Geneva: Miss Geneva Scott. She would finish high school in Wetumka and attend the teachers' college at Ada and the University of Oklahoma and endear herself as a social studies teacher to generations of junior high and high school students in Wetumka.

The year, 1933, was as dismal as any year of the depression in Wetumka. The Chevrolet Dealer declared bankruptcy before the year was out. It re-opened as Meadors Chevrolet. The Old Brick Hotel closed again.

There were three bus lines which made a combined total of nine stops in Wetumka daily. These were the Union, Pickwick and Greyhound. On some days there would five passenger trains that could take passengers in either direction.

Highway 75 was hailed as an "all weather road" from Galveston, Texas to Winnipeg, Canada. Mr. Melton, the Secretary of the Wetumka Chamber of Commerce, had joined a calvacade of boosters who traveled the whole distance of 3,500. He left posters and literature extolling the virtues of Wetumka at every stop.

This highway still had many gaps. It reverted to gravel just beyond Calvin. It stretched 272 miles in 1933 through Oklahoma. Only 178 miles had been paved.

At the beginning of 1934, more than half the warrants issued to teachers in Oklahoma during the year 1931-32 were still unpaid. The Wetumka school board had already announced that its resources would only afford a term of 4 1/2 months. The Federal government would ultimately pick up the tab for four months of teachers' salaries. The school district was given fifteen cents per day for each Indian student. The grant made it possible to hire two additional teachers. One of them ran a nursery school, a first for Wetumka. The other gave commercial courses at night for adults.

Central school had been completely destroyed by an unexplained fire early on New Year's day. By April a federal grant had been obtained and 40 to 50 men, selected from the drought relief rolls, were on the job of cleaning and stacking bricks and clearing away the refuge. Another crew built 200 yards of sidewalk at the high school and 100 yards at the Separate School. The tennis courts at the high school were built during this period.

On May 9, 1934, the American National Bank, in Wetumka, was robbed of $1500 and three employees taken hostage. They were handled roughly and thrown out of a car a mile from town.

The author's sixth grade teacher, her husband and a neighboring farmer were briefly held for questioning by law enforcement authorities. Evidently, the robbers had spent the night with them. These unfortunate people probably did not know about the crime. At any rate, they were never charged as accessories and were released shortly. The robbers were apprehended later in Oklahoma City.

Also, in 1934 the largest manufacturing facility ever in Wetumka was started by Archie Stout of the Stout-Walker Funeral Home. It was a casket factory that operated in a building on Main Street. Their line was moderately priced caskets (starting at $50) and vaults and their initial customers were funeral homes in the area. Within a year Mr. Stout had disposed of the business to two area automobile mechanics. They cranked up production and widened their marketing area. At their peak they were shipping 600 caskets a year. The Gazetteer, a reference work in Wetumka High School Library while the author was a student there listed Wetumka as a "Center of Casket Manufacturing." The Casket factory had ceased operations before the end of the decade.

It was revived very briefly by another New Deal program, The National Youth Administration (NYA) which provided modest work opportunities for needy youth of high school and junior college age. They constructed a few caskets each week for the County for pauper burials.

13

More Hard Times In The Great Depression

Will Rogers' famous quip about America going to the poorhouse in an automobile is apt in describing the lives of Wetumkans in the 1930s. The automobile developed as mass transit in the years Wetumka was realizing its ultimate size. Cars were a curiosity for only a short time. They became a personal necessity, a cornerstone of the local and national economy and an object for which the pride of ownership has seldom been equaled. They were also more deadly than anyone could have imagined.

Oklahoma did not have a Highway Patrol until 1937. In the preceding dozen years, there were more people killed, for the miles driven than during any comparable period, in American life. Statistics were not kept until 1928 and by then Oklahoma's experience was similar to that of the other states. It was estimated that 25,000 people were being killed in car accidents annually in the United States and that 70% of these were pedestrians.

The switch from a horse drawn to a motorized vehicle was not an easy transition for this generation. In July of 1930, Jack Murphy, of Murphy Tailors and Cleaners, panicked and allowed his delivery vehicle to go out of control on Main Street. He jumped the curb and headed down the sidewalk scraping the side of the First National Bank building and knocking down two men in conversation with their backs turned. He had one foot planted firmly on the brake pedal and the other on the accelerator. People at the scene said that during this time he was pulling back on the steering wheel and yelling at his machine like it was a runaway team of horses. He would have continued his path of mayhem and destruction if a concerned citizen had not jumped onto the running board and reached in to switch off the ignition. (The men knocked to the sidewalk were Nathan Lee and a Mr. Foster. They both required medical attention. Nathan Lee sustained a broken ankle.)

In the same year, a local farmer was strutting down Highway 75 south of town. The traffic was very light. The news accounts said "they had the highway to themselves." Yet, they were unable to avoid each other. The farmer, a father of eight, was run down and killed. To cap the irony, the coroner ruled that it had been "an unavoidable accident."

In the Age of The Automobile, people only slowly began to grasp the fact that accidents are not necessarily "an act of God." The speed limit on the highway was 35 miles per hour. The local Justice of The Peace, J. C. Laporte stated that he had never fined anyone unless he was convinced they were going fifty. (Speeding in an automobile at the time was called "scorching.") Stop signs were not even taken as suggestions. A group of citizens counted fifty cars that passed the stop sign at Main and St. Louis. Only two of them even slowed down. A motorist stopped to allow a passenger to alight and another to talk with another driver.

The police department had high school students hand out leaflets to offending motorists. They announced they would begin issuing court summons to lawbreakers. On the first day ten people were fined $1 with no court costs. The same person was fined twice in the same day.

Nathan Lee said that he averaged selling 10 to 15 new Fords each month in the Depression. He rarely had a used car to sell. Used cars were usually sold in private arrangements and some cars changed hands often.

By the summer of 1934 the Wetumka Lake had "settled" and it was clear enough for a second attempt to stock with fish. By this time the oil companies had mended their ways, somewhat, and fish had returned to the river as well. On June 1, 1934, Dr. C. A. Hicks who was one the first person to keep a motor boat at the lake, was offering rides to anyone in the crowd who felt brave enough to cross the lake. That day he made numerous trips across the lake. On the last trip he took on several children and young people. It was a large boat and was probably not overloaded. When the boat was within twenty yards of the shore, some of the kids stood up and caused the boat to capsize.

Horrified observers watched Dr. Hicks go completely out of sight. He finally did come up thrashing and grasped a long bamboo pole that had been extended to him from the bank. Fred Moore, a local grocery store employee and meat cutter, was the hero of the day. He swam out to the boat and uprighted it. Then he was able to help the children back into it and get them ashore. Dr. Hicks had to be transported to the hospital by ambulance. He had nearly drowned.

The Wetumka Lake road was very primitive until 1935 when thirty-three men were employed to improve it. Until this time there had been no culverts. Until that 1935 the lake access had been a road south of the golf course past the "fire boy's hut."

Technology was on the march in Wetumka, even in 1936. That year Wetumka got its first steel bodied school bus. It was purchased by the school district from Fleming Chevrolet and leased to its driver, J.

A. Cowan. From this time school groups had the option of not waiting for a train to attend out of town activities.

Also, in 1936 Lee Motor Company, with its Phillips 66 gas station, installed the first electric gas pump that automatically computed the amount of gas going into the tank.

Strictly speaking, Wetumka was not squarely in the Dust Bowl. But dust bowl conditions certainly did exist and wind erosion was severe. It was remarked that a barbed wire fence could catch so much dust that cattle could walk these dunes right over the wire.

The people of Wetumka thought their situation was as bad as it was anywhere. On April 12, 1935, a big "duster" blew into town. By 3:00 O'clock in the afternoon the howling winds were depositing huge quantities of dust on Wetumka. By 6:00 O'clock visibility was reduced to practically nothing. People who lived through it, said they could not distinguish a landmark less than a block away. Merchants closed their stores and went home. The business district of town was eerily deserted.

Wetumka was led by a pack of "incurable optimists" who thought things could only get better. In the summer of 1935, H. H. Darks, a pioneer Wetumkan who had been a lawyer, county judge and civic booster acquired 50,000 bricks at a bargain in Weleetka. He didn't know what he might do with them. But he always recognized a bargain.

He used the bricks to build a seven room bungalow a mile south of Wetumka

The 1930s was a long decade of unprecedented suffering. But business optimism was never extinguished. H. H. Darks was slow to give up on the dream of an ever expanding Wetumka. He had an opportunity to purchase a huge quantity of bricks in a bankruptcy in Weleetka. He didn't know just what he might do with them but he certainly knew a bargain. He used them to construct a new bungalow home for his family at the place he confidently predicted would soon be the suburbs of Wetumka. (He didn't have electrical service, yet, so he used a gasoline powered pump to keep his own water tower supplied.)

The elegant house he had built (still occupied) was at the Highway 75 curve a mile south of town. Since Mr. Darks had a huge quantity of bricks left over and being a real estate developer, he built a new store building on the premises of his six acre estate. This building was occupied by Chapman's Country Store. It was a very well stocked grocery store. The store was lost to a well publicized fire in the early 1940s. (Mr. Darks sold this home and built another two story home before World War II for his family in the 500 block of East Broadway.)

In 1935 a Civilian Conservation Corps camp was constructed on the northern outskirts of Wetumka on the former Mingo farm. It was one of just three segregated camps in Oklahoma for Colored Boys. (The CCC program was one of President Roosevelt's pet projects and he'd gotten authorization for it in his first 100 days.) There were only three segregated camps in Oklahoma and this was thought to be the largest. (The other two were located at Boley and at Konawa.) The City of Wetumka extended electrical service and a huge steel septic tank was brought in. During the time it was under construction, there were rumors that it would be soon be shut down. Actually, the camp at Wewoka was closed before it was finished and the buildings were dismantled and hauled to Wetumka. The camp would consist of seven buildings that were painted forest green and the grounds were very well landscaped by the enrollees.

About fifty carpenters worked overtime to get the camp ready. They were finished in a short time because the walls and other components had been prefabricated in factories. The government was building hundreds of these camps around the country.

While it was an all-Black operation, the officers and the camp doctor were White. Wetumkan, Burl Sanders, was appointed Camp Commander. And while Roosevelt had insisted that the camps be civilian organizations, in practice most of the supervisors were former military officers. The Wetumka location was the only Civilian Conservation Corps camp in Hughes county.

These "C-C-C" boys were fairly well equipped with trucks and tractors and they built hundreds of miles of badly needed farm terraces. They also built farm ponds.

One of the primary missions of the Wetumka C-C-C camp was to harvest hundreds of pounds of seeds of native grass and trees each fall which were used locally and throughout the West. The Wetumka boys re-seeded 333 acres of gullied land and returned it to pasture. They re-sodded 350 miles of pasture contour ridges. They planted windbreaks to reverse some of the effects of poor farming practices. They planted 173, 589 trees in the Wetumka district.

The color barrier was rarely relaxed during the Depression. It was apparent that Wetumka's C-C-C boys had few recreational or social outlets. Arrangements were made in November of 1935, to close the Nusho Theatre to all but these lads on Thursday evenings. They also had dances in the new armory.

The green buildings were vacant only briefly after the program was closed down in 1943. The camp had been mentioned as a likely detention center for Japanese-Americans forcibly relocated from their homes on the West Coast which was declared a Defense Zone in World War

II. This did not happen. The only other official use for the camp was as a barracks for German POWs during the war. After the Normandy invasion the United States took large numbers of German prisoners (including over 100 German generals). No suitable housing was available in Europe. There were large numbers of cargo ships returning empty. It was decided that these prisoners could best be transported to the United States and kept until the end of the war. There were 401 German prisoners of war at the Wetumka camp before the war's end. These unfortunates had been wounded or suffered severe privations of war and all of them were convalescing patients from a hospital at Okmulgee. Farmers were always desperate for help in the harvests. Most of the prisoners were pressed into service on the farms around Wetumka. They were delivered to farms in trucks and worked until mid-afternoon. They had to be back in camp by early afternoon because of medical necessity. The author has memories some of these poor wretches who on his grandfather's farm behind the Wetumka lake. They were only lightly guarded and one of them acted as their foreman. At the end of World War II the buildings were sold as government surplus. A couple of them were moved and converted into residences. One became a laundry building. One of them was moved onto the high school grounds. It was repainted white and used as the FFA building.

The white youth of Wetumka had the option of joining the CCC movement and several of them did. Forty-one Wetumka boys were selected in 1935. They departed from Wetumka on August 16 for Wilburton where a final examination would be given. (The physical usually consisted of determining if the boy had enough upper and lower teeth left to take solid food.) From Wilburton, they were assigned to various CCC camps in Oklahoma and throughout the western states. Some of the went to Nebraska. Those unfortunates that winter slept in tent cities on mattresses on the ground at an elevation of 8600. They wrote home of using seven blankets as a defense against frostbite.

There were numerous New Deal programs, aimed bettering the condition of the people and getting the economy to moving again, reached their largest extent in Roosevelt's second term after 1936. One of the noticeable monuments of those days is the drainage ditches in Wetumka. These rock-lined ditches, with their retaining walls, "tied-together with cement," were constructed by huge crews of men with very few tools. The rock was quarried from a farm just south of town and cut into exact sizes. Their stated purpose was to make sure there was no standing water where mosquitoes could breed. They were officially called malaria control projects.

The two-unit armory in Wetumka was identical with those in Holdenville and Wewoka, with a few minor trim differences. It was almost cancelled before it began. These massive projects did not meet the criteria of being labor absorbing endeavors because it required a considerable number of skilled workers. The citizens of Wetumka did all they could to get this underway before it could be cancelled. When it was learned that additional land would be needed, Charley Nichols rushed to Oklahoma City with a deed for additional land that was donated by the city and property owners nearby. Captain Bryan Nicks had requested that the entire armory be built of native stone because this would employ more people. He was overruled by his National Guard superiors. It was to be constructed of brick manufactured at the state penitentiary at McAlester.

The Oklahoma National Guard furnished the materials. In actuality, this was another state agency that got its funding from the Federal Government. The Wetumka school district had built the main wing of Central School with a tax increase and with a federal grant. The primary wing, or that wing which faces south, was a WPA project and the men hired were "drought relief clients." The nearby armory and this part of the school were under construction at the same time.

The Wetumka High School was destroyed by fire in the night of October 28, 1938. (See "Education" part for a complete description.) The school and its contents were well covered by insurance. Within sixty days, with the help of Congressman Lyle H. Boren, the school district had received a WPA commitment furnish the labor to rebuild the high school. The architect designed a building that would receive statewide and even some national mention.

The old building was torn down by WPA crews and every brick that could be salvaged was kept for the new building. Most of the inner walls were constructed of bricks from the first building. A considerable quantity of new buff colored bricks and ten-tons of steel were acquired for the building. No contractor was allowed on a WPA project; Mr. Leath, who had overseen the construction of the armory was the building superintendent at the new high school project.

The projected cost for the high school, auditorium and gymnasium was $108,000. WPA auditors kept a close watch on every possible expenditure and the project came in under budget at about $95,000. At this point the WPA scaled back its support. The Wetumka School District finished the project with about $5,000 in debt. The first graduating class of seniors was in 1940. The Depression had not lessened; everyone was still experiencing hard times. And although the teachers were obliged to work the last week of the school year without pay, nearly all of the building debt was retired before the term was over.

Several WPA projects improved the Wetumka Cemetery and its approach road. The four foot high rock wall in front was constructed with WPA labor. The main streets were graded and graveled. Before 1938, the cemetery chapel had been completed. Then it was decided that the cemetery should be landscaped and irrigated. George Williams, of The Coin Store, was chairman of this Committee.

It was a daunting problem. It was too far from town to install electrical lines. The solution finally decided upon was to drill a deep well and build a cylindrical water tower that would hold three hundred barrels of water. A gasoline pump would fill this circular tower and there would be a gravity flow of water through pipes throughout the cemetery.

The cemetery chapel quickly fell into disuse because the windows were often broken out by vandals. It quickly reverted to a tool shed. The irrigation scheme was never fully realized either.

The WPA was a factor in the life of nearly every Wetumkan in one way or another. There was a fifteen acre WPA garden that grew fruits and vegetables for school lunches. There were special classes for illiterate adults and the WPA provided professional correspondence courses. There was even a WPA fiddle band in Wetumka. The men who tried out for the fiddle band were required to practice five hours daily, six days per week. For this they were paid fifty cents an hour. After a few weeks they began to make goodwill visits to outlying communities. In 1940, the Wetumka fiddle band went to a convention at Shawnee and played in the WPA orchestra. (The Wetumka fiddle band was a quintet of old-time fiddlers: George Cato, Charles C. Lovell, Leon Jackson, Arvel C. Hobbs and Grover C. Hobbs).

Over 750 sanitary facilities (as outdoor toilets were euphemistically called) were constructed by WPA crews. (Indoor plumbing was still far into the future for many people in Wetumka at the time.) They could obtain one of these professionally designed units for $5. Or one could be custom built on their property.

Women who were unemployed heads of households were also eligible to be WPA workers. They had to put in 112 hours a month for their $32. In Wetumka they worked in the "Ladies Sewing Room" and produced hundreds of garments for distribution to the needy. (In January, 1938, one-thousand suits of clothing were distributed to needy children in Hughes County. According to the County Superintendent, Jim Ragland, this was about a third of the actual need. The clothing came from the WPA workshops and from the prison industries at McAlester. The women of the WPA Sewing Room also assisted in canning thousands of jars of fruits and vegetables for the school lunch program.

The National Youth Administration (NYA) was the youth component of the WPA. Its purpose was to provide employment for unmarried young people between the ages of 17 and 25. At first these young people did odd jobs at the schools. (Many of them were trying to earn their keep and pay the $75 per semester tuition at the Wetumka Junior College). There was a WPA bookmobile operated by these young people.

Before the end of the decade the "Old Mingo" school had been taken out of service. It was razed to the ground by NYA enrollees and rebuilt as a dormitory. They NYA tried to provide something of a social life for its participants. (That's why the dance floor was constructed at the dormitory) At the dormitory in Wetumka there was room for 25 boys and 25 girls and each group was very strictly supervised.

The Roosevelt Administration, and everyone else in the country was keenly aware that parental authority had broken down in countless households during the hard times of the Depression. Rebellious youth were turned out as families could not provide for them. Hundreds of thousands of them took to riding the rails. This was a dangerous way of life. (Two young hobos had shown up August of 1923 at a Wetumka restaurant just as the proprietor was closing. They proclaimed that they had not eaten in recent memory. He fixed them a hasty meal and they were on their way. They were seen clinging to a ladder on the side of a boxcar. A mile from town their bodies were found along the tracks in a horribly mangled condition. Dr. Fred Hicks, who was the railroad physician, pronounced one of them dead and said the other would be dead in a short time.)

The NYA was keen to the heart of Eleanor Roosevelt who traveled extensively for the president. It was difficult for him to leave the White House because he had never been able to walk after being stricken with polio in 1921. Wetumka was at the head of Eleanor Roosevelts travel agenda when she came to Oklahoma in the summer of 1938. She had heard of the Home Economics Cottage that had been constructed in "crazy stone" fashion by NYA boys and girls. (Townspeople who traveled customarily brought back rocks as souvenirs of their trips. Some of these were donated for this project and this small building contains rocks from most of the Western States.) As it turned out, Mrs. Roosevelt was thrown off schedule. She called from Bristow with her regrets. She was simply too far behind and too weary to come to Wetumka.

No group of Wetumkans were harder hit by the Depression than the first Oklahomans, the Indians. There were WPA projects especially for Indians. This is how the roads through the Mission Bottom were finally graveled. They still used a chapel at the site of the former National Boarding School.

A good many people were outraged by the low state to which the Indians had fallen. They petitioned the "Indian Service" to do something. And the Department of the Interior responded. The unfailing government was dedication to turning the Indians into farmers. No alternatives could be visualized. Seven miles north of Wetumka, the Indian service acquired a "Rehabilitation Plot" of 2,000 acres. It was intended to be a demonstration project for landless, distressed families. (The "Indian Service" had long employed Indian farmers who operated model farms to instruct their fellow Indians. There was an Indian Farmers Club and each year the Indians held their own version of the county fair on the church grounds south of Wetumka.)

At The Rehabilitation Plot there was a community house, a blacksmith shop, other repair shops, and several other buildings which had been hastily constructed. The laborers were Indian youths. And the plan was to accommodate 18 families and eventually divide the area into plots of forty acres in the forlorn hope of making the Indians self-sufficient.

It is indeed sad to recall the miserable circumstances of the Creek Indians who refused individual land allotments in Alabama a century earlier. In the early 1930s the Indian Service acquired warehouses of surplus U. S. army clothing. These castaway garments were distributed to the descendants of the people the U. S. Army had so brutally defeated. Some of the uniforms, especially the officers' trench coats, were of a high quality and were warm. They were also worth a few bucks. In 1940, in Wewoka, an Indian man who had a net worth of $200,000 was arrested for stealing clothing from a doctor's office. He had sold them for $2. He told the police that his guardian would not let him have enough allowance for him to sustain himself and that he was desperate. An unsympathetic jury recommended two years in the state penitentiary. (The self-image of the Indian had deteriorated to the extent that many of them dropped their Indian status and started passing as White. This may partially explain why on the annual school census reports there were twice as many Colored students as there were Indians in Hughes County.)

14

Months Before World War II

With the close of the 1930s, the people of Wetumka could look back at twenty years of floods, drought and the worst deflationary cycle ever. While the situation was a crisis throughout the 1920s, in just the first three years of the Depression Decade farm income again dropped by nearly 60%. There were faint signs things might be getting better for the farmer as the world seemed once again becoming enmeshed in war.

In 1940, Wetumka property owners were asked to pay $18.97 less per thousand of assessed valuation than two years before. Those who said taxes were unbearable in the Depression were certainly right. The worst was in 1933 when property taxes were a nearly impossible $117.75 per thousand. Part of the relief came in 1937 when Oklahoma enacted a 1% sales tax. This, in itself hit the general public very hard, but it enabled the State to bail out local education and meet many of its obligations. The Roosevelt administration had scrapped the terrible Gold Standard in a desperate effort to raise commodity prices. The money supply crisis had eased slowly in Wetumka. The merchants had quarter-cent tokens to make change on sales of less than a dollar when the new sales tax took effect. Sales tax on fifty cents entitled the customer to two quarter-cent tokens in change for the half cent of sales tax. A twenty-five cent purchase meant three quarter cent tokens in change. Three quarters of a cent meant a lot to the desperate consumer at the end of the decade. (Peixotto's Fine Foods would sell two dozen choice grapefruit for twenty-five cents in 1939).

Prior to the Depression the only way the Federal Government intruded into the lives of its ordinary citizens was through the U. S. Post Office. By 1940 the Government in Washington had become fundamental to every American in many ways they could never have imagined a few years before.

In January, 1940, the largest and most dependable taxpayer in Hughes County, The Frisco Railroad, was out of bankruptcy. The trustees had not authorized any outside purchases. The line announced that it was now ready to face the world with 21 new locomotives, 657 freight cars and 46 passenger cars that it had manufactured in its own shops while paying off debt of more than $25,000,000 of principal and interest. Governor Phillips had appeared before Congress and stated that one of the greatest obstacles to economic recovery in Oklahoma was the ever increasing freight rates. Farmers who consigned a carload of watermelons or cantaloupes realized almost nothing after the freight bill (Nevertheless, Oklahoma schools got more funding from the railroads than any other source during the Depression. It was said that Oklahoma was more dependent on railroad taxes than any other state.)

In 1940, the assessed valuation of Hughes County was over $12,000,000. Of this the Frisco railroad's holding in the county were valued at $767,173. The Rock Island line had its valuation set by the State Corporation Commission at $697,971. The Kansas, Oklahoma and Gulf Railroad's property was listed at $483,678. The KOG had the longest track in the county: 44.1 miles; the Frisco had 31.78 miles and the Rock Island 28.69 miles.) Only the Rock Island had streamlined, diesel-powered Rockets and only one was scheduled through the county. The first diesel powered Frisco train came through Wetumka—very slowly—in early 1949)

The dedication of the new High School building in Wetumka marks the end of an era in a real sense. The first high school was only fifteen years old and was a total loss from a fire in October of 1938. The Central Ward School was also lost to fire on New Year's Eve 1934. (It had taken two catastrophic fires, only weeks apart, to destroy that building.) School fires in the first forty years in Hughes County were like an epidemic. I've already mentioned the disastrous fire that destroyed the dormitory at the Indian boarding school. The early schools at Hannah and Dustin were destroyed during the course of their construction. Holdenville's five year old high school was burned in January, 1930, at a loss of $118,000. The Wetumka fire department rushed to Weleetka to assist in a futile effort to save the high school and gymnasium on January 12, 1940. The last big Depression Era school fire was in Dustin on July 25, 1941. The whole community was involved in trying to save the building, and the records, pictures and trophies were rescued. (There had been a previous attempt to burn Wetumka High School and on another occasion the City Hall and The Bank of Commerce were simultaneously arson targets.)

I have reflected on this epidemic of school fires and discussed it with people who were alive at the time and the unavoidable conclusion is that these fires were mostly caused by young arsonists. Anyone who believes that the Depression was "the good old days" when parents had a firm grip on their children and juvenile delinquency was yet to be invented, is rashly unfamiliar with the history of the time. The Federal government had recognized the problem as a national concern. There were hundreds of thousands of under age youth riding the rails. They were supposedly looking for some kind of gainful employment. Many of them were undoubtedly turned out of households because they represented one less mouth to feed. This was part of the mission of the Civilian Conservation Corps (CCC) and the National Youth Administration.

My own personal feeling is that while an iron discipline was maintained in the schools and everything seemingly was orderly; there was a seething resentment. Contemporary teachers would marvel at the exquisite control that even some of the old and frail teachers seemed to exercise over their classes. In reality the consequences of getting out of line were extreme. Parental wrath was something that never seemed to trouble any teacher. Part of the story is in the statistics. Students who had been honor roll participants dropped out in ever increasing numbers as they became old enough to find employment. Those who seemed to have fair prospects left after one or two years of high school. The senior class was usually just a shell of what it had been as juniors. Sixty and seventy years later many people who attended school in Wetumka say they felt there was a fundamental tension between town and country. They have told me that very few athletes came from farms. Part of this is a matter of how the person budgeted his energy. Most felt they could not plow fields and play football at the same time. But the bias ran much deeper and cannot be so blithely dismissed.

I do not know of a major school arson fire occurring since the hard times of the Depression . It seemed that a corner had been turned. (It was claimed at the time that Oklahoma had acquired more WPA schools than any other state. The WPA had helped build 23,003 new public schools in the nation between July 1935 and December 1939. At least 1,447 whole schools had been constructed in Oklahoma. A total of 4,095 educational buildings of one sort or another had been built mostly with WPA assistance on Oklahoma school campuses during this period.)

Wetumka's beautiful new school was dedicated on February 23, 1940. Senator Tom Anglin came and gave the main speech. Wanda Faye Lowder played a saxophone solo and was accompanied by Mary Lou Nicks. Wanda Faye Lowder, remembered by so many as a grade school teacher in Wetumka, also helped dedicate the new WPA school building at Fairview the same week.

Hughes County also got 285 miles of road with the aid of WPA. By the spring of 1940, No. 9 Highway was half completed between Wetumka and Dustin. A total of 110 men were employed on this $85,605 project. It should be noted that not a single foot of concrete of asphalt was laid down on this road before World War II. The complete right-of-way was not dedicated by property owners on the western segment to Seminole until after the war. The trio of bridges west of Wetumka were completed a full ten years before the road could be regarded even a good gravel road. Highway No. 9 was not paved through Wetumka until May of 1952. Throughout the era of World War II, it was just another dark, narrow and muddy street on the outskirts of town.

Another purely Indian WPA project was the completion of the road from Wetumka to Thlopthlocco Tirbal Town and on across the North Canadian. The first bridge here was factory built and was at the same place where the present bridge stands. It was considerably shorter than the present bridge; the entrance ways were narrow earth berms.)

One of the last WPA road projects in Wetumka was the removal of the Center Parkage on South Main street. (Holdenville's Main Street was being improved and widened at the same time.) Three blocks of South Main Street looked like Broadway does today. Forty-nine men were employed on this project and the cost was apportioned between the Oklahoma Highway Department and the city of Wetumka with the Federal government having the major role. Originally this had been a "bituminous mat" or rolled asphalt. It was badly delapidated with the passing of military convoys. The center whiteway of street lights was removed at this time as was a leaking water main. (In January, 1940, a motorist had been killed when his car struck the center curb and landed against a tree. Wetumka prevailed in a $50,679 lawsuit because the man's wife admitted that he might have dozed at the wheel.)

In 1940 white-collar WPA crews came through Hughes County and mapped the entire Wetumka township as to ownership. It was determined in a minerals survey that much Hughes County is underlain by coal at a depth of about 800 feet. (Another group did a historical records survey in the county and deposited hundreds of reels of microfilm at the Oklahoma Historical Society; this greatly aided my research.)

The men at the cotton gins of Hughes County remarked that the cotton was the best they had seen in ten years. The cotton harvest alone was expected to gross over a million dollars in 1940. This was a sign that the Depression was loosening its grip. The next year was the best for the county and the whole country since 1929.

In every way the 1940s was a new era. The Isolationists still held an iron grip on Congress but even they were losing their nerve. The World War was on in a big way in 1940. In September, 1940, Congress authorized the first time ever peacetime draft. In mid-1940 contracts were awarded for 45 new warships. This was in addition to 19 new submarines, cruisers and destroyers. Significantly, the Roosevelt Administration got authorization to build 35,000 new aircraft each year. (This was a tall order as it was more airplanes than had been cumulatively built of every sort since the day the Wright brothers first lifted off the ground when Wetumka was just three years old.) In another month contracts would be let for five new aircraft carriers. During the war this goal was broadly exceeded as 300,300 aircraft of all types were constructed before the end of the war. (The Armed Forces were hardly an outlet for men seeking military careers during the Depression. In 1940 men were enlisting from Oklahoma at the rate of about 600 a month. Bert Shaber, Jr., of Wetumka was nominated by Congressman Boren to be a cadet at West Point.)

This had an immediate stimulative effect on the national economy. And in 1940, the county treasurer Clarence Hastings, announced that Hughes County was in better shape than it had been since statehood and would soon be on a cash basis. The tax re-sales were one of the major reasons for this improved economic health. Over 100 pieces of property in the pavement districts in Wetumka were subjected to tax re-sale. (Lowell Cook recently remarked to me that he had read his abstract of title and learned that Mr. H. H. Darks acquired most of the 500 block of East Broadway when he decided to build his home there. He paid $5 for some of the lots and that was much more than some of the tax re-sale properties brought.)

A convenient dividing line between the Depression years and the era of World War II, in Hughes County, is the 4th Arkansas Day celebration in Holdenville. The parade was two miles long and took over an hour to pass any given point. There were 60 commercial and school floats, 400 horsemen, four high school bands, and a large number of trucks, cars, wagons, buggies, bicycles, tractors and livestock. The first place prize of $25 went to the Phillips Plant community for a float depicting an Arkansas apple orchard. That community had an entry typifying Lum and Abner's "Jot-Em-Down Store." A float of genuine Arkansas flavor was the prize winning school float was Hulsey's log cabin which was closely followed by a chorus of girls singing "Happy Little Home in Arkansas."

There were a number of Arkansas dignitaries present and they included a former lieutenant governor, state treasurer, a state justice of the Arkansas Supreme Court, and a State Senator. Holdenville mayor, John Ed Davis, introduced Oklahoma Governor Leon Phillips who resided in Weleetka. Governor Phillips wore a red neckerchief and blue shirt sleeves and in his speech urged Oklahomans and Arkansawyers to do their part in keeping America out of Europe's war. Governor Phillips declared that "Oklahomans and Arkansawyers could take care of that gang-but they had no business of crossing the pond to settle their war."

None of the postures taken by Congressional leaders and others to guarantee that America would not participate in the conflicts that were already a World War were reassuring. In September, 1940, the National Guard troops were ordered to Fort Sill for a year's duty. Wetumka's Engineers company boarded the train at the depot at 5:00 A. M. on September 21. The Headquarters company left at 9:00 A. M. T. J. Davis had requested a discharge because of his age and he was replaced by Captain Harlan E. Chase of Ponca City. Captain Bryan Nicks of the Headquarters Company, a veteran of the first World War, was also over age for combat duty but he wanted to complete his military career. (He served in Oklahoma throughout the war and was promoted to Major.)

Officers in the group were Lieutenant Howard H. Hart (formerly a principal in Wetumka and presently Superintendent of Schools at

Dustin), Lieutenant LeRoy Lambeth, and Logan Walker as First Sergeant for the Headquarters Company. The Engineers were short two officers. In addition to Captain Chase, there was the second in command, Lieutenant Glenn Chowins. (Chowins left three vacancies in the Holdenville school system. He had been the principal of two elementary schools and the high school football instructor. They denied him the title of coach because his services were voluntary as they could not afford to pay him anything for these duties.) Sergeants for the Headquarters Company were Everett G. Bowman, Quinton L. Hulstine, Wiley W. Wolverton, and as Corporal, Maurice D. Absher.

Privates First Class: Darl O. Absher, John W. Duke, William R. Flaugher, Ralph R. Franklin, Leonard L. Holford, Henry W. McElhaney, Fred W. Pippin, Ray Scott, Robert D. Sheppard, Thelmer L. Beavers.

Privates: James K. Arthur, Harold J. Bach, Robert P. Bach, E. J. Bamburg, Roy R. Barber, Wallace Barnes, James K. Bennett, Sam Brooks, Otto O. Campbell, Vernon E. Chastain, Matthew J. Cherry, Albert T. Decker, Richard S. Harris, Mose E. Holford, Mack G. Keithley, Leon F. Lee, Joseph L. Little, Charles L. Lucas, William T. Luman, Carl W. A. Morris, James K. Moses, Scott E. Sanders, Cecil R. Shaber, Elmer H. Stroup, Albert Thomas, Glenn E. Webb, Willie J. Wimes, Earl Badger, Eli Batt, Benjamin Harjo, Louis Harjo, Clyde E. Holmes, Albert N. Keithley, Raymond N. Kimbro, Jack P. Morris, James R. Payne, Roudy B. Smith, Harold L. Wilson, Otis, Welsh, Chales L. Ussry.

Enlisted men of the Engineers:

Staff Sergeants: Wayne J. Chowins, Homer L. Clawson, Wilbourn G. Neese.

Sergeants: Clifford Chastain, William E. Chowins, Marshall Clapp, Douglas C. Conley, Vernon E. Martin, John T. McGibboney, John Noggle, George A. White.

Corporals: Chesley A. Eason, Nolan J. Eason, John W. Cunningham, Harvey Hughes, Leland L. Ledgerwood, Charles E. Mooney, Merle L. Sanderlin.

Privates First Class: Rossie Andrews, William Biffle, Albert Burgess, Arnold J. Cissina, Raymond Clenny, Paul W. Dunzy, Robert L. Harmon, Audie E. Rollis, William E. Stringfellow, William F. Wolf.

Privates: William J. Ball, Bruce Barnes, Johnnie L. Blankenship, James Boylston, Curtis Bridges, Ray Don Brown, Kozy Buckley, Henry Buckley, J. B. Burns, Harland Clapp, Dexter S. Clenny, Porter Coachman, Billy R. Conley, Edward Cox, Wiley B. Davis, Lonny Finney, Jack Fuller, Raymond A. Gillespie, Mitchell Harjo, Paul Harwell, Edd G. Harvey, Louis H. Hayes, Arlin P. Hill, Howard L. Jones, James D. Jones, William M. Jones, Fred B. Kamplain, Neal Kamplain, James Mathis, Alfred D. Mannon, Chess R. Mangrum, Clarence Morris, Louis Morris, Bud J. Newson, Carl R. Penrod, James Ray, Burl Reid, Edd Richardson, John C. Robinson, John H. Rogers, Clifford A. Sanders, Hayden Sanderlin, Jack Seawright, Wilbert E. Sisson, J. D. Stringfellow, Walter Sumpter, Hershell Ticer, Jack Toney, Doyle W. Treadway, Alery J. Webb, Austin O. Webb, Thomas Ledgerwood, Thurman Johnson, Raymond Dunzy, Willie Harjo, Buster Brown, Thurman Jones.

One of the more interesting asides of my research of 1940 is that the disputed western boundary between Oklahoma and Texas was finally settled by a decision of The United States Supreme Court. About 400 landowners had been unsure of whether they were in Oklahoma or Texas. The high court ruled that the Act of Congress which admitted Oklahoma to the Union had to be upheld and the border would be the 100th meridian. A survey done in 1818 was in error and when it was corrected during the 1930s, 30,000 acres of wheat and pasture believed to be in Oklahoma was found to be part of Texas. The Texas legislature passed a bill where the former landowners could get buy back or get a clear title to their by paying $1 per acre before June 27, 1941.

Hughes County was still near its peak in population in 1940. There was a loss of only about 3.7% from 1930 and over half of this loss was in Holdenville (according to the 1940 Census, its 6,192 residents were 636 fewer than ten years before). Wetumka actually gained a net of 187 residents to stand at 2,340. Hughes County retained its standing of 25 among the counties as a pre-fix for its automobile license tags. (For the first time, in 1940, Oklahoma required a written test to obtain a new driver's license.)

The population drain from Hughes County did not actually begin during the Depression Years. It was the War years that re-distributed native Hughes Countyans all across America. By 1950, a third of the county's population had vanished. (1930, 30,334 to 1950, 20,664). By 1960 the county was only half as populous as it had been in 1930 with just 14,144 persons and just about half of them lived in Holdenville and Wetumka. The most noticeable population drop was from the rural areas as whole communities dried up and their names were no longer familiar). THE HOLDENVILLE DAILY NEWS reported that the community known as Wecharty before the county was organized and later called Bilby when it had a post office and was a stop on the Rock Island railway, was only a memory as the last building was razed. It had once had a cotton gin, post office and store and a boarding house. It was a place where Colored residents were welcomed. The late Mr. Bilby had "imported" them by purchasing tickets for the needed farm workers. (Coleman Atwood had been the deputy County Treasurer of Hughes County since 1928 and had served longer than any of the courthouse crowd. His parents had established the town of Atwood.)

Wetumka had gained some population and several businesses at the expense of Dustin. These included the Robert L. Meadors and Son dry goods store which moved to a building that was considered part of the Bank of Commerce building at the time. (The T. & P. Mercantile Company had only recently vacated that spot. They moved across the street to the place where the gap now exists on North Main.) Julian and Nellie Peixotto also moved their grocery from Dustin. Dr. D. L. Wenrick had also had his practice in Dustin until the fall of 1937.

Holdenville celebrated its 46th anniversary on October 10, 1941 with the town's founder, G. W. McShan, the guest of honor at an observance by the Pioneer Men's Club. Mr. McShan, a former lumber mill worker, rode out from McAlester on a work train as the Choctaw, Oklahoma and Gulf railroad was being built. He said that like others he had the express intent of starting a town. "I was looking for a place to start a town and saw this pretty stretch of prairie. I just liked it and got off here." He said that another man had already staked out the town site and he bought 11 lots at $40 each and one corner lot for $75 and set up a tent. He said that two other towns had been staked out in the area but he was able to attract the railroad to his and he named it after Jeff Holder, the manager of the railroad. The year was 1895 and Holdenville became a recognizable town in 1898. Mr. McShan operated a lumberyard and general store. His businesses were so successful that he practically monopolized advertising space in all of the early newspapers of the county. He even had ads on their front pages. Mr. Shan, a man of considerable wealth, had kept all of his original 12 lots, which were in the heart of downtown Holdenville.

The first collective move toward defense preparedness in Hughes County was the scrap drive for "defense" metal which was aluminum. Over a ton was collected in the first drive in 1941.

The year's training mobilization of the National Guard was extended indefinitely. They first moved to a new camp (Camp Barkley) at the edge of San Antonio, Texas. In September of 1941, the entire division of 16,000 men was on the move by road to Fort Pitkin, Louisiana.

In August, 1941, the Office of Production Management stopped the use of silk in all non-military applications. There was an run on stocks in all of the stores in the county. The use of rayon and of nylon was just coming into fashion but these fabrics were also declared defense materials.

During the Depression years it had been difficult for a boy to qualify for service in the Civilian Conservation Corps. He had to be from a
family that was receiving government assistance. In 1941 there was
nearly an unlimited quota system. By then applicants only had to get
on the CCC truck as it came through Wetumka. In a few months the
whole New Deal bureaucracy was devoted to defense preparedness.
(The New Deal operatives were housed in a courthouse annex in Holdenville. That $50,000 addition, alone, was larger than the whole
present courthouse.)

One of the earliest group of "selectees" as the volunteers for induc-
tion in the armed forces were called left Holdenville for Oklahoma
City in January, 1941. Of the 34 who reported, ten were rejected for
reasons that mirrored conditions in the Depression. The unusual number of men from Hughes county who could not qualify for military service were rejected for three principal reasons. First they were many who
could not read well. This time around the services would not accept
anyone unable to read at a fifth grade level. A second reason, so obvious to many, was that many of them were seriously underweight. (The
Red Cross had budgeted $50 in 1940 to purchase yeast to medicate
people with such poor diets they had been subjected them to pellagra.)
The third prominent cause was active "social disease" as it was referred
to in hushed tones at the time.

Cecil Kilgore, moved to Wetumka from Wewoka in 1934 and purchased the local bakery from Herman Darks. About five years later he
began baking fortified bread with essential trace nutrients. This was
one of the most important changes in diet that many Wetumkans
would experience before the war.

The Federal government, recognizing that it might be a long war,
moved quickly to remedy these deficiencies. Roosevelt, himself, had
said early in his administration "we may have to help the schools."
Every school in the county literally beefed up its hot lunch program
and made it available indiscriminately all year round. The WPA gar-

dens were still producing and the new element was the vast canning programs throughout the county. The WPA had already operated correspondence courses. It expanded into basic literacy. (By September, 1941, over 500 Hughes County men had been rejected on grounds of illiteracy. The new County Superintendent of Schools J. Grady Simmons, sent a letter to each asking if he would like to attend volunteer taught classes.) A group of doctors in Holdenville opened the first "VD Clinic." (Enrollees who failed to keep scheduled appointments were subjected to heavy-handed police harassment. Congress, at the beginning of the Roosevelt Administration had appropriated over $8 million to bring syphilis under control.

One of the great unrecognized contributions that places like Hughes County made during World War II was its crops of the lowly cantaloupe. Penicillin, the first broad-scope antibiotic, had been discovered by a British scientist over ten years before. It was the Americans who figured out how to get it into mass production. Beer and other intoxicating spirits were nearly taxed out of existence during the war. This meant that there was a vast unused complex of fermenting vats. Penicillin is extracted from a mold and it was discovered that nothing grew this mold better than cantaloupes. The services wanted as many million units of Penicillin as they could get and of course there was never a surplus. This is the miracle drug which gave sufferers of venereal diseases a fighting chance. And the reports were that Hughes county was as heavily afflicted as any county in the state.

In March of 1941 the entire medical staff of the Pryor-Johnston-Kernek Clinic-Hospital in Holdenville were called to army duty as First Lieutenants. Dr. Victor W. Pryor was sent to Fort Sill. Drs. L. A. S. Johnston and Clyde Kernek were ordered to Fort Sam Houston, Texas. Dr. Shaw who came to Wetumka as the part-time CCC physician also was called up. Henry Bowles and other prominent Wetumkans appealed to the Draft Board in his behalf but Dr. Shaw conceded that he was ready to go.

Oklahoma City was selected in April of 1941 as the site for the Army Air Corps Depot. It was to be five miles east of the city and $12,000,000 was appropriated for its start. Nearly 3,000 men would be employed in its early construction. (It would be named for Brigadier General Grant Tinker, a full-blooded Osage Indian who was the first general officer to be lost in the war.) Trainees from the Depot were frequent visitors to Wetumka's rifle range. It had been a WPA project and was located near the Wetumka air field (Boren Field) on the H. H. Darks ranch. Some groups lived in tent cities at the range. Many of them would be barracked at the CCC camp after it was abandoned in 1943.

15

World War II-Part I

Pearl Harbor, America's greatest military disaster, struck a sense of panic among Wetumkans as nothing else could have. Immediately, it was reported that the local airfield was under guard as was Phillips Plant and the bridges and overpasses of the Frisco Railroad. The railroads had been advised not to sell tickets to anyone looking Oriental. Actually, there was only one person of Oriental descent in the county, a Chinese cook at Holdenville. And he was even more bitterly anti-Japanese than most other Americans.

Wetumka was represented at Pearl Harbor. Johnny W. Smith notified his sister, Velma Herrington, by postcard that he had survived the attack unscathed although he'd been in the thick of it all. Young Smith was a Marine Corps sergeant and was recently featured in a television documentary in which 55 Pearl Harbor survivors tell their stories. (Mr. Smith, today, lives in Waterford, California, and his special California license plate to show that that he's a authentic Pearl Harbor Survivor.)

In a pattern that would be repeated dozens of times in Hughes county during the war, Mr. and Mrs. J. M. Carter of the Oak Grove community, were officially notified on December 17, 1941, that their son had been killed in action. A month later they began receiving letters dated in such a way that they developed real hope that he was alive. It turned out that he really was alive. On July 12, 1944, Mr. and Mrs. Chess Morris of Wetumka were notified that their son, Lieutenant Jack Morris, a B-24 pilot based in Italy, had not returned from a mission. On the following day they received another telegram in which they were assured, without elaboration, that their son had returned to duty.

Lieutenant Morris was a graduate of the Wetumka High School and Junior College. He took his basic CPT flight training at Wetumka's Boren Field.

The first really noticeable impact of the war on Wetumka was that all WPA jobs had to be wrapped up. No more projects would be authorized except those directly related to the war effort. Dozens of young men were being trained as motor mechanics at informal schools. Mr. Otis Adams oversaw the programs and the classrooms were at the local high school, at the Ford garage and other garages and even at a blacksmith shop. There were NYA schools at Holdenville and Calvin which trained men in "overhead welding." By March of 1942 the NYA school in Holdenville was training 54 boys and 18 girls in shifts around the clock. (Holdenville was one of twelve schools in the state that trained girls as well as boys. They were offered course work in sheet metal work, machine shop work, pattern making, electricity and radio.) Upon certification they were being shipped out in droves. Every week boy and girl welders were given train tickets, and a two weeks advance in pay to secure room and board, to strange places like Camden, New Jersey, Portsmouth, New Hampshire and Richmond, California. More people from Hughes County worked at the Kaiser ship works at Richmond, California than any other place. There was virtually a small colony of people from the county at Richmond. (On April 21, 1942, the first contingent of ten welders were sent to Seattle. From there they would be assigned to the Bremerton, Washington area as shipbuilders or to a private contractor. They were guaranteed a minumum wage of 75 cents an hour with a chance to make from $1.12 to $2 an hour.)

By June of 1942, boy and girl "overhead welders" were being trained in Wetumka and the girls outnumbered the boys two to one for a while. The National Youth Administration bought their train tickets and paid their apartment rent for the first two weeks. The wide dispersal of men and women had huge implications for the post-war migration that helped reduce the population of Hughes County by two-thirds.

There were two notable examples of aviation pioneers from Hughes County who couldn't wait to get into action with the American Army Air Force. Homer Berry, formerly of Wetumka, was a Wing Commander for Britain's RAF and he ferried planes to Britain under the lend-lease program. He'd been an eighteen year old pilot in the first World War. In February, 1942, Miss Grace Stevenson, a 23 years old, from Holdenville, took on a similar assignment in Britain. Eventually her sister, Majorie would become a Women's Air Service Pilot (WASP) as would Betty F. Martin of Wetumka. These women had to operate over 60 types of aircraft and their duties revolved around getting planes from the factories to the airfields or from one part of the country to another. They worked out of an all-woman airfield at Sweetwater, Texas.

During the summer of 1942, the U. S. Army recalled Wetumka's legendary Homer Berry as a Lieutenant Colonel for a high level job of evaluating American planes and their performance as compared to British planes and those which had been captured from the Axis powers. His reports were of interest to officials at the highest levels of the government.

Wetumka's Boren Field trained a surprising number of fliers. It was designated a Civilian Pilot Taining (CPT) facility and students who finished the basic course were promised a rating of Staff Sergeant. After their advanced training they would be commissioned officers. Before Pearl Harbor pilots were being trained in Wetumka for the Canadian Air Force and several of them became instructors in an advanced school that Canada operated at Miami, Oklahoma. About 100 combat pilots got their initial training at Wetumka. These include Jack Morris and the Holdenville attorney Oliver Stanley Huser. (All three of H. H. Dark's offspring were solo students: Willard, Max and Doris).

Mrs. Emily Duncan, owner-operator of The Redskin Theatre, still a Wetumka resident, told me that she had learned to fly at the Wetumka field at the insistence of her husband Cecil.

A best seller on THE NEW YORK TIMES booklist, this summer, has been THE WILD BLUE, THE MEN AND THE BOYS WHO FLEW THE B24's, by Stephen Ambrose. It is mainly about the experiences of George McGovern (the Senator and 1972 Democratic presidential nominee.) At 21 McGovern was a B24 pilot beginning his required 35 missions over Germany. He had never had a ride in a plane or even been close to one before the war. His basic training was at a lonely dirt field in the Dakotas. He took his advanced training at Hatbox Field near Muskogee. His experience parallels that of so many men from the Wetumka area.

I am just old enough to remember how busy Boren Field was. It seemed that sometimes there would be two planes landing at the same time. There would be several on the ground. It bore no resemblance at all to an airfield. The rocks had been gathered up into piles and the gullies were marked off by pieces of sheet iron that were arched like small roofs attached to steel stakes. No runways were ever graded and the pilots took off and landed in a meadow. All of the planes were of the open cockpit variety and the pilots waved to the passing motorists. The school owned three planes at its height although a good many Army set down there while enroute to other places. On one occasion a plane burned because the fabric in the wing ignited. Wetumka's facility was there before those at Holdenville or at the Oklahoma Baptist University at Shawnee. (Congressman Boren had literally put Wetumka on the aviation map.)

The patriotic trek of volunteers to the service began in earnest in April, 1942. Paul Ballinger, State Represenative from Holdenville, tried for the Navy but was rejected in his physical. He then enlisted in the army as a private. (Congressman Boren wanted to serve in the Navy but the Secretary of the Navy persuaded him to keep his Congressional seat where he could perhaps be even more helpful.) In another month there would be 816 Countyans in the armed services.

The McAlester site for the Navy Depot was confirmed in June of 1942. Very soon two-thousand workers were constructing the 30,000 complex which extended to the corner of Hughes County. Some of the architects who designed the buildings lived in Holdenville and the county became a rent control area. Rents could not be more than was being charged the previous April. This site was chosen because the politicians representing McAlester had engaged in an active campaign to obtain this defense facility but especially because of its inland location. It would be a place where TNT would be stored and where projectiles could be assembled and shipped to both coasts. It would virtually identical to the plant at Hastings, Nebraska. The explosives were to be stored in widely scattered "igloos" to localize an explosion and to provide some protection from an air attack. Construction continued throughout the war and its waning months rocket and torpedo production at McAlester peaked.

In the first two months of 1942, it was possible, in theory, to obtain a new car in Hughes County. The restrictions were such that even those who could afford one were reluctant to buy. The buyer had to be in a certain profession and he could not sell, lease, rent or loan the car without incurring a criminal penalty. Rubber was declared to be the most strategic of the war making materials. Nothing was more stringently rationed than new tires. In a month's time there might be two or three new tires available for the whole county. The paperwork was endless and there was a rationing board which interviewed prospective purchasers. Schools were reluctant to buy tires. If a bus had even one tire obtained through the rationing board, it could not be used for anything but transporting students on established routes during normal school hours. This really posed a special hardship for sports and other school sponsored activities. (I do not know how many new cars were available in the county; nationally, a third of the new cars on hand in 1942 were still held by the dealers when the war ended.)

The US government wanted to lease every typewriter in America. More government records would be created during the war that had been accumulated in all the decades leading up to 1941.

A large contingent of "selectees" left from Holdenville on October 19, 1942. They were led up Main Street by the Holdenville band and treated to a lunch at the Manhattan Café. Afterwards they were given a pep talk by local civic leaders. Then they were loaded down with cigarettes provided the various Chambers of Commerce. It was believed, at least at the time, that all great soldiers smoked. The virtues of smoking were that it was thought to steady the nerves and keep exhausted men awake. In the first World War, General Pershing had given priority to ships carrying cigarettes over those bringing rations. This practice intensified in the Second World War and raising money to buy cigarettes for the soldier boys became an ordinary event. General Eisenhower was a chain smoker as was the Commander-in-Chief, President Roosevelt, who liked being photographed with a cigarette. (In that crowd of selectees were at these Wetumkans: Eldon Osborn, Clyde Ray, Raymond Dunzy and John E. Bridges.)

Wetumka opened the first soldier's lounge in the county. It was in the American Legion Building just south of Neal's Drug store. During 1942 Wetumka was nearly always host to a large contingent of troops from Will Rogers Field and the Oklahoma City Air Depot. They took advantage of the rifle range near the airport and they were lodged at the tent city there and at the recently abandoned CCC camp. (The Selective Service and Training Act of 1940, to avoid mistakes made in the first World War, specified that sanitary facilities had to be in place before troops could be massed. The CCC camp was on a huge septic tank and it qualified.)

There were dances for the soldiers with a great number of Wetumkans acting as chaperons. There were games and various other amusements. The address of all the soldiers in the area were posted and anyone could got in and write a letter to a serviceman or woman.

The way servicemen overseas got their mail during the war is little known or understood. The post office accepted only "V-mail" and of course the "V" was for victory. It was a sheet of paper on which the letter was written and then folded into an envelop and sealed. The letters sorted and opened by high speed machines. Each was photographed and transferred to microfilm. It was said that 150,000 single sheets weighed 2,575 pounds but they could be reduced in weight to 1,500 pounds and the savings in space was even more substantial. They had already been sorted by unit and the man got a "snapshot" of the original letter.

The Douglas bomber plant opened "somewhere in Oklahoma" in August, 1942. I think that nearly everyone knew it was located adjacent to what would be known as Tinker Field in Oklahoma City. It was easily the largest building ever in Oklahoma and the production line was one mile long. My father's cousin, Mary Pace Andrews (sister of Wetumka's Joe Pace) who died in June, 2001, told me of her experience of being a war worker. She commuted from Bowlegs, Oklahoma and several workers rode with her as they pooled all their resources to keep a car in the road. (War workers could get gasoline.) Her job was to be in the cockpit of C-47's (the military version of the first widely used airliner, the DC-3) and attach the windshield wiper assembly. By the time the plant had been in production eighteen months, the 2000th cargo plane had been rolled off the assembly line. This type of plane was still used extensively by the American and Vietnamese air forces when I was there in the early 1960s. It was such a sturdy plane (overbuilt for the lack of wind tunnel testing) that to this day large numbers of them are still being flown all over the world by private owners.

Railroad traffic doubled in Hughes county early in the war. The interval between trains grew ever shorter and in November of 1942 a freight crashed into the back of another in the fog just before daylight a mile north of Wetumka. Four persons were seriously injured and four men were given emergency treatment at a Holdenville hospital and then rushed to a hospital in the railroad's headquarters, St. Louis, Missouri. A large number of rail cars burned up and about fifteen trains were thrown off their schedule.

The first Wetumka flier had been lost before the war had been on a year. Staff Sergeant Glenn Webb, son of Mr. and Mrs. Charles Webb, was lost when his plane went down somewhere in the south Pacific in November, 1942. He was one of many men who had transferred from the 45th Infantry Division to the Army Air Forces.

The effects of rationing can be seen clearly in one statistic. For the first time in living memory there were no road deaths in Hughes County for a whole year. The year was 1942. Gasoline was rationed although it was not critically short; the object was to save tires. The Roosevelt Administration recommended a national speed limit of 35 miles per hour. In the first six months of 1943, only two Wetumkan was able to get a grade one tires through the rationing board: Charles Nichols and James Norman. Grade Two tires were a little more plentiful and went to William H. Lee, Jess Goodspeed, James R. Ray, Earnest Ray Proctor, Mrs. Goldie Tunstall, George Rich, Carrol C. Martin, William G. Dilday, Goad S. Dilday, Earnest Gist, F. C. Garrett, J. W. Griggs, and Herman Logan. Truck tires were acquired by W. A. Brooks, George W. Hunter, and Virgil Hardcastle. Recap applications were approved for W. W. Wilson and Bert Hall.

Most of the Oklahoma Highway patrolmen were members of the original class of 1937; practically all of them went into the service. They were replaced by the AHP or "Auxiliary Highway Patrolmen" who were only slightly trained. They sometimes drove patrol cars and wore a simple khaki uniform with red patches on the sleeves emblazoned with AHP. They furnished their own uniforms, badges and side arms. T. J."Slim" Sanders, a post-war sheriff of Hughes County, had been an auxiliary highway patrolman. The were several prominent men who worked out of the Holdenville office of the highway patrol. Most of them were part-time and all were volunteers. They included Clyde Busey (county judge), Speck Broaddus (county clerk), Hade Harmon (county assessor). The auxiliary highway patrolmen from Wetumka was George B. Williams who could deputize others when the need arose.

In early January of 1943 a new CPT pilot class arrived in Wetumka. All fifteen of the men were from the Boston, Massachusetts area. At this point Ernie Stout was the ground instructor. The other instructors were Bill George, who was assisted by Raymond Jaggers and Joe Scott. Two weeks later the pastor of The First Baptist Church (Rev. J. H. Bradley) left Wetumka for Cambridge, Massachusetts. He would begin his training at Harvard University as an army chaplain.

Since 1941 the farmers of Hughes County had been urged to grow every peanut they possibly could. The price for non-quota peanuts was nearly as good as what was paid for the quota peanuts. In 1943 maximum food production really began in earnest. President Roosevelt proclaimed January 12, 1943, National Farm Mobilization Day and Day long meetings were to be held at eight county locations and every member of the family was expected to attend. Each farmer was expected to develop his own blueprint and set his production goals. Hughes county had also been selected as an experimental unit in pooling unused or out of repair farm implements. There was a huge effort to establish a county-wide parts inventory from every piece of equipment that could be cannibalized.

Hughes County was allotted five new tractors, one breaking plow and one disk in 1943. Agriculture was not mechanized to any appreciable extent. Official census statistics show that there were still 50 horses or mules for every 1,000 acres in cultivation.

Farm production was becoming critical to the war effort at the time manpower shortages were materializing in every line of work. The soil had been strained by ten years of drought and erosion. The State of Oklahoma (through the Prisons) was grinding mountains of limestone into agricultural lime that farmers could obtain for forty cents a ton. For the first time ever farmers could obtain peanut seed from the government on credit. No one had ever planted shelled peanuts before but that is what was available. The hulls were too valuable to waste.

Women did their part in the war. A surprising number of Wetumka women signed up for the uniformed services. Miss Odie Tims, sister of Mrs. Stona L. Fitch and WHS graduate entered Navy service in February, 1943. (She became a Storekeeper in the Navy and on leave stated that since there were no boys in her family, it was up to her.) Miss Helen Lewis began her basic training at Fort Des Moines, Iowa, in the same month. She was a graduate of Wetumka High School and the Wetumka Junior College. (Helen Lewis married a serviceman during the war: Sergeant Clarence Spier.) Mrs. Irwin A. Watson, wife of the Wetumka postmaster, joined the Women's Army Corps in June of 1943, at the end of the school term and was sent to Fort Oglethorpe, Georgia, to be trained to drive a variety of army vehicles. She had been an elementary teacher in Wetumka for 15 years. Many people remember her also as their high school English teacher. (The services were desperate for women and would gladly accept unmarried or married women (21-40) as long as they didn't have a dependent in the household under the age of 14.) Virginia Tomberlin, an instructor in the Wetumka Junior College joined the Navy WAVES in January of 1943. Miss Alene Hogue, a Weleetka resident, formerly of Wetumka, joined the Women's Army Corps in March of 1943. Josephine Duncan, daughter of Mr. and Mrs. Joe Duncan, became a WAVE and served at New Orleans.

One of the first Army men to come home from Europe on leave was Captain Glen Chowins. (There were plenty of transports coming from Europe; the trick was finding a ride back.) He gave a report on the war in England to the Kiwanis club in Holdenville in April of 1943. Chowins had transferred from the 45th Infantry Division to the Corps of Engineers. He told his classes that he spent most of the war involved in logistics at Belfast, Northern Ireland.

Franklin D. Roosevelt was the first American president ever to pass through Hughes County. (Most local people did not realize how completely paralyzed he was throughout his adult life. He'd contracted polio in 1921 and was unable to walk or stand without assistance.) He hated to fly because it meant he had to be carried aboard the plane and then it was very difficult for him to move about the cabin. He preferred train travel and specially adapted car that had railroad track in the floor and was armored to withstand just about any kind of attack.

In April of 1943 Roosevelt had to meet with the President of Mexico and this routed him through the county since his rail car was oversized and would not pass through many tunnels. His whereabouts were always classified information but many people knew that something unusual was about to happen when a military train came through and dropped off soldiers to guard every interesection. Despite the hushed secrecy it was a dead giveaway that the Roosevelt Special was on the track because it was preceded by a short pilot train. There was a crowd along the train tracks in Wetumka on April 20, 1943, when the Roosevelt Special rumbled through town. Some even claimed to have glimpsed his famous silhouette through the thick bullet proof window. One of the men in the contingent of soldiers from Fort Maxey, Texas, was PFC Oscar Smith of the Rush Springs community. He wouldn't talk to newspaper men until the train had passed. He said it was an honor. Rev. C. E. Venable, of Holdenville, said he recognized Roosevelt in the train's dining car. He seemed to be having lunch with two men and a woman. (Roosevelt was in Oklahoma more than once during the war. He actually reviewed the troops at Camp Gruber, near Muskogee.)

The Wetumka High School Class of 1940 was hard hit early in the war. Two days after Roosevelt had passed through the county, the parents of Elva McDowell were notified that their son had been killed in action in North Africa. (Young McDowell was survived by his three sisters, Mildred, Ruth and Wilma, all living at home and by his brothers Eldon of the home and Edsel of Tulsa. He had been according the honor of being "An Oustanding Graduate barely three years earlier.) TSgt Graham Wall Diggs, Jr., son of the pioneer doctor and the

Depression decade mayor of Wetumka, left a pre-med course at Oklahoma University to become a waist gunner on a bomber. He died during a mission over Germany as the plane was shot up so much it could not stay in the air. It crashed into the ocean and none of the bodies of the crewmen were ever recovered. (After the war some of the men in another plane, on the same mission, came to Wetumka to tell his mother than he had died a hero. They had watched his plane go down and said he kept pouring out machine gun fire as it descended. The Diggs house still stands on South Washita and is stately reminder of the kind of people who lived in Wetumka during the Second World War.)

I thought the people on the home front in Wetumka performed heroically. As in the first World War a large number of women were knitting army sweaters. In May of 1943, there were 119 Wetumka women who participated in making over 11,600 surgical dressings in that 30 day period. It is appropriate to give them the credit they have long deserved. This is the list as provided by their supervisor, Mrs. T. J. Davis:

Mrs. O. S. Adams, Mrs. Pete Box, Mrs. L. F. Battles, Bobbye Dorris Bare, Imogene Banett, Dovie Barnett, Juanita Burkes, Josephine Barnett, Mrs. R. C. Bicknell, Mrs. Ruth Brock, Mrs. Bradburn.

Miss Bertha Bloom, Miss Rebecca Bloom, Anna kBelle Burke, Mrs. Charles Burnett, Mrs. Lula Canard, Mrs. Roley Canard, Mrs. E. E. Cope, Mrs. Earl Chowins, Mrs. Lem Clingman, Mrs. Osie Crain, Mrs. H. H. Darks.

Joyce Davis, Mrs. G. W. Diggs, Mrs. Davidson, Juanita Evans, Mrs. Cecil Fair, Patty Fairman, Maxine Forrest, Mrs. Nora Fulks, Mrs. Orville Gammill, Mrs. Ida Gibson, Mrs. Jerry Golightly, Mrs. Joe Hall, Mrs. B. H. Harrison, Mrs. Anna Harriman, Mrs. Harlan, Mrs. G. L. Herring, Maxine Jackson.

Mrs. C. E. Jarrett, Mrs. J. E. Jarrett, Mrs. Harry Jackson, Mrs. Edna Kamplain, Louise Kamplain, Mrs. Klos, Mrs. Nathan Lee, Miss Mary

Leeper, Mrs. V. G. Lewis, Mrs. Curtis Lowder, Mrs. Gomer Laswell, Mrs. Rufus Martin, Betty Martin, Miss Margaret Mathis, Mrs. Wanda Malloy, Mrs. W. A. McCoy, Mrs. Jack McGee, Grace McConnell, Mrs. Ray Meadors, Reinette Meadors.

Mrs. Lloyd Meadors, Alene Melton, Mrs. Grover Morris, Mrs. Ida Morris, Jeanne Morris, Mrs. J. H. Morgan, Eula Faye Mullin, Mrs. Jack Murphy, Mrs. McGuire, Mrs. Turner McCoy, Wanda Nicar, Mrs. Kate Nichols, Mrs. Murvin Nicks, Delia Lee Nolan, Ledgel Old-acre, Mrs. W. D. Ogletree, Mrs. Julian Peixotto.

Mrs. M. L. Potts, Mrs. I. M. Preston, Imogene Proctor, Mrs. J. C. Puryear, Mary Puryear, Mrs. Peevey, Mrs. Arthur Ream, Jeanne Ritter, Adna Rahal, Myrtle Roberts, Dearis Ryan, Mrs. Anna Robinson, Mrs. Ray, Mrs. Burl Sanders, Mrs. Scott Sanders, Mrs. Bud Sanders, Mozelle Seawright, Mrs. Bert Shaber.

Mrs. Lois Shepard, Lucile Smith, Margaret Smith, Mrs. Mary Smith, Sybil Smith, Marie Sewar, Twila Studyvin, Genevieve Tippin, Velma Vendever, Mrs. Travis Watson, Mrs. June Wenrick, Lucile Westbrook, Alice Warwick, Mrs. George Williams, Mrs. M. H. Wol-ford, Mrs. Rosa Webb, Mrs. Juanita Yahola and Ethel Mae Young.

In May of 1942, two fliers from a base in Texas became lost in their advanced trainer. As they entered the airspace over Hughes County they realized they were nearly out of fuel. Being unfamiliar with the area, they made no attempt to crash land. The found a plowed field and bailed out. One of them came down in the newly plowed field and had a soft landing. The other landed in the brush and was scratched up a bit. They walked to the nearest farm house where a startled Walter Crawford agreed to drive them to town. The word was put out that local civilians were not allowed to search for the plane. They were not authorized to approach a crash site or to touch the bodies of anyone in or near the crash. This plane was eventually found and was left on a flat-bed semi-trailer at the curb near THE WETUMKA GAZETTE printing presses in the old First National Building.

Wetumkans did not always heed the advice to stay away from a crash scene when they thought they might be of assistance to injured fliers. On November 14, 1944, a Will Rogers Field plane crashed six miles west of Wetumka in Maynard Richmond's cotton field. Homer Kirkland's sons, Marvin and Ike, rushed to the scene and then summoned an ambulance from the Nicks Funeral Home in Wetumka. The pilot was killed on impact and the co-pilot was rushed to Physicians and Surgeons Hospital in Holdenville for emergency treatment. From there he was transferred to Glennan General Hospital at Okmulgee.

On that same day, Major Thomas Mackey, born in Wetumka 29 years earlier, was killed in a plane crash into a mountain during bad weather near Pasadena, California. He had graduated from Wetumka High School in 1932. He had just returned from a long tour in the South Pacific. (Major Mackey is listed among the Holdenville men killed in the War.)

16

World War II-Part II

It was 1943 before American planes dropped a single bomb on Nazi Germany. And Wetumkans were there to see that it was done. A farm boy, Lieutenant T. D. (Tom) Ledgerwood , was 23 years old when he became the pilot of a four engined bomber (presumably a B-24). He confided in his brother, Master Sergeant Leland Ledgerwood (later commissioned an officer on the battlefield) that the plane he flew over Berlin was the same one he had test flown from Sedan, Kansas, over Wetumka and Holdenville. (Pilots and their crews would often ferry their airships from the East Coast to North Africa and onto a field in Italy or England) Ledgerwood had been in the National Guard for several years when it was mobilized in 1940. He transferred to the Air Forces and earned his wings at Columbus, Mississippi in the later part of 1942. (He was a graduate of Wetumka High School and Wetumka Junior College.)

Lieutenant Ledgerwood was a pilot in some of the earliest American formations over Germany. He did not return from a raid that was conducted on October 8, 1943. It was nearly six weeks before his parents were notified that he had parachuted from his shot-up plane and was a prisoner of the Germans. He would be a resident of a German Stalag until he was liberated by the advancing American Armies in May of 1945.

Another man who has lived among Wetumkans all his life, Clyde Ray, was a POW of the Germans. Most people are surprised to learn this as he is a modest and unassuming man. He was a member of the US Army's elite Rangers and was in five major campaigns from North

Africa to the Anzio beachhead in Italy. In one battle his whole battalion was nearly wiped out and when there was no food, water or ammunition left he surrendered to the Germans as part of a group. He was a German POW for fifteen months and was taken to a place near the border with Russia. On a forced march back he and two other Rangers escaped into the forest. Attempting to escape is the soldier's frist duty when taken prisoner. But Clyde must have wondered if it was such a good idea. They were stranded in the forest of a hostile country for 45 days. They had to make their own shelter and all they had to eat was whatever they could catch with their hands.

Finally, Clyde says, he spotted a British tank outfit and managed to get to them to "surrender." He said he was still wearing the same tattered uniform and was covered with lice. He received a medal from the Brits for providing them with much useful information. The Americans awarded him a Purple Heart, five Bronze Stars and several other medals.

PFC Tommy Nolen, notified his parents Mr. and Mrs. Ed Nolen of Wetumka, that he'd been a prisoner of the Germans for four days. He said that his unit was overwhelmed in close combat and he and several of his buddies were captured and locked in a church building for four days without food or water. They were liberated when another American unit caught up with them. He said building was about to be demolished when they succeeded in yelling loud enough to be heard. He said they were given two days of rest before being returned to the front lines.

Private Sammie Fish, full-blood Creek Indian of Wetumka, was also a prisoner of the Germans. He had to arrived at Chickasha, Oklahoma, in June of 1945. Back in Wetumka in July, he told his story to Jue Miller who wrote it up for THE HOLDENVILLE DAILY NEWS work for 12 hours a day in an underground munitions factory with only a cup of tea for breakfast and a tenth of a loaf of bread for supper. He said he was marched east in front of the advancing American armies on April 6, 1945. He said it was a three day forced march without food and he had witnessed the starvation death of 79 American soldiers. On April 23, he was back in American hands. During the ten weeks of his captivity he lost 65 pounds. He was immediately hospitalized in three different hospitals in Europe and then flown to New York. He had not recovered from his ordeal when he returned Stateside.

Volunteers in Wetumka helped pack "kit-bags" for Americans held prisoner by the Germans and Japanese. On one occasion they knitted small squares and included needles and instructions on how to knit them together to make a comforter. The American Red Cross operated over 100 trucks behind the lines in Europe delivering supplies to the prison camps. They operated out of Switzerland and Sweden. There was even some civility between the American and Japanese during the war in the Pacific. American and Japanese ships rendevoused at sea to accept critical supplies for POWs. A citizen of the Philippines acted as an agent to distribute supplies to American prisoners in that country. A soldier from Holdenville said that he had help air drop supplies in the Far East.

Wetumka came to closely resemble a small military base. The rifle range was in constant use and the old CCC camp was barracks for many a unit from the Oklahoma Air Depot. There were troop columns marching in all directions from town as the army sent them on marches through the countryside to toughen them. It had been reported that a disproportionate number of American soldiers drowned in the early amphibious landings. Many American men and boys commonly had never really had a chance to learn to swim during the Depression years. (The WPA had built a swimming pool in Wetumka on land donated by Dr. C. A. Hicks. But it was really a wading pool because so many people were non-swimmers. It had rock walls for sides and a sandy bottom and was drained and refilled every week.)

In 1943 the swimming pools at Weleetka, Wewoka and Holdenville were taken over by the Army for training purposes. Troops were taken from Wetumka to these pools to give them some familiarity with being in the water with nearly a hundred pounds of battle gear. I am informed that the streets of Wetumka were thronged by army boys trying to relax after hours and they freely mingled with the local people. There were many heavily chaperoned dances and social mixers. (The largest community event was a regular Saturday night dance sponsored and chaperoned by the Wetumka Service Club in the showroom of the Lee Motor Company. And I am reliably informed that at least one local romance resulted in marriage. This was the marriage between Marie Nolen (Pee Wee Nolen's sister) and Ensign Richard W. Ice, which took place in Oklahoma City on July 17, 1944.)

On Sunday, the fourth of July, 1943, the largest display of military might ever seen in Wetumka culminated in a very colorful afternoon parade. Everyone was fascinated by the huge army trucks and jeeps. No less an authority than Hazel Bradberry, wrote up the visit of the 61st Air Depot Group for THE HOLDENVILLE DAILY NEWS. She stated that the band was made up of twenty soldiers and nine members of the Wetumka High School band. Lieutenant Eckstein had been working with them and they played patriotic military marches that really stirred the hearts of war-weary Wetumkans lining the streets. (There were also large groups of visitors from Dustin, Weleetka, and surrounding towns.)

The parade originated at the intersection of Highways 9 and 75. It moved north through Main Street and past the recently built reviewing stand in front of the Rogue theatre. In addition to Mayor Henry Bowles and American Legion Commander Otto Neal, the troop commanders who sat on the reviewing stand were Colonel Arthur B. Jones, Jr. and Major R. B. Palmer. (This was not the largest military crowd in Wetumka during the war. In addition to truck convoys that took hours to pass, in April, 1945, two passenger trains of soldiers were stranded in town for two days because of flood waters on the Wewoka Creek and The North Canadian River. There were over 1,200 servicemen caught on the streets of the isolated town. The American Red Cross, through its local representative, Bill Nicks, authorized the grocers to supply food. The cafes had already started closing on alternate days because of critical shortages. The War Price and Rationing Board at Holdenville agreed to provide additional ration coupons. Food supplies for the German prisoner of war camp, in the former CCC barracks, were trucked from Camp Gruber and brought across the swollen North Canadian by Army landing craft.)

Keeping the prisoners well fed was thought to be in the best interest of the country. They were free to write their own relatives in their homeland and it was thought this might affect the way American POWs in Germany were treated. Many of the 401 prisoners had nearly starved to death before their arrival at the "German Hospital" at Okmulgee. This was the only place German prisoners were kept in Hughes County. A smaller group was quartered at the armory at Okemah. (About 22,000 of the 400,000 German prisoners brought to American were lodged in Oklahoma.)

In another month Wetumkans would learn that their own sons in the National Guard (45th Infantry Division) had been committed to combat in Sicily. They had had five temporary homes and had left from Camp Pickett, Virginia. The first county casualty was PFC Richard Sullivan (a full-bloodied Indian) of Wetumka who died on shipboard, near Sicily, during an appendicitis attack. A soldier from Holdenville, Private First Class Elbert Hollingshead, came home on leave and told his sad story. He said he and his brother were serving in the 45th Infantry Division and had always been in the same unit. They were at the Anzio beachhead and later saw the historic Abbey at Monte Cassino bombed by the Allies to deny cover to the Germans. He said that in March, 1944, when the fighting was heavy: "I saw my brother fall in battle."

In truth, most of the men in the two Wetumka companies had left the National Guard upon the expiration of their terms and nearly all of them had entered other branches of the service. The former commanding General, W. S. Key, from Wewoka for a while had been the Provost Marshal of American troops in Europe, then he commanded the troops stationed in Iceland.

There would surely have been a General from Hughes County except for a plane crash in North Africa on September 7, 1943. Colonel Harold B. Wright from Calvin was killed when the plane on which he was a passenger developed engine trouble and crashed when the pilot attempted return to the airport at Accra, Gold Coast (Ghana). His parents knew about it several weeks before the official notification came. They had been telephoned by a close associate of their son. Colonel Wright was only 29. He had graduated from the University of Oklahoma and the Oklahoma Military Academy and was a member of the graduating class at the U. S. Military Academy at West Point in 1936. His mother said that he had been raised in grade every year after the war started. He seemed to have an unlimited future. He'd grown up in Calvin and married the daughter of a local doctor.

Before the massive invasion of Europe, THE TULSA DAILY NEWS reported that Hughes County ranked third in its battle deaths among the 77 Oklahoma counties. Thirty-eight were listed as dead, 12 were prisoners of war and 27 had been wounded. (At the end of the war this newspaper stated that 114 men from Hughes County had been killed. This number is open to question. One man was listed twice with different surnames. A missing soldier was not declared dead until he had been found or a year had passed.) There are many inherently difficult problems in keeping lists.

Overwhelmingly, the Wetumkans who died or were seriously injured in the war met their fate during or after the Normandy invasion of June 6, 1944. According to newspaper accounts, two Wetumkans, Arthur Cook and Private Burton Case died on July 3, 1944 and William Hatcher three days later. Johnny W. Smith died in Bulgaria on June 24, 1944. The fighting during the next three months was the heaviest of the war and it is borne out in the number of fatalities. Technical Sergeant Orrus T. Baxter, a recent football star in Wetumka, was killed over Germany on July 11, 1944. Private Wadie Buckley died on July 19, 1944 in the fighting in Italy. Ovie Young was killed in action in France on September 16, 1944.

Another Wetumkan at the Normandy Invasion was Flight Officer Henry C. Williams, son of Mr. and Mrs. Sol Williams had a very unusual and exceptionally dangerous mission. Every kind of craft imaginable came ashore at Normandy but the strangest were the gliders. Henry Williams was the pilot of one of these gliders which were flimsily built and meant for one flight. They were literally crash-landed on the beaches of France. Most of them carried 18 to 20 men and often at least one of them was a high ranking officer. (The first American General killed during the invasion was in one of these huge unwieldly gliders that had been towed across the English Channel.) Williams got his craft down safely in a French farmer's field. He said he was carrying a jeep, a trailer, and seven men. He said that he was in the area for 20 hours and was beginning to feel at home although shells were landing all around him. He said that he was actually numbed to the extent that he "didn't feel a thing" when he helped carry another glider pilot out of his craft. The poor fellow had hit the ground so hard that his feet were knocked off. He said his experience had been positive because the Americans had caught up to him and the only Germans he saw were dead or those that had been taken prisoner. He said when he made it back to the beach the whole area was cleared and an Admiral give him and four other glider pilots a lift on a destroyer. They got the air medal and a seven day leave.

The was an organization at Holdenville that called itself "The War Dads" and its function was to assist the parents of servicemen. A similar organization existed in Wetumka under a less formal set up. Since transportation was so difficult during the war years, they often pooled their resources to help.For Mother's Day, 1945, they made it possible for Hughes County wives and mothers to visit their convalescing sons and husbands in the hospitals at Chickasha and Muskogee. They provided transportation and accomodations. At about this time the Army started discharging all men age 42 and above who turned in an application.

In Wetumka manpower was becoming critically short in every sector. The postmasters of Wetumka and Holdenville served throughout the war as officers. Cecil Fair, clerk at the Wetumka post office, was recruited as a mail handler for the U. S. Navy. (Specific occupations like this were targeted by the service because there was not time to train and license mail handlers.) The Navy Seabees were mostly men who had been recruited from the civilian construction trades. Civilians could not work in the theatres of operation because they could be captured and accused of being spies; they were thus put into uniform.) Alex Noon, the former Principal Chief of the Creeks joined the Seabees and went off to Bermuda to help build ports and runways.

It was not just the service which heavily recruited from the streets of Wetumka. Wetumka men, free to travel, could sign up to help build defense facilities all over the country. There were even agents from lumber companies, on the West Coast, scouring the area for workers. The Frisco Railroad which had expanded into a truck line and was even planning a passenger airline at the end of the war, opened a wide campaign for manpower in early 1944. The railroad recruiters who came through Wetumka said they needed an additional 1,000 men and women for all kinds of railroad jobs and there were openings in nearly every city on its line. The railroad men told everyone who would listen that "railroad work was war work." Unskilled men and women would be accepted on a "learn as you earn basis." (In January, 1942, Wetumka's Chief of Police, Joe Bement, had left his elected job and went to work at a defense establishment at Wilmington, California. He left his assistant, Curtis Lowder, in charge. He thought the people of Wetumka would understand because he'd been elected so many times "and besides I might not like war-work."

Eventually, there would be a War Manpower Board located in Holdenville to rationalize the use of the ever dwindling pool of laborers. (In a few short years the county had gone from the situation of having a vast number of men unable to find any remunerative work to the greatest labor shortage in its history).

There was a severe labor shortage on the farms of Hughes County. This was especially the case in the fall when peanuts were harvested. It may have been a little easier to grow peanuts than cotton. They could withstand some hail and the farmer didn't have to worry about being wiped out by the bowl weevil. The harvest was a time of high anxiety and pressure for the farmer. A fine peanut crop could start sprouting in the ground or at any stage of the harvest.

No crop was more labor intensive at harvest than peanuts. In the 1940's there were only a few threshing machines in the entire county. They were wooden framed affairs with lots of chain drives and components that were apt to break down. The thresher ran off a long belt from a tractor.

The farmer felt triumphant just to get a peanut thresher into his field. It meant that his peanut crop had been dug and dried in the field. On a chosen day, the farmer would plow up the whole field of peanuts. Then a crew of men would move through the field "shaking peanuts" or picking up every vine and shaking the dirt off and turning the nuts up to dry in the sun. Since nearly every farmer, in those days, would experience some adverse weather before the peanut thresher arrived, the whole crop was pitch-forked into wagons and shocked around poles on raised beds of earth. On the day the peanuts were threshed there would be two to three dozen men and women who would haul the peanuts to the thresher. Burlap bags were really hard to come by. (This is the reason Congress authorized the growing of hemp within the United States. Marijuana is a type of hemp and there may be even a little truth in the saying "smoke a rope." Not many people knew of the hallucinatory characteristics of the hemp family.)

When the farmer's peanuts were bagged, he knew that he had to follow the thresher in its rounds to pay back the labor of every person who had worked for him. This was the only way a threshing crew could be pooled.

Most farmers did not think the German prisoners of war at the former CCC camp were good help. The main reason was that most of them had been injured or they came to the United States in a serious state of malnutrition. (The American soldier, on the average, was getting four times the calories on a daily basis as the German soldier.) Every one of them was a convalescing patient from "the German hospital" at Okmulgee. (This hastily built facility would be turned over to the Oklahoma Agricultural and Mechanical College (later OSU) to be a Tech School.

War time shortages were alleviated to a large part by community canning in Wetumka. Throughout 1945 an average of 2,500 quarts of fruits, vegetables and meats were canned at Vocational Agriculture area of the high school. Mrs. Jeff Biffle and Mrs. Bill Mullins were in charge of this project.

A small factory in Holdenville turned out two million tent stakes for the armed services. It was known as the United Manufacturing company and operated in a converted lumber yard. By August, 1945, it was converted to peace time production with an order to build 5,000 cedar chests. As was the case in producing tent stakes, this company went directly to the loggers for their raw materials.

The ranks of the teachers in Wetumka and Hughes county were thinned again and again by men going to war and women going to defense jobs. The situation became so desperate that most people with any college work at all could get hired as teachers. They had to attend two weeks of workshops and a weekend in a conference. These requirements were finally waived; the applicant could get an emergency teaching credential by completing a correspondence course.

Next to penicillin, the greatest medical breakthrough in World War II was in getting blood from civilians to soldiers. At the start of the war blood transfusions were done but the procedure was hardly routine; the technology for preserving blood and its components did not exist for civilians. It was still the responsibility of the patient's family to find suitable donors and get them to the hospital. In January, 1945, two young women from Calvin, Betty Jo Chaddick and Rosella Tharp answered an "SOS" for blood donors. They were rushed to an Oklahoma City hospital by Lieutenant C. T. Raley on a screaming trip to save the life of a woman from Calvin.

The first blood donations for soldiers from Wetumka were made a couple of months after the Normandy landings when the need was the greatest. It was necessary for the donors to travel to Durant to give a pint of blood to the mobile unit there from Dallas. At Durant they were given a quick medical examination and blood was taken from those who appeared to be in good health.

The Wetumkans who went to Durant were doing something noble in that it had not been done previously and they really did know what to expect. They were part of the 84 volunteer blood donors from Hughes County. This is the list:

Mr. and Mrs. T. J. Davis, Margaret Chowins, Mrs. J. E. Jarrett, Mrs. J. C. Puryear, Mrs. Bert Shaber, J. B. Kamplain, Mrs. Dorothy Thompson, Mrs. Juanita Uzzell, Mr. and Mrs. Turner McCoy, E. W. Cole, Henry Bowles, David J. McKinny, Wilburn Neese, Rufus Martin, Dick Martin, Ocie Crain, Mrs. Dorothy Stuckey, Mrs. Burl Sanders, Jack Murphy, I. M. Preston, J. M. Nicks, Ray Meadors, Marguerite Bicknell, J. W. Nicks, Mrs. Jerry Golightly, James McKinney, Harve Woford, Mrs. Elwanna Gibson, C. M. Murphy, Mrs. Juanita Yahola, Cannon Acuff, Sara Barker, O. S. Adams, Gordon Bradley, Mrs. W. B. Barnes, Wanda Studyvin, Bill Tankersley, Mr. and Mrs. John Harlan, and Mrs. Annie Thatcher.

These are the drivers in that caravan: Joyce Davis, Kathleen Murphy, L. F. Battles, Jack Murphy, I. M. Preston, Will Ogle, Henry Bowles, J. M. Nicks, H. H. Darks, and Ray Meadors.

After V-E day and V-J Day (May and August, 1945) there was a steady stream of Wetumkans returning to the States.

Major Glenn Chowins, was back in Wetumka by August and was working as the superintendent of the city light plant when he accepted the positions of head football coach and athletic director. (Mr. Ernie Stout was serving as the High School principal at the time.)

There were at least twenty-seven Wetumkans who died in World War II. Approximately the same number of men from Holdenville were fatalities. This accounts for fewer than half of the estimated 114 Hughes County boys who died in the war. The majority were farm youths or were from some the many small communities which have practically vanished from the map. (THE HOLDENVILLE DAILY NEWS and THE TULSA DAILY NEWS kept a tally of the war dead. Their list is not totally accurate and none ever can be because of problems of definition. Who is a Hughes County boy? The list contains the names of men who grew up in the county and enlisted, sometimes years later, in other states (which seems legitimate). If a man says he's from the county, he should be taken at his word. I have made no distinction between those killed in training accidents and those who died in combat. Some soldiers, that I know little of, were re-buried in the Wetumka Cemetery. This is the list that I have assembled by scouring the newspapers of the time:

Barnes, Wallace J., KIA with 45th at Anzio (Italy), 4-14-1944.(Indian)

Baxter, Orrus, Jr., T/Sgt., WHS Grid Star, KIA over Germany, 7-11-1944

Buckley, Wadie, Pvt., KIA, Italy, 7-19-1944

Burchell, Earl, son of Oscar L. Burchell, of Los Angeles, many years a resident of Wetumka, killed in plane crash in Nebraska. Graduated from Wetumka High School three years ago. A cousin of Mrs. Agnes Fuller, Mrs. Florence Adkins, and Miss Jeannette Franklin. (Another graduate of the WHS Class of 1940).

Case, Berton Ed, Pvt., KIA, France, 7-3-1944

Cheek, Benjamin, KIA, Italy, 8-17-1943

Cook, Arthur, T4. Killed in action during invasion of France on June 12, 1944.

Diggs, Graham Wall, Jr., KIA over Germany 12-3-1943. Son of the late pioneer Wetumka physician who served as mayor during Depression years.

Fisher, Andrew L., Pvt., KIA Philippines.

Gist, Lloyd, KIA Belgium, 3-2-1945. WHS Class of 1940.

Haddock, Benjamin, KIA, Italy, 9-14-1944

Harkins, Donnie S., Veteran of World War I, died when his Liberty Ship capsized. 12-2-1942

Harper, Franklin, Pvt., KIA, 3-30-1944 in Italy.

Harris, Omer, C/O.

Hatcher, William G., Pvt., KIA, 7-7-1944

Herndon, Loyal H., KIA,Germany 3-15-1945

Hulsey, Leon, Lieutenant, is declared officially dead on 2-5-1946.

Long, Noah, Pvt., KIA Germany 9-8-1945.

McDowell, Elva, KIA 4-2-1943 in North Africa.

McNeil, James S.

Ross, Whitson, Pvt., KIA Belgium, 1-24-1945

Scott, Ray, Cpl., KIA in parachute traning, 10-11-1942.

Sheppard, Ray, Cpl., KIA in Pacific, WHS 1940.

Smith, Johnny W., KIA in Bulgaria, 6-24-1944.

Sullivan, Richard, PFC, died of appendicitis aboard ship enroute to Sicily. 9-6-1944

Webb, Glenn, S/Sgt., first Hughes County flier to die. 11-29-1943

Young, Ovie, KIA France, 9-16-1944

(Benjamin Haddock was not a native Wetumkan. He was the son-in-law of Mrs. and Mrs. H. H. Darks. He had been married to their daughter, Doris, who died recently according to the Wetumka newspaper.) Some of the men from Wetumka listed their hometown as Holdenville. Major Thomas Mackay who was buried in the Wetumka Cemetery is an example.) Compiling lists is a difficult undertaking.

There is one irreducible fact. No county lost as many men except the metropolitan counties of Oklahoma and Tulsa. On a per capita basis, no county in Oklahoma lost as many men as Hughes County. There were over 3,000 men and women from Hughes County who served in the armed forces in the Second World War. No records are as confidential as military service records. I have tracked nearly every one of these persons and have at least a partial story for each one. Official U. S. Government records show that of the more than 10 million men and women mobilized between May 27, 1941 and January 31, 1946, 2.98% of them were missing or declared dead. The death rate was substantially higher for Hughes County, nearly a full percentage point higher. (It is correct to say that one out of every thirty boys from Wetumka and Hughes County who entered the service did not return.)

The figures for Oklahoma were 17,464 casualties: of whch 4,864 were killed and 9,801 were wounded. At the end of the war there were 1, 775 still missing and and unaccounted for. Over a thousand Oklahomans had been taken prisoner (1,041).

17

War's Aftermath and The Veterans

In January, 1946, there was a funeral in Holdenville of a quiet man who like dozens of other countyans chose to leave their elective position to serve in the Armed Forces. This was J. Grady Simmons, a long time rural school teacher who was the superintendent at Atwood when Jim Ragland resigned to be superintendent at Maud. The county commissioners had selected him to finish Mr. Ragland's term. Then Mr. Simmons was re-elected on his own but he heard his country's call. Like Paul Ballinger who left the state legislature to be a buck private in the Army, Mr. Simmons left to be an ordinary sailor. Before he could ship out to a theatre of action, he was diagnosed with a brain tumor. He died on the last day of 1945 in the Army hospital at Oakland, California. I admire his courage to become a sailor when he could have spent the war years in his office in the courthouse. (Early in the war there were eleven members of the Hughes County Bar Association in uniform.)

Then county commissioners appointed a Wetumkan to a position that was vacated by the heart attack death of Coleman C. Atwood, county treasurer and pioneer citizen. This man was Jeff Biffle who wore several hats in Wetumka. He was Secretary of the Chamber of Commerce (an important paid position then) and was Chairman of the Tri-County Labor Association, an organization set up to work German POWs on the farms of a three county area. Mr. Biffle was also a member of the Hobson-Gopher Hill school board. (He had been elected twice as county clerk in Polk county, Arkansas in the 1930s.) The commissioners were pleased that they could find a qualified person to step into a job in which the appointee would have to stand for re-election. It was a complicated and burdensome position that required a $75,000 bond. The salary was a modest $1,800 annually.

General MacArthur said it would have been a long war without DDT. This was the first effective pesticide and it enabled American soldiers to enter jungles and breeding places for mosquitoes and other deadly pests. The first peacetime application of this miracle substance was in Oklahoma. By January, 1946, it was already replacing cattle dipping that had utilized an arsenic solution that could be highly adverse to the health of men and cattle.

Returning soldiers often did not make a smooth transition back to civilian life. There were hordes of soldiers and defense workers trying to fit into the social scene. They thought that the Depression was over and they had dreamed of being back in Wetumka every night. This is where the dreams and aspirations drew them. The most fortunate ones came home and waited to be summoned back to get their discharges. The army had agreed to something called on-the-job training and twenty-four of the merchants and potential employers had been approved to accept these returning GI's as tentative employees. Many of the soldiers were mustered out and given their final pay in U. S. savings bonds. Of course the soldiers needed ready cash and the lines at the banks reached out to the street. As much was being paid out on a daily basis as had been paid out on a Saturday back in the heyday of cotton growing.

Very few men escaped military service in the Second World War. Governor Leon Phillips followed the lead of governors in surrounding states when he pardoned about 500 prisoners to the U. S. Army. It was commonly believed that convicts were being sheltered in prisons when they should have been subjected to the rigors of combat. The U. S. Army had no experience at all in gathering such a large body of fighting men and convicts and those with serious police records were at first accepted. It was a disaster because men who fail as citizens in civilian life seldom make good soldiers. The Army was nearly overwhelmed by the number of men who had to be court martialed and released.

The feeling that "nervy" men made good soldiers must have been common in Hughes County as well. In October, 1941, a soldier on leave. John H. Gordon, became intoxicated and went on a rage through the streets of Dustin telling everyone that he was going to kill the town marshal. No one took him seriously but he hunted down the well respected lawman, Jake Henderson, and unmercifully shotgunned him. The lawman died within a few hours and the sobered soldier was arrested for murder. But he was remanded to the Army after just a few days. A year later he was returned to the county to stand trial for murder. The jury declined ton convict him on the abundance of evidence and testimony. There seemed to be a feeling at the time, among some of the citizenry, that the country needed manpower so badly that there was no way this fellow was going to get out of going. If he was sent to prison, it only meant that another farmer's son would have to be drafted in his place.

This mentality manifest itself in other actions. In early 1940, John Anglin, a former Justice of the Peace at Calvin (no relation to the Senator) was deserted by his wife. When he learned that she had gone to visit a male friend, he went to the man's house, called him outside and shot him to death. Then he called the Sheriff and told him what he had done.

Mr. Anglin was taken into custody and booked for first degree murder. Mr. Anglin had been disfigured (perhaps by smallpox) and made a sympathetic defendant. A jury was seated but they were a group of sullen men who only opened their mouths to cite Biblical phrases. The prosecutor, sensing the futility of a trial, asked the judge to dismiss them. The defendant got away with murder.

Hughes county had never permitted women jurors until February of 1952 when two women were seated, unintensionally, on a civil jury. A bingo game device was used to randomly select names. The women called were Mrs. Ray Peavy of Wetumka and Mary Ingram of Holdenville. I knew that Mrs. Peavy was the type of person who would stand her ground and introduce the woman's perspective into legal proceedings. The same jury would hear the entire docket of eighteen cases.

The most ridiculous of the antics of the veterans occurred right after one soldier's discharge. Loy T. Shields of Holdenville casually robbed a bank in Oklahoma City without benefit of a disguise or get away car. The bank employees ran him down on the streets. He was smiling when he said, "that whole dang town was chasing me." He got a very light sentence because it was not a bank robbery in the usual sense of that term. He had removed the powder from the bullets in his pistol because he was jittery and thought he might accidentally shoot someone. Technically he was not an armed robber.

Cpl. Pat Parker, of Calvin, was released from a Japanese prison camp after thirty-three months on March 14, 1945. In December he was tried and convicted of a forgery that netted him less than thirty dollars. Judge Howell, a former GI himself, gave him a ten year prison sentence which he suspended in light of the time Parker had already served in prison.

Five years after the war a War Claims Commission was tying up loose ends and decided to pay every American soldier who had been a POW $1 for every day of captivity for his rations as if he had been on leave. The newspapers incorrectly hailed this as a bonus. H. D. Malloy, the John Deer Implements and Studebaker dealer in Holdenville got $333. The veterans I talked with said they got nothing because they didn't know about filing a claim.

The most bizarre of all the incidents took place at the Oklahoma State capital on May 7, 1947. Jimmy Scott, Holdenville resident, served as a storekeeper in the Pacific during the war. He came home and got into politics as part of the "GI Slate." (Some of the ex-servicemen even wore their uniforms while campaigning.) He was elected the Oklahoma House of Representatives. His life was seemingly normal but his recently divorced wife would have said differently. That day in

Oklahoma City he confronted his legislative colleague, prominent Senator Tom Anglin, with a pistol and despite the Senator's shout not to shoot he managed to get off a round which struck the Senator in the abdomen. Spectators first thought he had fired two shots. The second shot came from the gun that the Senator had always carried. Representative Paul Ballinger, also of Holdenville, finally persuaded the Senator to put down his weapon.

Representative Scott was apprehended in the Men's room and Senator Anglin was taken to a hospital where he spent a month. His injury was more serious that he admitted. It was months before he returned, even part time to his office. Jimmy Scott got exactly what Senator Anglin recommended. At his hearing he was found incompetent to stand trail and was confined to a Naval Hospital.

I personally found the death of Major Jack Kelley very sad as his brother, Mack, was with my father when he was killed on the job in 1954. The major was a graduate of Fairview High School and had spent three and a half years in the thick of the fighting. He came home and started a new career with the Army Reserve Officer Training Organization (ROTC) at Louisiana State University. In early 1946 he died going to his job on a foggy highway near Lake Charles, Louisiana. His brothers were Ted and Mack Kelley. (In 1945 alone, nearly 100 former servicemen were killed in Oklahoma road accidents.)

The death of Sammie Fish after midnight on the train tracks on January 21, 1952, shocked the whole community. He had served 19 months as a prisoner of war performing during slave labor in an underground munitions factory in Germany.

Police Chief John McGibboney and his deputy Bass Moore had placed Sammie under arrest. Just before they entered the city hall he broke free and tried to cross in front of a train. Police Chief "Mack" McGibboney said they did not pursue him and did not immediately realize that he'd been hit by the train. They theorized that he was blinded by the light of the oncoming southbound freight and could not determine which track it was on. The engineer said he saw the man running along in front of the train and thought he would get off the track.

Another very tragic event took place at Doc Rupe's gas station and store near the stop sign on Grand Avenue and Main Street. A thirty-one year old Creek Indian, winner of the Silver Star in World War II, confronted a 25 year-old Indian who had just been discharged as a paratrooper in Korea. Raymond Dunzy slashed at Robert Lee Thomas laying open to the bone his left forearm and right elbow. The injured man fled in panic. First he ran to the city hall and then crossed the street and ran to the stairs leading to Dr. Morris's office. It was here that he collapsed. The trail of dried blood looked like something leading out of a slaughter house.

The witnesses, Doc Rupe and Everett Neese (the taxi driver) could not make sense of what had happened. Dunzy's half brother Felix, a friend and National Guard associate of mine, would only say: "Nobody knows." That, in itself, is probably a valid explanation of these tragic and unexplained events. The mental debility suffered by men in the first World War was medically recognized and the problems of many Vietnam veterans are believed to have had a medical basis. It seemed that so many veterans of World War II had a difficult time getting their lives back on track and someone of them never did. It may have been beyond them.

18

The Paving of Highway 9 and Wetumka's Transformation

For the first two decades of its existence Highway 9 through Wetumka was as primitive as any county road. While it marked the southern boundary of the town, it was a very dark, narrow and muddy street of seemingly bottomless obstacles to traffic. The intersection with US 75 was an especially dangerous spot. Highway 9 was nearly a foot lower and during wet weather it was possible for automobiles to hit a "high center" at the edge of the pavement. During dry and dusty weather it was not unknown for cars to have "roadbed collisions" with the pavement in this intersection.

Oklahoma was able to build roads after World War II primarily because of a five and a half cent per gallon tax on gasoline. Governor-elect Raymond Gary was in Wetumka in 1955 to attend one of the many conferences to discuss the future of Highway 9 and he stated on that occasion that Oklahoma was already reaping the benefits of a billion dollars a year spent by tourists and other travelers in the state. Oklahoma was well positioned as a crossroads for interstate traffic.

Doc Grisso, is often called the "father" of Highway 9. I am doubtful of this paternity claim although he was instrumental in getting the road that passes in front of his mansion paved. Mr. Grisso is often erroneously called Dr. Grisso and by people who knew better. He was an early resident of Tidmore, a community that stood near present day Seminole. He got his medical title as the proprietor of a drug store where he was known for his skill in mixing potent patent medicines for his customers. He was one of the greatest beneficiaries of the Seminole oil pool. In the 1920s he was truly rich as he could only estimate his worth. His mansion which still stands at the edge of Seminole was variously estimated to have cost $600,000 to a million in 1926. In later years he devoted much of his time to civic projects and served on the State Highway Commission.

In the summer of 1949 work in earnest began on paving Highway 9 west from the US 75 intersection in Wetumka. A quarter of a million dollars was allocated to six miles. The right of way to widen the road had already been acquired. (This practice was a new one but was necessary before any Federal aid could be sought. For several years there was hope that Highway 9 would be designated US 366.)

Road building was entering a new era. Nearly sixty-four thousand tons of crushed rock was laid down as a roadbed. On top of this went a nine inch stabilized aggregate base and then a hot mix of asphalt an inch and a half thick was applied. About $480,000 was spent on the road in Seminole county. But it would another ten years before the gap between Wetumka and Seminole would be closed. Asphalt roads were held in very low esteem before the war. Part of US 75 was a "bituminous mat" through south Main Street in Wetumka and was unsatisfactory from the start. By mid-1950 $2.5 had been spent between Haskell county and Norman and Highway 9 was not anywhere close to being an all weather road in current parlance.

Downtown Wetumka seemed to revitalize within a few months of the end of World War II. There were two motion picture theatres (the Avalon and the Time) and a third was under construction. The new theatre, The Redskin would open in 1948 and represented the largest private investment on Main Street since the building of the Meadors' Hotel twenty-three years earlier during the Oil Boom. Over $100,000 went into the construction of this new entertainment palace which could seat 499 persons. No building in Wetumka had ever been so ornate and modern. It's huge neon sign was highlighted by a 25 foot marquee that had a sequentially blinking neon center. It's festive appearance extended to the sidewalk with its concentric rings of colored cement. Persons familiar with the entertainment complexes of Oklahoma agreed that this building with its luxurious velvet-feel seats of red and green outdid any theatre in Oklahoma City of Tulsa. For several years the theatre would draw patrons from a large radius as first run movies were always featured.

Five years after the opening of The Redskin, it was apparent that the business district was shifting to Highway 9 and the Oklahoma Highway Commission had a large hand in it. During the summer of 1953 there was more business construction than had been seen in Wetumka in its half-century life. The last five miles of the highway was to be paved from the east to the junction of Highways 9 and US 75. The State did all but draw the blueprints for the motels, gas stations and resturants which would result from the widening of Highway 9 within the city limits. Highway 9 was now a 44 foot wide slab seven inches thick with six inch curbs. And this was courtesy of the State. Two months after this concrete addition to Wetumka's street grid (August, 1952) was made the State paved 1,100 feet of Dustin's Main Street.

Early in 1953 a committee from Wetumka (H. H. Loard, Stona Fitch and Bryan Nicks) approached the State Highway Comission with a request to improve Highway 75 through Wetumka's Main Street. Senator Paul Ballinger got an estimate and the Commission approved it. There was no need to wait for warm weather because the hot mix asphalt could be applied any time. The project covered .8 of a mile from Grand Avenue to the 9-75 junction. It was a three inch overlay of asphalt that really was a lot smoother than the brick which had developed many corrugations due to the passage of so much heavy traffic.

Benny Kirby purchased the southeast corner of the 9-75 junction from Robert Kay and proceeded to build what he intended to be a tourist court of 9 units. A house had to be moved and Mr. Kirby experienced several changes of heart during the course of construction. His complex of buildings would become an apartment building, a grrocery story (first operated by O. K. Ramsay) and a gas station and cafe operated by Glenn Blackburn and Robert McConvil from Holdenville.

Raymond Davis, a Holdenville resident, moved to Wetumka, temporarily, to build a motel on the opposite corner. He had purchased this corner from Frank Eastep. Actual construction started in August of 1953 and the new 17 unit motel and coffee shop were ready for a grand opening in February of 1954. The Ranch-O-Tel name was adopted shortly before the neon signs were to installed. Ten of the motel rooms were fully carpeted and seven had tile floors. A feature of one of the rooms was bunk beds. Three types of wood were used in the decoration scheme: mahogany, maple and walnut.

The Coffee Shop consisted of five booths and ten stools at the counter. There was a lavish use of stainless steel with the perma-stone style of the outside walls extending inside to form a seperation between the booths and stools.

The Ranch-O-Tel was predicably a success. The traffic through Wetumka was increasing rapidly and customers were willing to drive distances to dine at the coffee shop which quickly acquired a reputation for cleanliness, wholesomeness and outstanding restaurant food. (Many of the local resturants had an image problem because so many citations had been issued for unsafe and questionable food handling practices. Ten years before the County Health Officer, Dr. Kernek, had publicized conditions of cafes in the county. He said that most of them did not wash their drinking glasses between customers and he had seen glasses with so many fingerprints that they were no longer transparent. This became the "public dipper" issue and may have contributed to better resturant sanitation.)

Within a few months of its opening the Ranch-O-Tel had been acquired by Cecil and Della Kilgore and a consortium of Wetumka business people that included Mrs. James Taylor. The coffee shop and motel had a 35 foot drive-way before the dining room was built a couple of years later by Wetumkan Levi Clendening.

During this road construction, Charley Baker, Wetumka's chief electrician, and his crew had installed thirty-two mercury vapor lamps on high reach light poles. Herman Darks, now the mayor, considered this one of the greatest achievements of his tenure. He touted the new lights in a ceremony as the finest in Oklahoma and congratulated the city crew for their work of installing the new whiteway without the necessity of hiring a contractor. (In his speech he kept reminding the crowd that only two cities in Oklahoma had this kind of up-to-date lighting: Hugo and Wetumka.)

For such a brief period in the 1950s, Wetumka seemed to be a thriving place. The automobile dealers seemed to do well. Gammill's service station, one of the longest lived businesses in town, was also the Pontiac dealership and the showroom was in the front of the present building. There were always several new cars parked in front. Gammill's had long been the agent for International Harvestor farm equipment. After the war International Harvestor trucks and pick-ups were added and proved very popular with farmers and others.

The Wetumka School District allowed the use of two addmittedly unsafe buses during the war. These were the operated by Charlie Wells and Fred Hooper. They were "wooden body" buses with flat roofs. Instead of having dents, they had broken planks on the sides where they had collided with ditches in bad weather. I rode Fred Hooper's bus from the first grade when my parents share-cropped in the Mountain Grove area. Fred's two teenaged sons, Vernon and Vester, took turns driving the old bus which was really a rattle trap. The roof often leaked and a window was always missing. The passenger door was opened and closed manually and the windshield wipers were cranked by a high school student who sat on a box. At the end of the war, Oklahoma outlawed this type of equipment. Fred Hooper, also the head school custodian, took a hand saw and turned it into a flat bed truck one weekend. His brother-in-law, Oliver Elzy, operated an ancient bus that was legal because the body was of metal. He ordered a new International chassis through Gammill's and a crew of men with cutting torches and welders attached the old bus to the chassis.

Harry Jackson, brother-in-law of Stona Fitch, had served on the school board, been the Census Taker and runner up in the exams for Post Master. Before the war he'd been the salesman for Fleming Chevrolet. After the war he operated his own Chevrolet-Oldsmobile agency just north of the City Hall.

Dalton Fuller was the Chrysler-Plymouth Dealer and Carlos Garrett, who earlier had been the shop foreman at the Ford garage, became the owner when Nathan Lee retired in 1950. Jim Ed Hansford, the barber, had gone to defense work at Santa Barbara, California. He was right when he said that it was one of the most beautiful spots in California. But he came back to Wetumka and it seemed that he was leader of a trend. Everyone wanted to come home.

Wetumka, in the 1950s, was a busy place. There was a grocery store on every block and every one of them had a pick-up truck and would deliver. Wetumka was ringed by gas stations and nearly everyone of them had a small stock of groceries. All of the stores were open until nine o'clock on Saturday night and also on every weekday evening for most of the month of December.

19

Sucker Days

I n the annals of Wetumka no event has ever generated as much good natured publicity as the events that led to the annual celebration known as Sucker Day. Mrs. Jim Ed Hansford published an excellent account in THE READER'S DIGEST and THE WALL STREET JOURNAL and various other national publications have taken note. My own personal favorite is the account that was written by the veteran news manager and commentator at the Tulsa radio station, KVOO, Ken Miller that appeared in THE SATURDAY EVENING POST on June 16, 1951 under the title "Where They Celebrate a Swindle."

Mr. Miller always had a big part in the Arkansas Day celebration in Holdenville. I do not believe he was present at the first Sucker Day although everyone tried to find him. (Without a doubt his voice was the best known and trusted in Oklahoma.) His article captured the true essence of what really happened. Accuracy was always his foremost concern and it is mine. So much has been written by persons who weren't there and are not all that concerned about historical accuracy.

I am a self-appointed bearer of the truth and although I was only twelve-years-old at the time, I was a most passionate observer. More important than that, my patient research has uncovered the official minutes of what actually transpired that on Saturday when Wetumka was only half its present age.

Ken Miller, in his account, artfully showed how a town of 2715 citizens could be so completely bamboozled. In the aftermath everyone can see the folly of accepting F. Bam Morrison, the loveable flim-flam man, as the genuine article. I don't think any merchant in town today would cash a check comically signed "F. Bam Morrison." I've always thought that was one of the funniest names I ever heard.

But the man had a method and he was hometown sincere. He must have gone to the Wetumka Cemetery and memorized names on the tombstones. When he breezed into town he was a such big hit as he spoke familiarly of respected Wetumkans long gone. The Chamber of Commerce swallowed his line whole, "hook, line and sinker." Julian Peixotto stocked up on hot dog weiners and Argie Taylor agreed to supply a vast quantity of elephant hay. The Meadors Hotel spruced up for their expected guests. After a couple of days of local exposure the "old con" developed a sore throat which Dr. Morris fixed up for a handful of circus passes.

It went so well for F. Bam that he left town and in a few days made a second coming. This time he made his biggest haul. He offered a circus sound truck to visit not only Wetumka but Holdenville and every town and settlement in Hughes County. For this he got an advance of $300. (I was young but I knew at the time that that was real money.)

The appointed day that the circus was to appear came and went. Argie Taylor received a package at the Post Office and he was suspicious before he even accepted it. There was postage due. It contained a small sample of "elephant hay" and a note signed F. Bam Morrison. Soon the merchants were telling one another: "We've been plucked." In those days there were several wholesale grocery salesmen who came to town to take orders from the merchants. While everyone was licking their wounds and deploring their bad luck, one of them saw the bright side and said: "You fellers ought to have a "Sucker Day." This seemed like such a good idea. They could have their own circus without even the chance of anyone being stepped on by an elephant.

Mayor Tom Smith proclaimed the first Sucker Day and it took place on August 18, 1950. The parade was one of the longest ever. The Wetumka and Weleetka bands led the procession. Horses made a real comeback in Wetumka that day as the Round-Up Clubs of Holdenville and Wetumka vied with each other to show which had the most members with the best horses and the most prized saddles. There were lots of Wetumkans like Floyd Callison and Jim Ed Hansford who lived in town but they could not live without owning a saddle horse.

F. Bam Morrison had laughed himself to death and his grave was transported through town on a truck. Just his big feet were sticking out. A hay wagon in the parade was pulled by a new Studebaker from the H. D. Malloy agency in Holdenville.

The parade ended abruptly and the milling crowd surged into the street. Traffic waiting for Main Street was able to move only a short distance before it was mired in a sea of humanity. A truck from The Holdenville Rendering Company was completely immobilized long enough for a good many persons to get a nose full of its cargo. The dead animal wagon, grossly overloaded with many frozen legs and hooves in the air, took longer to pass than any other float in the parade.

The food and treats were free on the first Sucker Day. I got a popsicle and an ice cream bar and other items for a value of thirty-five cents. I considered it a sensational haul. Thousands of candy suckers were given away; the streets were littered with them.

In the Sucker Day contests, Jimmy Winters was the pop drinking champion. James Wilder was the best rooster crower. Paul Byrd was declared the best in the pie eating contest. Mrs. Lillie Richmond was the winner in a long line of hog callers. Mrs. Bob Fish was the best husband caller. Kenneth Adkins had the fastest terrapin and Joe Lowder was the best bubble blower of the day. (During the hog calling contest Cecil Kilgore, standing in the crowd, had made a remark that was picked up by Brian Nicks, the Master of Ceremonies. "If there are any loose hogs in this part of the county, they should be arriving shortly!")

Richard "Pee-Wee" Nichols was the only boy who could climb one of the greased saplings, set up on a West Broadway Median, and get the ten dollar bill at the top. There were lots of boys who tried. They rolled in the dirt to get themselves gritty to perhaps get a little traction.

Their only succeeded in ruining their clothes. About this time Mr. Red Jet arrived in his truck with a couple of runty little pigs that had been covered with great gobs of axle grease. When he raised the tailgate, these terrified little pigs took off running for their lives. Several boys tried to latch onto them but all they got were fists full of grease. No one caught the greased pigs and they disappeared through a high stepping crowd.

It was as hot as the middle of a cotton patch on that first Sucker Day. The crowds were tightly packed but no one seemed to mind. Very few men even wore short sleeves and T-shirts and shorts were absolutely unknown. Women of all ages wore long dresses and blue jeans were exceptionally rare. But the people tolerated the heat very well and only a little grumbling was heard. Most remarkably, they were willing to stand shoulder-to-shoulder for long hours. The crowds did not diminish as the day wore on. Dr. Wenrick's office was full of people looking down on the spectacle. The microphone was set just below in front of the Chamber of Commerce office.

A skit managed by Mrs. Lloyd P. Smith was presented to show how Wetumka merchants were duped by F. Bam. Bryan Nicks starred as the notorious F. Bam. Patti McGee helped direct this production and other characters were A. B. Clement, the Rev. I. Smith, Joe Davis, Hoot Gibson, Jack Herring, John G. Nicks, E. J. Early, and the Rev. W. B. Timberlake, Bob Marsh and Dalton Fuller. Two men played themselves in the skit, Dr. C. W. Morris and James Robertson. They were the only ones who got something out of F. Bam. He paid Dr. Morris with a blanket for a prescription and he purchased the blanket from Robertson. Dr. Wenrick would have gotten the blanket but decided to wait for an authentic fringed circus blanket.

This past fall a parody of this Wetumka event was presented by students of the La Jolla Junior College, La Jolla, California. It was scripted from the account given in a popular book intended for children.

That evening Kenneth Wilhite was forced (yes forced!) to push his newly acquired wife, the former Betty Little, the full length of Main Street in an iron wheeled wheelbarrow. This type of vicious hazing of newlyweds was a long standing tradition in Wetumka.

There was another hoax being perpetrated on the people of the vicinity at this time and I believed at the time that not even F. Bam Morrison could have thought it up. Wetumka was always a fertile field for rumors and I'm convinced that some people started outrageous rumors for their own perverse amusement.

Not many people remember the legendary "Slippery Sam" the snake. Just before the arrival of F. Bam Morrison on the Wetumka scene, there was a story making the rounds in Hughes County about a snake that had supposedly been sighted by the county commissioners' road crew. He was "as big around as a man's body and as long as two pick-up trucks." Something that was unbelievable was being heartily believed (seemingly) by about everyone. Slippery Sam made headlines in the Wetumka and Holdenville newspapers as additional sightings were reported. For several weeks it was even a national story covered by United Press International.

He was called Slippery Sam because no one could corral him. And there were lots of search groups who went out after him almost daily. Outsiders got involved. A man from Wewoka came with a pickup load of crushed ice. His plan was to pursue old Sam into the bogs and ice him down to keep him immobilized.

It seemed that more and more people really believed that Slipper Sam existed. There were unconfirmed reports of baby calves turning up missing and mothers began watching their children extra carefully. A woman from Konawa said that she had seen snakes like this on the King Ranch in Texas. According to her, they had been imported from Siberia to keep down the varmints.

My recollection was there was lots more hysteria than laughter about the errant snake. One of the most popular entries in the very first Sucker Day parade was a colorful cloth model of Slippery Sam. No credible sightings of Slippery Sam were made although one Wetumkan claimed to have run over him on Highway Nine. He may have hit something slippery but his account does not ring true because "he didn't look back."

The national press took note of the Slippery Sam hysteria as an "urban legend" or a story that has great staying power although no one ever confirms it. Slippery Sam was completely eclipsed by Sucker Day and was forgotten in a few years.

Another ridiculous story going around at this time was a rumor that was authored by an unnamed Wetumkan who claimed that he had witnessed, in the middle of the night, a bizarre practice by the Mackey Funeral Home in Holdenville. He said they threw bodies of the deceased from a second story window onto the concrete below. His steadfast conclusion was this was to "tenderize stiffs" or make the bodies more flexible and easier to prepare for the casket. This story also had its passionate defenders.

In my humble opinion, the most regal of the Sucker Day celebrations was the second one because it involved the citizenry of Wetumka's namesake, Wetumpka, Alabama. A delegation of Wetumkans had caravaned all the way to Alabama to be a part of their Founder's Day Celebration. The favor was returned when many prominent persons from that town came to the Sucker Day affair. Never had so many cars bearing the Alabama license plate been seen in this part of Oklahoma. One Wetumpkan came to Wetumka by Greyhound bus. (The Wetumpkans had gone to a candy factory and special ordered a giant sucker so large that it was cast on a stick the size of a broom handle.)

The original Sucker Day was a silly season and a valuable diversion from events on the world stage. South Korea had been invaded in June and things had not gone well for the United States and its Allies. The people who celebrated the first Sucker Day had no way of knowing that the first Wetumkan to fall in battle in Korea, had already been killed in action. PFC James M. Carter had died on July 19, but it would be September before his parents, Mr. and Mrs. J. O. Carter, who lived on West Broadway , would know. They had first been notified that their son had been awarded The Silver Star for gallantry in action. The wording of the citation made them suspect that he had also forfeited his life. Congressman Tom Steed finally got the Army to verify their worst fears. I knew three of the nine Carter children in school: Martha, Nick and Nin.

Before the next Sucker Day, First Lieutenant Arnold Bamburg a graduate of Wetumka High School and an honors graduate of Oklahoma A. & M. College, had died of wounds suffered while leading his platoon in Korea. His untimely death changed the history of Wetumka in ways that can't be fathomed. His parents were Mr. and Mrs. Leonard Bamburg who were farmers. Their son had majored in agriculture and was briefly employed as a vocational agriculture teacher. He had earned his officer's commission in the R.O.T.C program at Stillwater.

On August 1, that year of the First Sucker Day, the Oklahoma National Guard had been notified that the 45th Division was one of four to be mobilized and sent to the Far East. Company A of the 180th Infantry Regiment, the Wetumka unit, was already drilling three days a week and had assumed a large role in the first Sucker Day celebrations. Within a month the Guardsmen, their vehicles and equipment, would be loaded onto ships at New Orleans for the trip to a training base in Japan. That Fall, Coach J. B. Badgett wondered aloud how he could win any football games with most of the men of his starting line-up in the Far East.

The bodies of fallen soldiers of World War II were still being returned to the United States for re-burial. Sergeant Johnny W. Smith, a tail-gunner on a B-24, who grew up in the Fairview area and graduated from Wetumka High School had been killed in a bombing run in

Bulgaria in 1944. His body was brought back aboard a "funeral ship" and returned to Wetumka in the first week of May, 1950.

The population decline in Wetumka and Hughes County was well underway before the 1950 Census was taken. Yet, over a thousand people were drawn to the H. H. Darks Ranch for a Quarter Horse sale in June, 1950. Mr. Darks had a modern racetrack with the latest model starting gates. The pedigree of his horseflesh was known nationwide. His partners in this endeavor that he casually referred to as "my hobby" were Argie Taylor and John Campbell.

20

Tornado!

On May 28, 1924, Wetumka was struck by the greatest tornado disaster in the history of Hughes County. Three eyewitnesses have told me that it came out of the Northwest from the darkest cloud they had ever seen. Most survivors agree that it struck Wetumka's south end (near the present 9-75 junction) at about 5:30 in the afternoon. Several said that their clocks stopped at this time. (All of the tornadoes that have touched down in the county have done so in the evening or early evening: this according to records at The National Storm Center at Norman.)

Official records say that it was a mile wide and and was part of a breakout that affected Hughes, McIntosh and Muskogee counties. Nine persons were reported killed and 37 injured. My research indicates that seven persons were actually killed.

About three dozen persons were seriously injured. At the time, the Frisco railroad had a number of employees living in Wetumka. An officer of the line had a passenger car set out of a train and another train, stopped at Yeager, was summoned to push this carload of injured people to the hospital at Henryetta.

The tornado actually allowed the healing process to begin between the two towns over the viciously fought courthouse issue of a decade earlier. A "corps of doctors" from Holdenville and other communities helped the local physicians locate and treat victims. (People from both towns had sworn never to set foot inside the other and although I'm certain that some people were true to their vow, this occasion did alleviate much of the hard feelings that existed in the professional classes.)

The National Guard Companies set up a temporary morgue at their armory which was first located at the Lodge building just south of the Gammill corner.

Ivon Osborn Williams told me that her parents (John and Helen) rushed from the Lone Oak community to check on his brother and his wife, Elam and Bessie. They were at the time living about half a mile from town on the cemetery road. She said it was a fearsome looking scene. The house and outbuildings had been completely flattened but no one was injured.

Mary Pace Andrews said that she was only about thirteen but what she remembered was the chaos that came with one of the biggest downpours anyone had experienced. All of the gas mains were sheered off but there were no fires and this was probably due to the heavy rain. Gille's greenhouse sustained major damage but the two-story house across the street escaped completely unscathed.

Within twenty-four hours some Wetumkans were out digging to build a storm shelter; nothing like that was known before the tornado.

The American Red Cross disbursed about $11,750 but the entire amount was repaid by the merchants and people of Wetumka within a short time. About $450 was expended for emergency clothing for families most affected. The medical aid which was reimbursed came to about $2,700 and $313 was contributed to the burial of the victims. Five of the victims are buried in a row in block seven at the Wetumka Cemetery. Five thousand dollars was spent to help families rebuild and another $2,700 went for household goods.

A tornado that caused widespread devastation in the Big Springs area on March 25, 1948 at 8:30 P. M. was not rated by the National Storm Center for its intensity. But comparison to comparable storms leads me to believe that it was an "F4" or the most powerful classification. (The intensity or power of tornadoes is rated on a scale of F1 to F4 and can only be measured after the event by the destruction left behind.) This path of this twister was a mile wide and it caused damage in Hughes, McIntosh, Muskogee and Sequoyah counties.

In Hughes county the destruction reached from the Pecan Grove community, near Holdenville, and travelled in a northwesterly direction through the Big Springs, Greasy Creek and Big Prarie communities and reached to the edge of Dustin.

Seven persons were killed outright that Thursday night. The greatest loss of life was in the Bill Harris family. Five members of this family were killed by the tornado or by the ensuing fire which reduced the farm house to ashes. One of them was a two-day-old child. Three persons (a daughter of the Bill Harris family and two children who were visiting relatives) were spared when they were blown free of the house.

The other two victims were from the Woodrow Stringfellow family. Mrs. Woodrow Stringfellow who was thirty years old and her three week old son were killed. Mr. Stringfellow, 34, their six year old daughter, Patsy Sue, and three year old daughter Betty June were injured. A fourth child, two-year-old Carol Sue was seemingly uninjured. The Stringfellow home was scattered over an area of fifty square yards.

Howard Laneer, the Wetumka Chief of Police surveyed the entire area and reported that twenty families had been seriously affected. He counted 98 homes that were seriously damaged or destroyed in the Big Springs, Greasy Creek, Big Prarie and south Dustin communities. The roof of the Dustin school was blown off and the teacherage (district owned teachers' residence) sustained serious damage. The Red Cross's final report showed that 388 homes, barns and outbuildings were damaged or destroyed in Hughes County.

The tornado which twisted through Holdenville on April 28, 1950 at 7:07 P. M., caused five deaths and injuries to about 125 persons. An eighteen block area was leveled and 215 homes were damaged or destroyed.

As fearsome as tornadoes are, my opinion is that the people of Wetumka would do better to watch the road more closely than the skies. The number of people killed in traffic accidents is huge and there have been very few deathless years. The stretch of road from Calvin south to the Coal county line was often dubbed the bloodiest stretch of road in Oklahoma. The spot that I always feared most was the banked highway leading to the underpass near Wetumka. There have been as many people killed and injured there as in the disasterous tornado of 1924.

On the first day of October, 1946, a man and his wife died on the underpass curve when their car went out of control and was broadsided by a Union Transportation Company Bus. Their names were Jennings and they were both Assembly of God ministers from Okmulgee who had ministered in Wetumka.

At the beginning of 1952, the future Governor of Oklahoma, State Senator Raymond Gary and his wife were injured there when they collided with a truck loaded with a crane that was being inched through the underpass.

There were other Wetumkans who were killed or seriously injured there and at least one Weleetkan died at that hazardous spot on U. S. 75.

21

Oklahoma Govenors and Wetumka

The governor most intimately associated with Wetumka and Holdenville was Leon "Red" Phillips who practiced law at Okemah and
lived near Weleetka. So many people from Wetumka knew him on a
first name basis that he hardly caused a celebrity stir when he was in
town.

Mr. Phillips was not from Weleetka nor was he a native born Oklahoman. (The first Native Oklahoman to be Governor was Robert S.
Kerr.) He had played football at Oklahoma University and after law
school he opened a law office in Okemah. But he took a great deal of
pride in being a farmer and stockman although he hired all of the work
done and and his unorthodox approach to farming probably kept him
from realizing much profit.

His gift seemed to be for politics. He was certainly a powerhouse as
Speaker of the Oklahoma House of Representatives. He belived that he
could use his considerable prestige to enlarge the governor's office
which had been designed to be constitutionally weak.

In 1938 the Weleetkan was elected with a voter mandate that was
unprecedented and never since equaled. He carried 73 of the Oklahoma counties. (He lost only in Alfalfa, Beaver, Major and Texas
counties.)

Governor Phillips wasted no time in trying to assert himself and
aggrandize the office he had so handsomely earned. His announced
hallmark was clean government and he practically shut down the state

with his audits to prove where the money was going. The legislature, of which he was so recently a member, was always feisty with the governors. (The textbooks claim that in the years prior to World War II, Oklahoma had impeached more governors than all of the other states combined. They often did this over trivial issues. One governor earned their ire when he would not get rid of his personal secretary who was detested by key legislators. They summarily impeached him for "general incompetence.") Oklahoma paid its governor only $525 a month when many of the department heads who reported to the Governor were much better compensated.

From the beginning Governor Phillips was at odds with his own party in Oklahoma and he never missed an occasion to blast President Roosevelt and The New Deal. Occasionally, Congressman Lyle Boren would chime in to criticize the administration in Washington.

He openly feuded with Ron Stephens, the WPA administrator for Oklahoma. Stephens often reminded Oklahomans that their Governor had cost them millions of dollars in grants because he had so slow to sign onto projects.

Governor Phillips especially disliked the Civilian Conservation Corps (CCC). He gloried in calling it a hotbed for juvenile delinquency. He could not have had much evidence to sustain such talk.

Before the end of his term Governor Leon Phillips had alienated many people in government. It appears that his enemies arranged to have him indicted for conspiracy to solicit a bribe. A prominent doctor had been imprisoned for several years for performing illegal abortions and when he was pardoned it was claimed that several officials had been bribed including the governor. Supposedly, Governor Phillips had gotten $500. (In his farewell speech to the legislature, he bitterly denounced his successor, Robert S. Kerry who arguably was the first really effective Governor of Oklahoma.

Governor Phillips went to trial a few days after the expiration of his term. The trial was a very short one and he was acquitted by a jury that was out for five minutes but he was hardly exonerated. This further embittered him and in a couple of years he actually changed his party affiliation temporarily to Republican.

His Wetumka associates worried about the health of the former governor. He chewed more tobacco than ever and became a very portly man. He had joined a law firm in Oklahoma City after he left politics but he spent most of his time in Weleetka.

Like his predecessors, the governorship had become a political graveyard for Mr. Phillips. Like them, he was never seriously considered for a higher elective office.

Governor Phillips even divorced his wife and in 1952, he married the woman who had served him as a secretary for 17 years. This marriage lasted three days. She said that he fussed, fumed and nagged and within 72 hours she knew she desperately wanted out. Governor Phillips died at Weleetka in 1958.

There was another Oklahoma Governor who lived at Holdenville and this was Senator Tom Anglin who wisely contented himself with being acting governor for weeks at a time. He was one of the longest serving members of the Oklahoma legislature. He had first been elected as a Representative in 1918. He is probably the only man ever to serve in both houses and to be the leader of each. As the Senate *pro tem* he acted as governor when the Governor and Lieutenant Governor were out of State or incapacitated.

In 1934, Senator Tom Anglin did stand for election as governor. In the Democratic primary he was the biggest vote getter and he became very uncomfortable when it looked like he would inevitably win. With no explanation, he withdrew his name and in effect caused the election of Governor Marland. Marland was as erratic a Governor as Oklahoma has ever been. He had started the Conoco Oil Company and had no experience in politics. (His company executives were often promoted because they played Polo well.) While he campaigned for governor, he was building his mansion at Ponca City. By the time he was elected he had been ousted from his company through stock manipulation. Whispers that he had paid Senator Anglin to withdraw from the race were never credible. When he became governor, he was broke. His mansion was never finished and he could not even pay the light bill.

It should be added, paranthetically at least, that Governor Marland was hardly a fit man for public office. Not many people realized the mess in his personal life. He and his wife had never had children. They adopted a boy and a girl and then a few years later Mrs. Marland died. He had his lawyers get an annulment of the adoption of the girl so they could marry.

Dixie Gilmer was from Oklahoma City but it was his choice to practice law in Wetumka from 1924. From Wetumka, he moved to Tulsa County and entered politics. He became the elected County Attorney (1937-1945) and managed to survive many a scandal. In 1946, he campaigned for governor and came in very closely behind the man who would be elected, Roy J. Turner. Unlike so many candidates before him, Mr. Gilmer did not continue to attack the man who had defeated him. He sounded a very concilitory note and helped the Democratic nominee win. His efforts were rewarded when Governor Turner made him the State Director of Public Safety. He was in charge of the Oklahoma Highway Patrol and several other agencies. He was known as an efficient administrator with a future. But he died before his appointive term was over. This was the closest a Wetumka resident had come to being elected governor.

Prior to the election of the first Republican governor (1960) no governor had ever been elected without winning Wetumka. I don't know if they were aware of this as a myth but none of them ever neglected Wetumka. Governor "Alfalfa Bill" Murry was in Wetumka so many times before, during and after his governorship that ledge at The Meadors Hotel should bear a placque denoting that fact. Robert S. Kerr was in Wetumka an astounding number of times as Governor and also as a U. S. Senator. His campaign for the Senate in 1946 was modern in every sense. He made use of the radio and spent a lot of his own money. He was the first to have celebrities appear for him. Gene

Autrey, to my knowledge, was never in Wetumka although he had plenty of relatives living about the town. He was in Wewoka to entertain in behalf of Robert S. Kerr in 1946. (During World War II, Gene Autrey served in the Army Air Force as a flight officer. In February, 1945, he flew a big government plane into Holdenville. He and his wife came to spend a night with friends. Perhaps, only a celebrity in uniform could perform such a stunt.)

I do not believe that any governor, in the time frame of this book, was a better governor than Robert S. Kerr. He was unlike all the other governors. He became very close to the President of the United States, Franklin D. Roosevelt and even made the keynote speech at the convention in 1944. He was one of the earliest of Roosevelt's supporters to urge him into a fourth term. It is said that Robert S. Kerr could have had a position in Roosevelt's cabinet. He could have been Secretary of the Interior.

Robert S. Kerr was governor during World War II and this enhanced his effectiveness. Oklahoma is a landlocked state and yet no less than 13 naval installations were located within the State. No other governor left such an indelible stamp on Oklahoma.

22

Herman "Red" Darks and His Wetumka

I n all the history of Wetumka there was never a person comparable to Herman Darks. His personal rise and fall parallels the fortunes of the town that he loved so well. He was elected to the state legislature in 1932 when he was only 23. In the only term he served, he was widely known as the hardest working member. He left the legislature because the compensation was so abysmal. Nearly all of the other lawmakers were lawyers or had another source of income. (It was felt, at least at the time, that the wage earner class should not serve as lawmaking should be left to persons of means. During World War II there was an effort to oust the sixteen members of the Oklahoma legislature who were teachers or school administrators on the dubious grounds that they constituted a lobby for their profession.)

1932 is also the year that Jim Ragland was elected County Superintendent of Schools. On his second try, he trounced the incumbent by over 1,000 votes. Glen Chowins, familiarly the Wetumka High School principal, made his only foray into politics at that time. He stood for election as County Commissioner and although he ran a vigorous and clean campaign, he failed to win a single ballot box.

Herman Darks was not just the 1950s Mayor of Wetumka. He had worn many hats. As a young man he had been a company clerk in one of the local National Guard companies and at the same time was a bookkeeper at the Bank. After exiting the legislature, he acquired the Wetumka Bakery and a reputation for making very good pies in addition to baking the loaves of WETUMKA MALTED MILK BREAD. He had a good many positions in the 1930s and 1940s. He was the acting postmaster and then an insurance salesman. For several years he was a scrappy little Deputy Sheriff for Hughes County. During World War II, he served in the U. S. Navy.

After the war, he was variously the director of The Chamber of Commerce and City Councilman. In March, 1951, he became the Mayor of Wetumka. In those days the Mayor was in effect the city manager and his pay was in line with the other city employees. (Usually, the city electrician earned about $25 a month more and was the highest paid city employee.)

Herman Darks had a wide network of friends (as well as enemies). Bill Tankersley, said that when he was a city councilman, the Mayor would not hesitate to call anyone at the state capital. He called the Governor whenever he felt like it.

The most obvious thing about Herman Darks was that he really lived up to his nickname. He became very ruddy-faced due to his excessive drinking. (His good friend Tom Phillips, publisher of THE HOLDENVILLE DAILY NEWS referred to it as his affliction. Darks was not the only person so afflicted in Wetumka although the whole state was supposedly dry.

In January 1950, occurred one of the strangest trials ever to take place in Hughes County (and there were many strange court trials!) A man that everyone referred to as "Pap" but whose last name was Bamburg was a notorious bootlegger. He flouted the law; in fact he thumbed his nose at the law. In that month the County Attorney (Stanley Huser, Jr.,) had him jailed on a charge of vagrancy.

Pap Bamburg was not a vagrant or a bum. He had a reliable income which enabled him to wear nice clothes and to drive a late model Chrysler and live well. Of course he never broke a sweat but he was hardly a member of the idle unemployed.

This was the last trial before a Justice of The Peace in Wetumka. The JP was W. H. Pangle and the jury was made up of six locals. That Pap Bamberg was not actually a vagrant is evidenced by the fact that he could afford to hire Frank Grayson as his defense attorney. One of Mr. Grayson's duties was being the Mayor of Holdenville. In some strange sense it was like the rivalry between Wetumka and Holdenville of the first decade of the Century. The jury in Wetumka was not going to bend just to please those people from Holdenville.

The first trial ended in a hung jury (3-3). The retrial with a new jury ended the same way. The second re-trial finally resulted in a guilty verdict and the spectacle was over. (His apt defense was that he had been improperly charged. He was not charged with bootlegging but he was finally convicted. (At this time in Wetumka's history, the Mayor was Tom Smith who was "Mister Church of Christ." He held every job and position in the church except that of the pastorate. But he did not like people from Holdenville running his town. He had interferred in the serving of warrants and failed to safeguard the evidence which happened to be illicit whiskey.)

Pap Bamburg paid his paltry fine as he should have in the first place and avoided attorney fees. But he liked being ostentatious. In a very short time Dick Martin had apprehended him again and this time with a fresh shipment of merchandise. This was significant because it attracted the attention of the Federal Marshal who seized the liquor and confiscated his nearly new automobile. This effectively ended the public career of Pap Bamburg.

A little later, Sheriff T. J. "Slim" Sanders openly engaged in harassing the bootleggers who hoped to avoid Bamburg's fate by purchasing a Federal liquor stamp. He had no trouble in finding them or staying current on their addresses. Tom and Milt Phillips publishers of the newspapers in Holdenville and Seminole published the names, addresses and particulars of those who had purchased a federal license. He often bragged about cutting their phone lines or following them around. Sheriff Sanders thought it was good politics to have high-pro-file enemies. Whenever he was in Wetumka, he would find Bennie Kirby and shadow him for a few hours.

There were other bootleggers around Wetumka. (Decades earlier the Ku Klux Klan had beaten bootleggers so badly that someone of them were disabled. This did not prove a real deterrent.) Ted Kelley, an erstwhile farmer, was often mentioned as a bootlegger. He drove a 1936 Ford coup and was otherwise rather discreet. But eventually he was caught. Since he was such a young man and a World War II veteran, the judge wanted to impose jail time to get him squared away. Fifty prominent Wetumkans signed a petition offering to be his "guardians" if the judge would be lenient. Their main professed concern was that they did not want him to lose his GI benefits.

There were always things amiss at City Hall. Howard Laneer became the Wetumka Chief of Police in 1947 after campaigning as part of the GI slate. He had been a teacher and school administrator before the war and had done course work at the University of Arkansas. He seemed a fair choice for such a job.

At first it was family problems that enmeshed him with the County Attorney and a Deputy. In May of 1948, Mr. Laneer's brother-in-law R. L. "Bob" Ganaway, the long time Men's Department manager at The Coin Store, was attending Commencement Exercises at The Wetumka High School when the Chief of Police filled his auto's "oil chamber" with sand. For this he was arrested and charged with malicious mischief. Ganaway was Laneer's brother-in-law before he divorced his wife, Lois Sheppard. (John McGibboney, the future Chief of Police, was serving as constable and assumed the Chief's job on a temporary basis.) In the strangest incident I was ever told about in Wetumka, the following month Mr. Ganaway committed suicide on a muddy stretch of Highway 9 near Stigler. His associates said that he had been profoundly subdued for a comple of weeks. His method of suicide was almost unbelievable. He severed his jugular vein with a box opener. He had told his wife that he was stopping to check a tire before this took place.

Mr. Laneer probably would have kept his job a little longer except for a matter of police violence. In August 1948, Laneer arrested William T. Phillips and confined him in the Wetumka jail. When Mr. Phillips would not give up his billfold, the Chief of Police twisted his fingers to the extent that he lost use of one of them and was partially disabled. This matter cost Wetumka the $1,000 bond that was carried on employees and officials.

Police roughness seemed to be part of the culture of the time. When Herman Darks was campaigning for Mayor he made the same speech often and one part he repeated so many times that no one could have missed it: "If need be, I will meet anybody in any alley in this town and we'll settle our differences one way or another." He shook his body and his fist and the point seemed to have been pretty well made.

The trophy job in Wetumka was that of Post Master. It was the one local federal job that carried real benefits. Wetumka had many temporary post masters but only a few could claim the job in their own right. Travis Watson was Wetumka's Post Master from 1937 until 1948. He had won this supposedly nonpolitical position by scoring highest on the Civil Service Examination. His score was 84, and the runner-ups were Dixie Hall 82, Harry Jackson 75, and Herman Darks 71.

Travis Watson must have become complacent in his sense of job security because everyone has political persuasions. In May of 1948, a group of Wetumkans signed an affidavit to the effect that they had seen him engaged in political behavior. They alleged, among other things, that they had witnessed him tacking up political notices and had even heard him speak approvingly of a candidate in the post office building. At first Mr. Watson was going to make a stand. Then, at a Civil Service "trial" in Holdenville, he was confronted with this affidavit. He was so astounded that he asked to be relieved of his duties as soon as possible.

The Congressman that Wetumkans had known for five terms or ten years was Lyle H. Boren. (He was the father of the Oklahoma Governor and U. S. Senator and present President of Oklahoma University.) In the first election after the War Mr. Boren was challenged by one of his loyal lieutenantsl, Mr. Glen Johnson of Okemah. Johnson won but held the seat for only one two year term. He was defeated by the man who happily referred to himself as the Kaiser-Frazier Dealer from Holdenville. Tom Stead was not from Holdenville. He and his son had served in World War II. He was the survivor. This is undoubtedly the reason that he became such a strong advocate for the GI's. (Mr. and Mrs. Steed were kept in the dark for an unconscionably long time about the fate of their son. He made the case that the Army was sloppy in its notifications process and he never allowed the Army to forget it. He really got on their case as a Congressman when the Army again started making unreliable reports about whether a soldier had been killed or wounded.) In the peacetime boom he was able to get the franchise for a new line of automobiles from the war contractor, Henry J. Kaiser. This line of cars survived only about five years because they were more expensive than a Ford or a Chevy and they just didn't have the styling or the reputation of an established brand. The people of Hughes County had great affection for Fords, Chevrolets and even Plymouths. Following the war there were three Plymouth dealerships in Hughes County. (There was a Chrysler-Plymouth agency across from the City Hall in the white building on Main Street which presently houses a laundry.) Mr. Steed kept his seat in the U. S. House of Representatives a lot longer than he'd kept the Kaiser-Frazier dealership going. He was always looking to the future and while I was in high school he made an unannounced visit which prompted a special assembly. He was obviously recruiting the next generation of Democratic voters.

There never was a politician in Wetumka quite like Herman Darks. He had a great many admirers and no small number of detractors. His showing was always strong with the Colored section of the electorate because he knew he needed them. He once embarassed The Oklahoma Natural Gas Company so much that they laid a new gas line in that part of town. He said the gas main they replaced was just junk and never been buried properly and was dangerous because it had leaks. (The original gas lines were laid out in 1918 by a private company that was controlled by X. S. McGee and W. C. Farmer. I am informed by Mr. McGee's daughter that these individuals also gained control of the First National Bank.)

Joe Roberts had become the elected Street Commissioner of Wetumka in 1946. He ousted Mance Franklin who had been the only commissioner most Wetumkans could remember. At that time Wetumka owned only one small grader which Mr. Franklin used constantly to keep the roads passable. The city was able to get a real grader and a one row Farmall tractor and a cart. The tractor was used to spray the alleys with DDT. Walter Meeks was in charge of this crew. There had been two large outbreaks of polio in Oklahoma in the 1940s: 1943 and 1946. The vector for polio was unknown and priority was given to the spraying job.

When Mr. Roberts notified the city council that he was unable to spare a men to sweep Main Street and Broadway, Herman Darks spoke up: "No problem, I'll do it myself." Herman Darks was a man of his word and everyone knew it. He would start sweeping sometime after midnight on Saturday night and he would still be pushing a broom long after the sun came up. No matter how cold and windy the weather, the streets got cleaned by the mayor. There was more mud that had fallen off the undercarriages of cars than there was trash. He picked up most of it with a scoop shovel. I was with my mother when she drove my dad to town to catch a ride to his temporary laborer's job on a nearby pipeline job. I saw it for myself. What civic pride!

Herman Darks was always contemplating his political comeback at the State level. In 1955, in the final year of his life he actually filed papers to run for the State Senate and then changed his mind and withdrew his candidacy. Then, he told his closest associates that he thought he might make a run for the Lieutenant Governor's office.

In practical terms, he had to keep himself politically alive as Wetumka's mayor. He was re-elected in March of 1953 in a strange little election. His cousin, Armand Gibson, who had come home from Korea as a Warrant Officer chose to run against him. Gibson, like his dad "Big-Hoot" Gibson, was in the service station business but he thought he could run the town while he ran his business.

The Gibsons and Darks families had the same common origin in Arkansas. Armond and Herman had always been rivals. Back in the 1930s, their uncle, H. H. Darks, held family get-togethers that featured outside events like "Who can slice a watermelon the straightest and fastest." Then, the main event was having the cousins put on boxing gloves and sparing with each other until someone got a bloody nose or got mad or both.

To some people the election between first cousins was unseemly. But Herman Darks was the incumbent and the seasoned politician and he spoke an earthy language that a lot of down and outers could relate to. His gestures were well practiced and he could really shake his fists in a way that amused a crowd.

Darks retained the Mayor's job and got twice as many votes as his cousin. The talley was 446 to 205. (A previous Mayor, Tom Smith was also a candidate but he only got 110 votes. (Mr. Smith had quit Wetumka because he said he couldn't live on the local salary available to him. On his way to the West Coast he had a mile heart attack in Arizona and had to turn back.) The voters returned the whole slate of office holders with the single exception of Councilman D. F. Burns who was beaten by a new comer, Bill Cunningham. (Many people remember Mr. Burns but not as many recall that he was also a Reverend. His church was the Church of God which met in a small but attractive church on Tiger Street. The congregation withered to a very small number and the church building eventually was abandoned. It was dismantled sometime in the early 1960s.)

H. H. Loard (propreitor of the Junction Tourist Courts) had failed to get elected to the Council. Earl Chowins also failed to get a seat.

David Peixotto, city treasurer and Haskell Brock, city clerk were unopposed but they got 539 and 596 votes, respectively.

The only notable thing about that election was the closeness of the contest between the Chief of Police J. T. McGibboney and challenger John Campbell. The Chief prevailed by a margin of six votes. (There is no provision in the law for a re-count in such a small scale election and John Campbell had to accept the first results.)

The other Councilmen re-elected were Bill Tankersley, Ed Nolen and Lawrence Massey. Tankersley defeated John Harland. Lonnie Pangle and E. H. Daniels had also vied for the Chief of Police position. They got 69 and 85 votes, respectively.

On the day of the election the man who had headed the list of "the usual suspects" in petty crimes in Wetumka, Jack "Torch" Forrest was arrest yet again for arson. In the 1930s there was a succession of residential fires or as they were called at the time: "insurance sales." Jack Forrest's name was bandied about as freely as the names of well known bootleggers. In 1937, he was arrested on a charge of arson. It seems that his confession came about through police trickery. He was told that a kersosene can found at a house fire bore his fingerprints. His reaction went like this: "If I'm going to the Pen, I'm going to name my clients." The county officials would have none of that. After all, you can't take the word of a confessed arsonist.

Jack was paroled in a coule of years to another part of the state but he violated the conditions of his parole by stealing a hog. Then he returned to Wetumka where he resumed his career as a very sloppy criminal who covered his tracks poorly. He was arrested several times in the period following the War for burglary and the like. On one occasion he called the Wetumka police to ask them about his mother whom he had heard was quite ill. When asked were he was calling from, he answered that he was at the bus station in Sapulpa and that he would wait there for them to pick him up.

But in 1955 the mood of the citizenry had changed. Jack Forrest, who had returned from California a couple of years earlier, named his client and this time he was arrested and charged. This was Ben Williams (of Wewoka) who had hired Jack to make repairs to the frame dwelling that he wanted to have torched for insurance payments. Jack had only been returned recently from Richmond, California, at tax payer expense. In Richmond, he'd been arrested for drunk driving and and it was discovered that there was an outstanding warrant for his arrest from Holdenville. Jack had been doing time in the county jail and had escaped from that second floor facility by going out a window. (People who consulted with me on this project asked me to mention Jack Forrest. They found him to be a contrary, sympathetic figure who always did the wrong thing, incorrectly.) Mr. Alvin Jack Forrest died in 1978 and is buried at the Wetumka Cemetery.

On the day of that 1951 city election it was announced that Robert L. Meadors had died at the age of 79. I am advised that he was the brother of the first Turner Meadors. He was to Dustin what Turner Meadors was originally to Wetumka. He had been a pioneer merchant in that town when its prospects seemed at least as bright as Wetumka's. It had a railroad and was the home of the largest wagon factory in Oklahoma.

R. L. Meadors and Son was one of several businesses which relocated to Wetumka during the Depression. When I was a youth, R. L. Meadors, as he was known professionally and "Uncle Bob" to his customers, was semi-retired. He came to the department store every day and when the store got busy he would wait on customers. My family was waited on many a time by "Uncle Bob" and I regarded him as the best mannered and kindest person I'd ever met. He was an excellent merchant and an expert in public relations as this was required of every businessman who might be a success; every one of them had keen competition in Wetumka. I was told recently by one of his long time employees that he was always a gentleman but he really knew how to "strip the bark off" someone that he thought was not being as productive as they could be. Apparently, no one ever took a break on Uncle Bob.

I decided that 1955 would be the terminal year in this local history essay. Herman Darks, a man that I personally admired, was detested by a good many because of his alcohol dependency. Not many people were then willing to look upon the alcoholic as a sick man. Addiction was not well understood at the time. The days between November 11 and December 5, 1955 must have been the most awful time in the life of Herman "Red" Darks.

On the 11th of November he was arrested and charged with drunk driving. His cousin, Max Darks, filed the charges and jailed him but set the bond at $500. Herman Darks made bond and was out of county jail and in the offices of THE HOLDENVILLE DAILY NEWS by 4:30. He penned a paid advertisement (in a blatant effort to tamper with the potential jury pool). He acknowledged that he was guilty of hitting the car of Mr. Early, the rural mail carrier. (For some strange reason he was driving the Chief of Police McGibboney's maroon 1949 Plymouth and it was totaled.) Herman Darks loudly proclaimed that despite all of this he was "absolutely sober." But any fair minded person who read that ponderous column realized that its author was not really very sober. Probably, Mr. Darks could not remember being absolutely sober.

In retrospect, it is obvious that his cousin should have recommended a bond so high that Herman Darks would have had to sit in jail for a while. In his paid advertisement Mr. Darks blamed his political enemies for his predicament. He then did something out of sheer desperation: he announced that he would once again stand for election to the State legislature.

Three weeks after the accident with the mail carrier, Herman Darks was involved in a doubly fatal accident on a calm Saturday morning near Dustin. (I was a mere lad of sixteen and was washing cars for Armand Gibson at his Conoco station across from the funeral home. When there was a lull in business, I'd go over a bring a car from the funeral home and wash or dust it off. That morning I was vacuuming out an ambulance and didn't hear Arthur Spiller shouting at me. He tugged on me with such force that I knew something terrible had taken happened.)

Herman Darks was following too close behind a slow moving truck on a straight stretch of Highway 9. He pulled out to see if he could pass and smacked head on into a car. A Shawnee banker and his wife were in that car. She was instantly killed and he was seriously injured. (Both of them were ejected from their car) Herman Darks sustained massive injuries and lived for a only few hours at the Saint Francis Hospital in Holdenville. He was 47 years old.

Mayor Darks' genius had been in making friends and that was reflected in his funeral services. His casket was borne by Fred Berry, Bryan Nicks, Webb Fulks, Ray Meadors, Cecil Kilgore and David Bloom. The honorary bearers were Ovie Webb, Nathan Lee, Hugh Sandlin, Tom Phillips, Dick Jones, Argie Taylor, Harve Ball, Bud Hayes and the city council and city employees.

On the evening of the day that Herman Darks was buried, Senator Robert S. Kerr made his final visit to Wetumka. He came, as he had before, to attend the annual meeting of the Wetumka Chamber of Commerce. That evening the comedian, Frank Streetman, "the Mayor of Sasakawa" was the Master of Ceremonies and he found it very difficult to get laughs.

It was the end of an era (and of this study) but not entirely. Another of Herman Darks' cousins, Willard, had been appointed to the city council and his fellows selected him as acting mayor. C. H. Baskin, city attorney since the 1920s, said that the city charter required a special election.

It was a very special election, indeed, and was held on December 20th. There was speculation that Floyd Callison, the local Oklahoma Natural Gas manager would run but he had taken himself out of consideration early. Bill Cunningham and Lawrence Massey declined to be drafted to run. Herman Darks' widow Ora Jo, a very strong and capable woman at 39, became the first serious female candidate for office in

Wetumka. At the time she was running the Chamber of Commerce as her husband had done earlier.

Bill Nicks, brother of Bryan Nicks was the candidate who would win. He had owned and operated the funeral home in Wetumka before the Spillars arrived. Like his brother, he'd been the acting postmaster.

Mrs. Darks carried two wards and Nicks carried the other two. Nicks came out the winner with a slim 53 vote margin. She conducted a vigorous campaign and drew nearly as many votes as her husband had in the March election when there were four candidates. Gender was an issue in the election and of course scurrilous things were said about her "being out of her place."

Mrs. Darks did better than Willie Murray, wife of Governor William Murray, who had tried to succeed him as Governor in the previous year. During the Democratic primary Mrs. Murray campaigned in Wetumka in a unique spectacle. It had been announced in the newspapers that she would be arriving on Wetumka's Main Street via helicopter.

It didn't take much to draw a crowd in Wetumka: there was usually already a crowd there and many a politician would arrive in Wetumka, without any notification, by automobile, and set up his sound system on the streets of Wetumka.

I was in the crowd on that slightly windy morning when Mrs. Murray descended from the sky to speak. She was a few minutes late and people were wondering about whether or not she could land in such conditions.

Hers was the first actual helicopter I'd ever seen, and I presume that was true for most of the Wetumkans standing around. The helicopter was heard before it was spotted. As it got closer to the street level, it appeared to really be huge. I thought it was an exceptionally dangerous and daring stunt to land such a craft in the middle of a surging crowd. I had my doubts about whether Bass Moore, John McGibboney and Gene Abney could push the lines of people back far enough to clear a landing zone on West Broadway. As the craft got close to the crowd its huge rotors kicked up dirt and trash and created the biggest whirlwind that had hit downtown Wetumka in a while.

The rotors finally did stop spinning and Mrs. Murray stepped out and began her little speech. But most of the people in the crowd came to see the helicopter, not its occupant. The length of the rather primitive helicopter looked like the lattice work on the side of a bridge. It did have a glass cockpit bubble which gleamed in the sun.

I did not believe, at the time, that many people in the crowd were listening and even fewer understood what she was trying to convey. Her voice was hoarse from all the speechifying she'd done (and perhaps from riding in a drafty helicopter).

The take-off was just as terrifying as the landing had been. It was really difficult to compress a crowd that backed up to the buildings on both sides. The pilot cranked the rotors a couple of times to see if there was an operating radius. Wonderously, it seemed, no one was decapitated. He then started the somewhat reluctant engine. It spit and belched smoke and finally came to life in an ear splitting roar. As he lifted off, another sand storm struck that part of Wetumka. A man standing nearby me said: "At least she's cleaned the street!" Another replied, "Yeah, but most of that dirt is in our eyes!"

Mrs. Murry only got 253 votes in all of Hughes County. This was the smallest number any candidate for governor had ever received. The people thought they just weren't ready to be governed by a woman.

23

Never Again!

Never again will there be a hog calling contest for women on the crowded streets of Wetumka. Nor will there ever be a variant which was a "husband calling" contest. Nor will there be greased pigs to catch or poles to climb. For that matter there never will be over-crowded streets in Wetumka.

Until some unknown date in the mid-1950s, the people of Wetumka were as comfortable sitting for hours in their cars as they would have been at home on their porches. The streets were never completely deserted any day or night of the week.

Many Wetumkans recall how they would park their car early in the morning at some vantage spot and leave it so they would have a place to sit that day to see the procession of the world in front of them. No one was more faithful than Elam and Bessie Osborn who managed throughout the 52 Saturdays of the year to get the first space north from the Redskin Theatre. They had done this for years and long before there was a theatre there. It was in front of Peixotto's Fine Foods (later Peixotto's IGA). There was a reason for this preference but I did not find out until they and Julian and Nellie Peioxotto were all dead. Nellie was their first cousin. (Her father was Elam Severe McCracken and the namesake of Elam Osborn.) They were friendly and sociable but I never knew them to associate as family. (My grandfather, John Osborn, was a brother to Elam and Joe Osborn and Mrs. Myrtle Gay and Mrs. Gus Pace.)

Saturday night in Wetumka may have been eclipsed by television in the early 1950s. Until about the time of the first Sucker Day television stations only broadcast in the evenings for a few hours. The picture was small, grainy and the reception varied from bad to no picture. Herring Hardware and The Coin Store were early venders of television sets which were beyond the reach of most Wetumkans. Herring's had rigged up an outside speaker and at dusk the night watchman would turn on the television with a switch above the door. There would already be an eager crowd sitting in cars and on fenders.

Whatever inroads into motion pictures television achieved in the early years were very slight. There was little programming that made much sense. There were endless variety shows like Ted Mack and Milton Berle but most viewers did not comprehend the humor. They came to see the flickering light. Televised prized fighting was a big draw for crowds of old and young. WKY-TV featured two hillbillies ("Wiley and Gene") for fifteen minutes each week. They were eagerly anticipated. There was a news roundup once a week that resembled a home movie. The people who regularly came to Herring's finally saw wonderous scene from the first Sucker Day. It was a little difficult to discern just who was in this flim clip but it was stock for conversation for some time.

Eisenhower's inaugeration was a first for television. Jack Herring installed a television set in the high school auditorium for the historic occasion. "Installed" was the correct term. He spent the better part of a day hoisting up the antenna and wiring the tiny set which was placed in the middle of the stage. (About sixteen inches was the limit of television screens in those days.)

The entire student body of the High School and Junior High School was present to witness history. Everyone watched as President Truman rode with Eisenhower on a Cadillac convertible to the Capitol Building. The big moment of oath taking was completely snowed out by poor reception which "snowed" out the entire screen. Trying to watch the television's image in a crowded auditorium was very similar to watching television in downtown Wetumka with the traffic passing by and people strolling down the sidewalk.

My suspicions are that it was television which dispersed people from the streets of Wetumka and kept them in their living rooms. The change was gradual but ultimately it was nearly complete.

For all of my life the merchants had kept their doors open until six in the evening and until nine in the Christmas season. There had always been a grocery store in the middle of every downtown block. Each one of them had a pick-up truck and they would cheerfully deliver a shopper and their groceries to their homes. Usually the grocery store had a butcher; they were all eager to purchase eggs from the farmers. (Back in the 1930s, The Coin Store, in one week, shipped out over 100 crates of eggs in a railcar. This was the surplus they couldn't sell.) Merchants admonished the farmers to pen up the roosters. Each egg would be candled and fertilized eggs were rejected because they easily incubated in the warm weather.

Before the advent of television there was hardly a single vacant building in downtown Wetumka. Just before television hit the downtown, parking was permitted in the middles of the streets. On a busy Saturday the cars would reach for several blocks in every direction. They parked in the middle of West Broadway all the way to the railroad.

Never again will a tourist find lodging in Wetumka. As late as the 1950's there were people who lived, at least part time, at the Meadors Hotel. There were rooms available at The Ranch-O-Tel and H. H. Loard's Junction Courts just across the street. (The first "tourist cabins" had been built at the present site of the Jack McGee residence. They were detached rooms and were primitive indeed. Before that tourists were discouraged from spending the night in their cars on Wetumka's streets. They were herded to a camping area on the old Mingo school grounds.)

Downtown Wetumka was a place of arrivals and departures. Sometimes there would be four or five Greyhound or Union buses in Wetumka at once as the café at the Meadors Hotel was a rest stop. Red

Aultman was the dean of Taxi operators but in his time he saw lots of competition come and go.

LaLoise McGee Wright (daughter of one of the town founders, X. X. McGee) recalls a scene that were familiar to my own memory. She said that the train depot was always a popular gathering place because there was always a coal stove doing its best in the waiting room and outside there were wide eaves where people could stand to get out of the rain. Some of the people actually bought trip tickets but most of them were just there to see who was coming and who was going. Mrs. Wright remembered Indian women with colorful and warm blankets bundling themselves and the baby they were nursing. The banks also had long benches and were popular places where people took shelter. There had been a plethora of witnesses when the American National Bank was robbed.

Nothing was like a train ride out of Wetumka. The coaches had really high ceilings and the seats were wide. The trip to Holdenville was unmercifully short. It didn't seem to last any time at all. The train never got up to a good speed before it began slowing down for the station at Yeager which seemed almost as large as Wetumka's. In Holdenville the Frisco and The Rock Island had a Union Station. Both railroads used the same building. They took turns in operating the depot. For four years the Frisco would be in charge. Then at midnight at the end of the fourth year the Rock Island would take over.

New Fords were unloaded at the railroad station several times a month prior to the War. There were special double decked boxcars and Nathan Lee, himself, would often go to the station and help drive the cars off at the loading dock.

Historians are not supposed to traffic in nostalgia. It's unprofessional. But in the final chapter of a personal history it should be permitted.

I attended Sucker Day in 1996. (I was there for several months as my mother was terminally ill.) I realized that never again would there be a crowd in Wetumka like those that were commonplace in my youth.

It was a different era in the 1950s. By 1962 I had the beginning of a college education from the University of Oklahoma and two tours of duty in Vietnam. (Absolutely the best years of my life from every aspect.) I was drawn away from Wetumka because of dire necessity. A man does not easily desert his birthplace to move the the western edge of the Continent. My story is like those who once peopled the streets of Wetumka. We believed, very wisely in my opinion, that there was a better economy in places like California. I believed, at the time, that it was a place of unlimited opportunity and wealth. I believe that more firmly today than ever.

The export product that Wetumka has always excelled in is its people. I am continually amazed by the accomplishments of expatriot Wetumkans. Yet, it was this forced migration of the masses which has impoverished Hughes County and Wetumka. I consulted the recent Census figures which show that there are 3,110 counties in the United States. There are over 3,000 counties which are better off than Hughes County in terms of per capita income.

In my own estimation, the reasons for this are obvious. Hughes County has lost over two thirds of its population since World War II. Wetumka is hardly half of what it once was. In statistical terms, the city and county are worse off than they were in the Depression. There were 3,601 Social Security recepients in the county or just about one out of every four persons in a recent year. The postal payroll and veterans benefits are absolutely essential to the local economy. In one way or another the Federal government spent about $64 million in Hughes County in the most recent year for which statistics are available. This is nearly $7,000 for every man, woman and child.

Recently, THE HUGHES COUNTY TIMES reported that for the first time in decades, no peanuts were purchased at Wetumka. The first big peanut year was 1942 which coincided with the outbreak of the war. Farmers could plant as many acres as they wanted. Quota and non-quota peanuts brought about the same. Before the farmers were half way through the season they had exceeded the storage capacity of the armory building. At least 32,000 acres were harvested in the county that year. By the end of the War, James Taylor was boasting that he was the largest purchaser of peanuts "West of the Mississippi." His warehouse was four stories high and was served by a rail spur that came to within a few feet of U. S. 75. Nearly every evening box cars of sacked peanuts were shipped out by rail. Ed Adkins, who is 91 and a resident of Wetumka, reminded me that in the 1930s there was more cotton than the gins could buy. On some Saturdays buyers would purchase up $10,000 worth of cotton from wagons on Main Street. I knew a man who had been a cotton buyer; I mowed his lawn when he was retired. His name was Clyde Jarrett and he had been a cotton buyer. He would buy loads of cotton and have then ginned and shipped out.

Before World War II there were about 3,200 farms in Hughes County. And in those days people who lived on farms really were farmers. About a thousand farms were lost, mainly due to manpower shortages, before the war was over. Today there are only 800 plus farms in Hughes County of all types and sizes and the Agricultural Census shows that off-farm income is a large factor in farm life.

Why shouldn't I be nostalgic for the "not-so-good" old days when a person could go into Herring Hardware and buy anything from a horse collar to oil cloth? Oil cloth! Or they could buy a complete set of clothing from any one of several local stores.

I know, kind reader, that it's just a small town in Oklahoma, but there are those who still love her! But I realize, now, that NEVER AGAIN shall I spend a day or night there.

APPENDIX

Wetumka Timeline

1905—Newspaper Ads: Calico per yard 5 cents, Meadors Brothers &Busey

Hot or Cold Baths, 25 cents, Richardson's Barber Shop (Agency for Ada Steam Laundry)

J. R. Dutton, The Leading Druggist, Phone No. 3.

February 23—First Balloon Ascension in Wetumka is a success despite the fact that it had earlier caught fire. Ascension made from lot east of the City Bakery.

May 23—Carrie A. Nation, possibly the most famous person ever to speak in Wetumka, lectured at the Baptist church on the evening of May 23. She was the widow of an alcoholic doctor who became famous when she and her women's group started going into saloons in Kansas and smashing everything in sight with hatchets. She spoke in favor of the nationwide movement to outlaw the manufacture, transport and sale of intoxicating beverages. She was nearly mobbed by admirers everywhere she spoke. Even in Wetumka, it was necessary to limit the crowds by the sale of tickets at Crank's and at Dutton's Drug Store.

June 1—Mr. and Mrs. C. B. Williams are rejoicing over the advent of a new boy, born last Friday. He was named George, in honor of their business partner, George Appling, who"bears his honors like a soldier."

June 29—THE MONTGOMERY (Alabama) ADVERTISER states there are people still alive who witnessed the "the sad features of the removal" of the Creek Indians. Editor's opinion is that Oklahoma statehood will mean "adieu" to the Indians.

December 7—President Murray, in the opinion of THE WETUMKA NEWS HEARLD has started things off right by putting a curtain between the Whites and Negroes at the Constitutional Convention.

Newspaper Ads: The Celebrated Studebaker Wagons at Doak & Mackey's.

1907—Constitutional Convention decides against "Jim Crow" laws in the state's fundamental law, the Constitution. They are advised that the President might seize upon it to withhold statehood. It is said that if the state wishes to have separate schools, and suffrage tests that will tend to discourage the activity of the Negro in politics, all these ambitions can be achieved by legislative enactment.

August 1—Lamar, Oklahoma, is touted as a place where a fortune can be made quickly. Soils are of inexhaustible fertility, said to be located over pools of oil and fields of coal.

August 8—Assessment of real and personal property in Wetumka area is $335,492. This will create a fund of $2,686.23 for the school and $2,350 for the incorporated town.

September 7—Long list of Indians who have successfully petitioned Interior Department to have restrictions removed from their allotted lands is published in THE WETUMKA GAZETTE.

September 26—Concrete crossings on Main Street to be started.

October 24—Transmississippi Congress for Indians hosts 1,000 delegates at Muskogee. Claim is made that every Chief of the Five Civilized Tribes is already a bank director.

Wetumka's School has an enrollment of 233-136 boys and 97 girls.

1908—County Seat Vote, First Election:

	Holdenville	Wetumka	Calvin	Lamar
Holdenville	457	0	2	2
Wetumka	6	497	0	5
Yeager	90	41	15	8
Dustin	67	49	55	12
Calvin	6	1	164	0
Newburg	19	0	133	0
Guertie	71	7	41	1
Spaulding	65	1	8	0
Hanna	38	22	1	21
Trenton	8	10	0	2
Carson	13	35	0	40
Lone Star	3	65	1	7
Mountain View	16	51	1	0
Valley View	8	35	7	1
Butner	27	66	8	1
Pecan Grove	112	6	0	0
Coston	82	0	0	0
Prarie View	74	0	1	3
Edmondson	117	1	0	0
Greenleaf	36	0	10	0

Gum Springs	10	1	26	0
Spring Creek	18	1	34	7
Lamar	2	0	1	126
Wecharty	37	0	9	0
McMahan	52	5	18	24
Rag Town	25	18	12	7
Big Springs	17	59	0	6
Round Prarie	9	0	54	0
Bakers Branch	8	2	79	0
Citra	4	4	59	0
Non	7	2	62	1
Stuart	50	7	49	1
Tandy	6	1	22	0
Rock Creek	13	1	50	0
TOTALS	1563	988	917	275
	(41%)	(26%)	(24%)	(7%)

County Seat Contest, Final Election

	Holdenville	Wetumk
Holdenville	487	6
Wetumka	8	515
Yeager	100	66
Dustin	101	87
Calvin	57	121
Newburg	104	57
Guertie	87	49
Spaulding	76	4
Hanna	54	48

Trenton	23	16
Carson	35	70
Lone Star	4	98
Mountain View	16	64
Valley View	11	63
Butner	52	73
Pecan Grove	125	19
Coston	90	14
Prairie View	113	1
Edmondson	113	7
Greenleaf	66	19
Gum Springs	27	5
Spring Creek	31	31
Lamar	84	78
Wecharty	31	3
McMahan	92	36
Rag Town	45	38
Big Springs	19	87
Round Prairie	25	44
Bakers Branch	39	30
Citra	42	45
Non	31	34
Stuart	57	47
Tandy	16	21
Rock Creek	59	40
TOTALS	2320	1936
	(54%)	(45%)

1908—January 28—Indians ready to dedicate new church on thirteen acres south of Wetumka.

January 28—The City is having 256 bricks lettered and numbered which will be placed on the corners of each of the blocks in the cemetery.

November 10—John Tabner, Wetumka Deputy, kills one and seriously injures another when he is fired upon while trying to break up a street fight on Main Street. Mr. Tabner is also fatally injured. He was asleep at the Old Brick Hotel when he was called for. He was an orphan from Arkansas who had been sponsored by the C. B. Williams family, founders of The Coin Store.

1909—July 6—New School costing $11,872 and only days from completion in Dustin is total loss in fire. Insurance covered only $5,000.

1910—October 21—Honorable W. H. Murray speaks for the first time in Wetumka. He would often be in Wetumka before, during and after his tenure as Oklahoma govenor.

1911—January 17—Three rooms at Mingo School are used for the first time.

January 27—Special Agriculture Train Due in Wetumka on Saturday. Livestock car will contain specimen of the beef and dairy cattle; two common cows for comparison; an 18-month old A. & M. college bred colt that weights 1500 pounds, a shoat for demonstration in vaccination against hog cholera; four types of hogs. The flat car will also carry an 8-foot model silo and other dairy equipment. In addition to displays of corn and cotton, these exhibits will include scientific instruments from the engineering department, samples of students' work in wood and iron, models of bridges, designs, paintings from the classes in art, sewing from the domestic science department and dissecting models from the veterinary department.

February 3-Official reports show that 906,186 bales of cotton have been ginned in Oklahoma up to January 16, as compared to 522,803 bales last year.

February 24—Horse Thieving on Main Street on Saturday evening. Dr. G. W. Patterson's team was stolen from the hitching rack in front of Jarrett's Drug Store. Early Sunday morning, Monroe Reed, Charley Darks, Roy Chowins and Burney Gilkey left town on the trail of the thief. He'd already been apprehended near Indianola.

March 10—C. J. Dickerson let the contract to build three stone and brick buildings on West Broadway between the First National Bank and the Brick Hotel. The total cost will be about $4,000.

March 24—Sheppard's Gin Reduced to Ashes. The gin stands and main building were completely destroyed and twenty four bales of cotton were badly damaged.

June 18—Public election determines location of new town hall. Chowins brothers have the contract.

January 17—A birthday party was given in honor of Rebecca and David Bloom on Thursday, January 9. Games were played and refreshments served. Many pretty and useful presents were received. Those present were Rebecca Bloom, Mabel Pevy, Louise Tiger, Thelma Turner, Aldine Young, Thelma Horsely, Nettie McCoy, Beulah Young, Floy Bennett, Gladys Geren, Inez Bennet, Bertha Bloom, David Bloom, May Blankenbaker.

January 24—Obituary. James C. Chowins was born in Devonshire, England, February 23, 1865 and immigrated to America in 1865. He was married to Miss Julia Marshaley, to which union seven children, four of whom are living and were present at his funeral.

February 7—Assessed Valuation of Hughes County is $12,169,066. Total tax to be collected from all sources is $269,236.

February 28—Frisco demonstration farm, one of 36 on its line, is established near Holdenville. Purpose is to provide best seed suitable to the soil and climate and to give minute instruction in making the crop.

Expenditures for the Wetumka Colored School ending June 30, 1913: Wood, $30.00; Crayons $2; Globe $4; Chart $5; Map of Oklahoma $2; Maps of the World $4; Erasers 60 cents; Brooms $1; Janitor $15; Stove Pipe $1; Sanitary Work $18; Rent $60; State Association expenses $11.

May 28—An Old Landmark is torn down. It had stood at the rear of A. W. Smith's drug store and for several years and held empty boxes. It was first erected as the store and post office run by Jackson Dunzy in Old Town. The late J. C. Chowins had cut it into halves and moved them to hold his lots on Main Street where the American National Bank and Smith's drug stores now stand. The two halves were later placed entirely on lot 2. It was then called the "Little Red Front" and Wetumka's first mayor, Frank Shires, had his office there. There, too, H. H. Holman, Wetumka's second mayor presided at the first jury trial held in Wetumka.

November 7—"Back to Africa" meeting was held at Clearview

(near Weleetka) . According to THE WELEETKA AMERI-CAN, the Negroes of this county are selling everything and turning it into money. The Clearview meeting, itself, raised $12,435.50 for the movement.

December 19—It is announced that Guthrie has opened a $100,000 municipal bathhouse. Govenor Cruz and his daughter head a capital guest list.

1914—January 1—Mr. J. F. Busey sold his interest in department store. The store is now owned soley by Turner Meaders and his son Frank.

February 13—Chief Sam Disappears. A dispatch from New York, dated February 10, states that a shipload of Negroes, mostly farmers and their wives from Oklahoma, are waiting there for Alfred C. Sam to lead them to a new Negro utopia on the Gold Coast of Africa. Chief Sam has disappeared and his whereabouts are unknown to his followers. Word from Weleetka is that 500 to 700 Negroes from various parts of Oklahoma gathered there, and the news from New York created consternation among the colonists. It is reported that Sam carried with him between $65,000 and $75,000, subscribed by his followers to finance the project.

February 25—The Battleship "Oklahoma" is launched in Camden, New Jersey. Governor's daughter, Miss Lorena Cruz, will christen. Said to be the world's greatest battleship and consecrated to a mission of peace.

May 29—Those graduating from the Wetumka school are Charles Appling, Gladys Busey, Drayton Burke, George Deere, Virgil Fulks, Leona Long, Grace Masterson, Charles Rice, Agnes Wells, and Roper Williams. Those finishing the eighth grade are

Hattie Hayman, Nina Rushing, Cecele Crawford, Georgia Crawford, Murray Edwards, Jennie Smith, Clifford Hays, Alva Haag, Clark Fulks, Rose Lee Holman and Merle Busey.

July 5—A fourteen year old boy was stabbed last Sunday at Yeager and almost instantly killed by a boy only twelve years old.

December 4—Wetumka Cotton Gins Report 7506 bales have been ginned. The F. & M. Gin Co., 2497 bales; Wetumka Gin Co., 1813; Ogletree Gin Co., 1333; Planters Gin Co., 1228; Independent Gin Co., 635 bales.

May 7—A deal was pulled off this week whereby Bass Moore takes over the dray business formerly owned by Roy Gammill. (Bass Moore was also the City Night Policeman for decades.)

1915—May 7—Confederate soldiers can apply for an Oklahoma pension. The law provides that no one person can receive more than $10 per month, the whole state appropriation being limited to $20,000. (Union soldiers were already eligible to receive a modest Federal pension.)

June 4—Confederate Reunion at Brick Hotel. They were guests of James Williams. Those present were D. J. Davis, Stewart Oklahoma, Ben D. Calvard, Wilberton, Oklahoma, and Ben B. Chism, Pans, Arkansas. Three of them were members of the same Company-Capt. John Titsmouth, 5th Arkansas Infantry-in the early part of the war. D. J. Davis was a member of Capt. John Walker's Company.

1915—May 15—First Trades Day in Wetumka draws crowd of 3500. This is a partial list of the premiums offered:
The Hays Store-Panama Hat and pair of ladies silk hose to youngest married couple. The Coin-100 pounds of flour to the

person bringing in the largest wagon load of people. Herring Hardware Co.-One, 1 gallon ice cream freezer for best Jersey cow. B. F. Scott-One 42-piece dinner set to the largest woman. Mastin Barber Shop-Hair Cut and shave to man with the longest hair. Vanderpol Brothers Fixit Shop-One $2.50 rocking chair to largest baby under 1 year old. M. Bloom-One pair $5.00 pants to man with the largest waist. Billie Fields-$4.00 meal ticket for man pulling a split log drag second farthest. X. X. McGee-First annual premium on $1000 life insurance to the man getting married in bandstand.

June 18—Wetumka 8, Holdenville 7. "A rattling good game (baseball) was pulled off at Holdenville last Saturday and as usual, the Wetumka boys 'brought home the bacon.'"

June 18—Harrison-Haulk-A pretty wedding was solemnized at the home of Mr. Ben H. Harrison last Monday, when Miss Lucille Harrison was joined in matrimony to Mr. Lloyd Haulk of Hanna. She was the sister of Ben Harrison who was a Depression era Mayor of Wetumka. (Mr. and Mrs. Ben Harrison were lawyers with a joint practice. Their home is in the 200 block of East Broadway (next to Mr. Absher).

June 25—Twenty-five carloads of peaches are shipped out of Wetumka.

July 2—Farewell party. A number of young folks were entertained at home of Turner Meadors last Wednesday, in honor of Miss Gladys Busey who moved to Holdenville. Those present were Misses Beulah Crawford, Velma Foster, Gladys Busey, Lavacca Kirkpatrick, Atha Meadors, Ruth McCoy, Ruby Evans, Nancy Harrison, Nellie Jones, Gladys Blakely, Irene Appling, Vivian Hemphill, and Leslie Wiggins, Messrs. Jeff Jarrett, Kenneth Lucas, Burton Malone, George Cook, Noel Hays, Dewey Foster, Ray Meadors, Roper Williams and Charles Burrow.

July 14—Mamie Pippin is struck and killed with an iron bar in her garden in Wetumka. Her husband is convicted and sentenced to 49 years at McAlester.

August 13—Herring Hardware, Co., De Laval Cream Seperators, Revonos Oil Stoves, Ice Cream Freezers.

Sept 1—Wetumka to Have Ice Plant. A deal was closed last week between Charley Appling and the town council whereby Mr. Appling will install an ice plant in connection with the city power plant. Mr. Appling's intent is to manufacture ice utilizing exhaust steam that is presently going to waste. Mr. Appling agreed to charge no more than 69 cents per hundred weight for ice delivered in town and no more than 40 cents per hundred pounds at the plant.

June 22—Booster trip is a great success. Thirty five cars full of businessmen and ladies left Wetumka to visit all the nearby towns. The first stop was Weleetka. Then came Dustin, Carson, Lamar, Holdenville and Yeager. They were cordially received by crowds everywhere. Only one incident marred the trip. Mr. Kitchen's big Case auto ran off a bridge and turned over and had to be left behind but there were no injuries.

August 16—Three wagons given away in drawing during December Trades Day.

August 16—Wetumkans for Camp Pike. The following will entrain for Camp Pike, Ark., on or about August 26. Eleven are of the new class of 1918.

Henry Melton, John W. Nicks, Lewis King, Amos Lowe, Ralph Mayberry, Daniel W. Moore, Percy P. Penrod, C. B. Burnett, John Rash, F. D. Smith, N. E. McDonald, Edward Bear, Bill A. Cline, C. Deer.

February 14—The County Agent Vanderpool, and T. A. Milstead, The Frisco Demonstration Agent accompanied by some of the businessmen of the town will visit seventeen school houses adjacent to Wetumka to talk to farmers about growing peanuts.

May 2—City of Wetumka is sued for $20,000. D. Y. Burkes was electrocuted by coming into contact with exposed wiring at the Red Cross Drug Store. (The City prevails.)

October 9—Fourth automobile garage in Wetumka is opened next to the City Hall.

November 12—Wrestling at the Majestic Theatre.

December 19—40,000 pounds of pecans shipped by Fate Dickerson, manager, Wetumka Produce House.

May 28—J. L. Skinner, last Monday, sold 400 acres of land, adjoining Wetumka, on the east, for $50,000.00 cash. Tom Long, a wealthy Indian, is the purchaser. Mr. Long, according to THE HOLDENVILLE DEMOCRAT increased his fortune in oil royalties and is supposed to be worth more than a half million dollars.

July 14—The regular examination for teacher's license will be held in Holdenville, July 27, 28, 29. All planning to take this examination must be present at 8:00 O'clock. H. S. Mathis, County Superintendent.

July 14—ELMO SMITH, public weigher, Transfer.

1920—July 9—Mrs. Rosa Bloom and Mr. Nathan Lee went to Okmulgee and were married.

September 24—The contract for erecting the consolidated school building for Districts 19 and 25 was let a few days ago to Harry Chowins for $28,500.00.

Preliminary announcement of Census Bureau for Hughes County is 26,045, in 1910 it was 24,040. Calvin 700, a gain of 130; Dustin 713, a gain of 134; Gertie 251, decrease of 54; Holdenville 2,032; decrease of 264; Wetumka 1,422 an increase of 272; Yeager 286; increase 55.
September 30—Cornerstone of the county courthouse will be laid today under the auspices of the Masons of Hughes County.

December 24—A lynching took place in Holdenville last Saturday night according to THE DALLAS MORNING NEWS. Johnson E. Tiger, of Wetumka, reported this item in an interview. C. S. Darks, Wetumka Chief of Police was in Dallas with him. (Mr. Tiger believed it was the first such occurrence in the county and said the "peace records" of Hughes County were good.

April 29—The heavy rains have put the river and the creeks out of their banks in the highest flood since 1908.

April 29—Rev. and Mrs. John Smith arrived home Saturday from Fort Lauderdale, Florida, where they had been missionaries to the Seminole Indians.

June 3—Eighth Grade Commencement was held at the Methodist Church and forty diplomas were given, the largest number ever in Wetumka. The following composed the graduating class. Pauline Peevey;, Waltie Parks, Cressie Mills; Mattie Moses; Edith Casey; Florence Farmer; Roxie Mae Gillispie, Nellie Osborn; Lucy Light, Alma Powell, Ethel Blankenbaker, Roy Chaney, Barbara Crabtree, Gussie London, Harry Withers, Bessie Louise Busey, Sonn Lee, Neva Thompson, Downey Waltmire, Amos Combs, Try Rae, Fred Booze, Lora Mae Whitfield, Flora McKinzie, Geory Sheppard, Marguerite Mayfield, Helen Nichols, Lucille McLeod, Lono Head, Henry Lee Brazil, Alice Winters, Fairley Wheat, Oliver Roberts, Eldred Ostrom, William Cowan, Irl Brady, Paul willie Mackey, Alice Reed, Del Ramsay, Beryl Ozment.

June 1—Wetumka National Guard contingent sent to Tulsa because of "race riot." Captain Charles Rice happened to already be in Tulsa. He send a message to get 25-30 men together and depart immediately. There were twenty-eight men from Wetumka who did duty there. They were 1st Lieutenant Milton F. Thompson, 2nd Lieutenant Edward L. Morrison, 1st Sergeant Birch Walker. Sergeants Kermit Smith, Robert McCoy, Lawrence Ostrom, Bill Mullins, K. V. Lucas. Corporals Paul Powell, Freeman Crowles, Curtis Lowder, Clyde Busey, and Clarence Penrod. Privates George W. Cowan, Virgil Harris, Gladney Mackey, Daurice Palmer, John D. Jones, Melvin Brock, Oliver Young, Harry Withers, Raymond Stone, Winfield Price, Will F. Johnson, Elmer D. Stuckey, William A. Grisson and Ed Hansford.

June 3—High School Graduation. Eleven were awarded diplomas: Mimmie Troop, Grace Streeter, Oliver Nicks, Castle Mackey, Velma McEhannon, Ona Pack, Lyra Richardson, Paul Gille, George Morrison, Lester Williams, Hilda Franklin.

June 3—Memorial Day fittingly observed. A military service was held over the returned body of Alvis Hubbs, who was killed in France in October, 1918. The Clarence Kitchens Post of the American Legion and Company "I", 2nd Oklahoma Infantry participated.

July 21—Saturday, July 30th: "The Son of Tarzan" is showing at the Majestic Theatre. Admission Matinee and Night, 10 and 25 cents. Ladies free at matinee.

July 21—Gas mains extended and 79 new meters installed.

August 5—Chief Motey Tiger dies. Was aged 87 and lived at Sharp, near Okmulgee. Was elected Second Chief of the Creeks in 1897 in the last Tribal Election ever held. He is survived by his wife and one son, Johnson E. Tiger, the latter of Wetumka. (He had been named "Motey" in honor of Motey Canard, once a famous chief of the Creeks. He had been a Methodist minister and had engaged in raising cattle on an extensive scale. He was a member of the Tuckabacha clan which was composed entirely of full blood Indians in pioneer days and was one of the most powerful clans in the Creek Nation.

August 12—Next Tuesday Good Roads Motor Club will begin two days work on road from Mission Hill to the Cemetery. A free barbecue is also planned.

August 12—Bertha Bloom, daughter of Dry Goods Store Owner Morris Bloom, has completed work at Ada and at O. U.

August 26—The following is a list of those working on the road last Tuesday:

B. C. Robinson, L. M. Ross, G. L. Herring, Geo Waggoner and tractor, Henry Lee, S M Blevins and car, Ray Meadors, Birch Walker, M O Vaughn, H M Brazil, John Klein, T N Knight and team, Lem Clingman, Fate Dickerson S M Puryear, M L Sims, Nat Williams, C L Collins, J M Watkins, Carl Haubold, J A More, C B Williams, J H…, Lafe Knight and two teams, Charley Palmer, W. A. Geren, Arthur Woolverton and team, J. W. Woolverton and team, Will Thompson and team, Bob Kendall and team, A N Brown, A. B. Knight, E. A. Smith, L V Palmer, R. R. Martin, W B Chaney, H E Wise, P M Powell, , H C Griswold, Bob Mastin, Ed Hicks, Thomas Ipcock, J R Knight, A B Kelley and team, H. H. Conley and team, J B Irby, JB Powell, J P Rash, Don Phelps for Ray, Raymond Kirkpatrick, C. W. Norris, N C Barry, Harry Sturdevine and horse, I H Cagle, T. M. Norris, P A Bolin, Frank Hurley, G. F. Barret, J C Tomberlin, J A. Malhewe, Gladny Mackey, Walter Glissen, Jake Grotis, John Harkins, Ralph Busey, Roy Rice, R. A. Conley, J. E. Burris, Charles Evans for D S Mitchell, Ed Kelley, Glenn Young, W. N. Dilbeck, Buford Carrol, P. E. Mitchell, Paul Nicols, Milo Lucas and Don Darks. The following who could not work on the roads last week paid two dollars, which will be used on that road. H J Days, Davis Drug, Nathan Lee, W. C. Kline, A P Steed, J E Jarrett, G. L. Carroll, H H Woford, J F Busey, J H Kennedy.

August 26—The American Legin is building "log cabin" from telephone poles secured from the telephone company at a reasonable price.

September 2—Gas Plant sold. The gas franchise for Wetumka, which was granted to the Gladys Bell Oil Company last year and who installed the system which is furnishing gas for the town, has been sold to R. H. Williams, of Wetumka. For the past four years he had served as deputy county treasurer but is an "Old

Wetumka man."

September 30—Wetumka Eagles win football game over the Henryetta Hens, 20-7.

October 21—Statistical Report of Work in Wetumka Schools-Enrollment for month ending October 7th:

	High School	
Freshmen		63
Sophomore		31
Junior		22
Senior		22
1st grade, high school	36	
1st grade, Mingo	28	
2nd grade, high school	30	
2nd grade, Mingo	19	
3rd grade, high school	27	
3rd grade, Mingo	18	
4th grade, high school	35	
4th grade, Mingo	35	
5th grade, Mingo	40	
6th grade, Mingo	55	
7th grade, Mingo	42	
8th grade Mingo	40	
	395	
Total Enrollment		533

Those students who have made a grade of 90 or above are placed on the Honor Roll. The following students are on the honor roll from the high school:Bernice Arnold, Sr., Berdie Dickerson, Sr., Rebecca Bloom, Jr., Thelma Sheppard, Jr., Ima Marsalas, Jr., Dale Ozment, Jr., Ura Thompson, Jr., Lucille Taylor, Jr., Blanche McElhannon, Jr., Eunice Brown, So., Margaret Farmer, So., Marie Ramsay, So., Bessie Louise Busey, Fr., Ella Lee, Fr.

Those students on the Honor Roll from the grades are:

Cora Arnold, Eunice Robinson, Laloise McGee, Lorene Busey, Goldie Gorhum, Henriette Giswold, Alye Tomberline, Margaret Brazil, Cloyce Mastin, Arthur Collins, Ira Bryce, Kenneth Tiger, Joe Cavanaugh, Elvin Hixon, Lynere Casey, Mary Elinor Couch, Velma Louise, Moore, William Brady, Homer Henley, Otis Kendall, Mattie Moore, D. M. Casey, Thelma Meadows, Cecil Hamilton, Thiril Jaffett, Grant Jones, Roy Alexander, Zuma Coleman, Agnes Crabtree, Agnes Hixon, Melba Jones, Nora Jones, Pauline reed, Mary Robinson Vivian Brady, Arcel Duet, Eulah Lucas, Hubert Osborn, Roberta Burkes, David Jamison, Ruth Berryhill, Wade Fulks, John J. Grotts, Emma Lewis, Juanita Mayfield, Gussie McElhannon, Perlie Wilson, Lonzo Yahola, Margaret Haubold, Ruth Ryan, Laneva McElhannon, Charley Gorham, Margaret Jackson, Mike Ledbetter, Woodrow Osborn, Gillie Reed, Daisy Weson.

November 4—Wetumka Ordiance issued regarding rules of operating automobiles in town.

November 18—List of Parties opposed to Pavement Bond Issue:

Party	Lot	Block
Mrs. W. W. Masterson	4&5	17
William Buck	7&8	40
W. J. McElwee	1-12	18
Mary F. Hawks	9&10	46
W. H. Freeman	9&10	46
Pearl Jackson	16	40
Kate C. Mackey	7&8	46
G. H. Wilkerson	18	40
E. M. Roberts	1-4	60
Henry Bowles	15	40
C. O. Wilson	6	39
Kate C. Mackey	7&8	32
Nathan Dunzy	6	39
Henry Shaber	7&8	39
B. Parker	1	39
Kate C. Mackey	5&6	47
A. S. Umbenhour	1&2	45
Geo. Knerium	1&2	45
Hester Bristow	1&2	45
Mary Turner	3	46
J. M. Towery	13&14	39
J. F. Lucas	9&10	40
Eula Burkes	10	40
R. F. Blackburn	16&17	39
R. B. Blackburn	18	39
J. A. Smith	5&6	39
McIntosh Lumber Co.	1-4	38
McIntosh Lumber Co.	16-18	46
Lee Woford	11	31
Lee Woford	11	31
W. D. Yocum	13-15	32
W. C. Yocum	13-15	32

W. N. Dilbeck	S1/2 6	54
Fate Dickerson	15	39
I.O.O.F. Hall	4	54
J. A. Grotts	7	39
J. A. Grotts	7	39
Frank Meadors	5&6	67
Herring & Haubold	7&8	45
Carl Haubold	7&8	45
Geo. Appling	11&12	45
Ray Meadors	17&18	45
Turner Meadors	15&16	40
C. I. Clanton	5&6	40
Joe McCann	6	54
J. S. Ledbetter	13&18	38
John Turner	3	53
H. M. Brazil	7-12	26
H. M. Brazil	5&6	59
Darks Brothers	18	39
Mayfield & Jackson	15	45
A. W. Smith	2	46
A. W. Smith	2	39
Tennie Hawks	9-11	46

October 7—The boys and men have agreed to wear overalls or just plain clothes and the women have agreed to wear house aprons or common clothes at services to encourage the less fortunate to attend services at the Baptist church.

October 21—B. Harris of Sallisaw buys jewelry store in Wetumka.

November 18—Wetumka Eagles are defeated by Tulsa High

School Braves (in football) at Lee Stadium in Tulsa.

July 8—Raymond Saxon arrived Saturday from Fort Sill, on a short furlough to visit his parents, Mr. and Mrs. J. R. Saxon.

July 25—Preliminary work has been done to mark The Cotton Belt Highway through Hughes County north of the river.

September 2—Premium is paid for the first bale of cotton marketed in Wetumka. Those contributing were First National Bank $2.50; Bank of Commerce, $2.50; American National Bank $2.50; A. W. Smith $1.00; H. J. Hays $1.00; G. L. Carroll $1.00; J. H. Kennedy $1.00; Davis Drug Co., $1.00; Nathan Lee $1.00; A. P. Steed $.50; Mackey Hardware Co., $1.00; J. M. Watkins $1.00; J. E. Jarrett $1.00; W. N. Dilbeck $1.00; C. W. Mayberry $.50; Laidlaw-Moore $1.00; Herring Hdwre Co. $1.00; The Coin $1; Mrs. J. A. Ostrom $.50; Mayfield and Jackson $1.00; M. L. Waggener $1; Hicks & Hicks $1; Palace Drug Co., $1; T-P Mercantile Co. $1; R. D. Morris $1; Lucas & Sons $1; W. H. Burkes $.50; P. A. Bolin $.50; G. T. Gibson $.50; J. A. Hemphill $.50; Billington Lumber Co. $1; V & R Garage $1; Virgil Murphy $.50; Jack Murphy $.50; T. L. Neal Drug Store $1; City Grocery $.50; William Nicks $1; Liberty Café $1.00; City Grocery $.50; William Nicks $1; Liberty Café $1; J. H. Shaber $1; J. A. Cain $1; R. F. Vaughn $.50; Wetumka Trading Co., $1.00; J. M. Allred $.50; Darks Brothers $1; Chas. N. Hamilton $1; The Fair Store $1; Live Oak Gasoline Co., $1; Bow-Dunson $1; Shaber & Son $1; H. H. Darks $1; Hugh White $1; Ind. Oil & Gas Co., $1; W. T. Berryhill $1; Nat Williams $1; M. Meadors $1; C. P. Hicks $.50; C. L. Hughey $1.

February 3—Ray Meadors and Helen Gille are married.

February 10—The 1920 Census shows Wetumka at 1442. Recent census by W. H. Freeman shows 1576, an increase of 134 in two years.

March 3—S. M. Blevins puts up "oil map" at The Bank of Commerce to plot the progress of the feverish oil drilling in the area.

March 10—The "Airline Road" is marked. This is the future path of State Highway 9. The marking crew sets up steel marking posts from Oklahoma City to Fort Smith, Arkansas.

October 6—A radio broadcast (of a distant baseball game) is demonstrated for the first time in Wetumka at The Red Cross Drug Store to an amazed crowd.

October 13—Ex-Governor Cruz will speak in Wetumka.

January 19—Methodist Indians are building church six miles north of here on the Okemah road. The building is of native stone and of such dimensions as to accommodate a large congregation.

February 16—Kiwanis Club is organized.

July 7—National Guard to encampment at Fort Sill. Capt. Charles Rice, with seventy-five men of Company "I" 179th Infantry, and Capt. D. J. L. Walker with sixty men of Company "A" 120th Engineers left Wetumka in special train coaches. Their equipment consists 100 horses and of other things necessary.

July 7—Pioneer dentist, Dr. J. P. Gille becomes naturalized as citizen of the United States. Dr. Gille was born in Germany.

July 13—Nusho Theatre installs cooling system. Big blow fan changes the air inside every minute. It is blown over vats of melting ice and gentlemen can wear their coats on the hottest day of the year. Manager says he uses 1,800 pounds of ice weekly. He says it is not a novelty but the type of cooling used in many metropolitan theatres.

July 13—J. H. Williams, father of C. B. Williams, passes away. Had come to Wetumka in 1891. He was a Confederate veteran. The body was taken to Etna, Arkansas, where it will be laid to rest. He was 81.

August 31—Carload of broomcorn is shipped out of Wetumka.

December 21—Over $20,000 is paid out for pecans in a "middling" year.

December 23—Mrs. Gille is operating modern greenhouse. At first she was a hobbyist who like having a yard full of beautiful flowers. When she started making her flowers commercially available she realized that she could satisfy markets nationwide with modern green houses. She is the first person to use thermostatically controlled heating in any form in Wetumka. She is now able to supply the market on a year round basis.

January 11-THE WETUMKA GAZETTE converts to electrical power. For nearly twenty years the presses had been run by a gasoline engine. The school population has increased by 400% in five years. Number of students exceeds the number of Wetumka residents counted by the 1920 Federal Census.

March 3—Meadors Brothers sell half interest in royalty for $95,000.

July 24—Forty-three families receive assistance after tornado devastes Wetumka. Cash disbursements were: Clothing 455.64; Household goods 2,766.50; Maintenance 97.56; Cash grant 76.50; Building and Repairs 4,818,23; Medical Aid 2,697.06; Burial expenses 343.50; Livestock 75.00; Labor 20.00; Miscellaneous 20.51; Repairs and Implements 100.00; Stock for store 100.00. Total disbursements $11,750.00. The Red Cross was fully re-imbursed by local contributions. The "cyclone" hit Wetumka on May 28, 1924.

August 29—$100,000 paid for eighty acre oil lease to Tom Ryan by the Independent Oil and Gas Company.

September 10—New Buildings for Wetumka. I. E. Fleming is completing a rent house on his lot just north of the high school building. Harry Chowins will soon have a new home on his place north of town. Mrs. J. C. Wiggins' splendid six room modern home will be completed in a few more weeks. It is located just north of Dr. Hemphill. Chas. Hamilton will begin in a short time to erect a modern home on South Main Street, just south of T. T. Rice. W. B. Kirkpatrick has sold his lots in the southwest part of the city to Earl Chowins who will build a home, beginning right away. Workmen are making splendid progress on the twelve room apartment house of Dr. J. P. Gille, just across the street from his home on south Main Street. Otto Moses is building on his lots on South Main Street. Mrs. S. M. Bradbury's new apartment house on South Main is completed and occupied.

October 10—Contract to pave Main Street awarded Park and Moran.

October 17—Bank Deposits in Wetumka total $1,384,645.86:

American National has $519,899.43 on deposit; The National Bank of Commerce has on deposit $544,899.43 and The First National has deposits of $320,114.02.

October 24—City plant is profitable. The city power plant showed a profit of $5700 in the first two months of the fiscal year.

October 31—Henry Bowles becomes the owner of the White Front Grocery and Market. Will open Saturday with his brother, Wesley, in charge.
December 19-Postal Receipts have doubled over last year's according to postmaster W. A. Geren.

December 24—Paving fever hits Wetumka. Two blocks on Main Street now open for traffic. Within a few weeks both Main and Broadway will be paved. The city council has passed a resolution for pavement on Alabama and St. Louis Avenue.

1925—January 13—Only two members of the original volunteer fire department of Wetumka (organized in 1904) are still on the job: Roy Gammill and Roy Chowins. The original equipment was hand drawn chemical wagons. In 1911 a horse drawn fire wagon was acquired and a modern fire truck was acquired at the end of 1924.

February 2—75 Cars of corn are shipped out of Wetumka.

February 20—Chamber of Commerce organized in Papoose City with 65 members

February 27—W. H. Burkes, City Clerk completes census and finds 3118 persons living inside Wetumka's corporate limits. There are 298 homeowners and 333 rent houses and a number of

houses under construction. He found forty-one mercantile estab-
lishments and other businesses as follows;

Drillers-	78	Nurses	3
Rig Builders	104	Shoemakers	4
Truck Drivers	109	Postmasters	1
Teamsters	112	Engineers	2
Housewives	386	Landladies	1
Farmers	58	Supt. Del.	2
Laborers	569	Printers	4
Café owners	29	Porters	9
Barbers	22	Plumbers	11
Clerks	82	Seamsters	8
Merchants	79	Lumbermen	37
Painters	16	Businessmen	98
Blacksmiths	13	Mechanics	34
Oil Workers	48	Tailors	13
Teachers	27	Hotel Prop.	16
Lawyers	5	Contractors	61
Law Officers	7	Carpenters	62
Mail Carriers	5	TaxiDrivers	9
RR employees	18	Cotton buyers	6
Retired men	16	Supt. Supply	14
Gas Distillers	4	Undertakers	2
Florists	3	Florists	3
Undertakers	2		
Supt. Supply	14		

March 20—Chamber of Commerce lists accomplishments for
the past year among which was building two houses for the

needy: one for Daddy Gorham and one for Mrs. Sims.

May 8—Wetumka ice plant has storage for 135 tons and can manufacture 15 tons per day. It has a stone wall 21 inches thick with a four inch thick cork lining. The plant is owned by F. W. Abshire of Tulsa and his brother George Abshire of Wetumka.

June 25—Work on Highway. The grading is finished from Holdenville to Horn's store and is now open. Within three weeks the grading will be finished from Horn's store to Wetumka.

July 10—Radio Station KFRU of Bristow begins enrolling men in the National Radio Farm School. A ten-minute class is held every weekday at 1:00 PM.

July 24—The First National Bank and Bank of Commerce are each completing $15,000 additions, while the American National Bank is building a $20,000 addition.

July 24—City sells oil and gas leases. Mayor Charles N. Hamilton and the council sold two leases: a twenty acre tract located in the SW corner of the corporate limits and twenty acres belonging to the cemetery. The first was at $55 per acre and the second was at $92.50 per acre.

September 25-2400 pound shipment of Dental Powder was made to the Peace Dental Supply Company of Wichita, Kansas. The raw material is perlite which exists in huge quantities near the surface north of Wetumka.

September 25—Post Office is in new home in the beautiful Meadors Hotel.

1927—March 25—M. C. Moore arranges to ship out 100 bushels of peanuts to Ada.

April 6—Gasoline Plant is located here. The Forrest E. Gilmore Company of Tulsa, with headquarters in Portland, Oregon, manufacturers of natural gasoline, have located in Wetumka. The deal for the ground was consumated last week and material is now being received to erect the plant. It will be located on Wm. Buck's land just west of the city. (In June 384 carloads of gasoline will be shipped from this plant, not far from the railroad.)

July 1—High School streets are now graveled. In the past several functions at the school have been called off or postponed because cars could not get to the school building.

July 15—Brinson Motor Co., in new quarters in The Chowins Building on East Broadway, one door east of Post Office (just across the alley from the Meadors Hotel complex.

July 15—Roy Gammill's filling station installs new air gauge which can be preset at any pressure so that tires are not overinflated.

August 19—Wetumka Telephone Exchange sold for $40,000 to Mr. R. Crawford of Sulphur. Exchange had been installed in 1903 by Mr. T. L. Lumley (who also established hardware store that year that would become Herring Hardware).

August 19—Herman Darks, Company Clerk of Company "I" writes to say both companies arrived safely after train trip to Fort Sill.

October 14—School Attendance Increased. School attendance is better this year. The attendance for September were: Miss Ima Lora Allen, 10th grade, 97.5 %; Miss Mabel Taylor, 12th grade 97.4%; Mrs. W. E. Jones 11th grade, 95.6 %; Mrs. R. B. Knight, 9th grade 95.5%; Miss Maude Kitchens 7A grade, 97.2%; Miss Mary Long, Grade 7B, 96%; Miss Waltie Parks, 4th grade, 94.5 %; Mrs. Grace Klein, 2nd grade 93.9%; Mrs. W. W. Ferguson, 3rd grade, 93.2%. Mrs. Jack Murphy, 5th grade, 92.5%; Miss Alma Mayfield, 8B grade, 92.3%; Mrs. Gertrude Freeman, 4th grade, 90.5%; Mrs. Pearl Jackson, 6th grade 90.5%; Miss Flossie Allen, Primary 90.2%; Miss Vida Crumley, 2nd Primary, 90.1%; Miss Rebecca Bloom, 5th grade, 90%; Miss McAllister, 3rd grade, 89%; Mrs Burla Wilson, 1st grade, 87.5%.

February 3—An attempt to burn City Hall and National Bank of Commerce. The work was undoubtedly that of an incendiary and his plans were well laid.Damage to City Hall runs to $1,000. This is third attempt to burn bank building in past several months and no substantial damage has been done.

March 2—After long continuous labor, the Church of God Bethel has been completed and is open for worship.

March 23—Cornerstone of the Baptist Church is laid.

August 19—Baptist Church to be opened to public.
November 9—Two are killed in automobile accident. The car carrying Roy Chowins, Earl Williams, Pete Parker and J. P. Law, went off the embankment on Gopher Hill. Roy Chowins was killed instantly and Pete Parker died shortly thereafter.

December 16—New Christian Church is dedicated.

1929—March 1—Wedding in Coin Store draws big crowd. This is the third wedding to take place in the store.

July 26—Hundreds of Indians attend their fifth annual B. Y. P. U. Convention, at the Indian Church south of Wetumka. Thousands of white people visit the site and say it was one of the most orderly programs of that kind they had ever witnessed. One of the interesting numbers was a demonstration of the early white missionary, as he preached the Gospel to the Indians while an Indian standing at his side repeated his sermon in the Indian language. The convention was opened by a parade through Wetumka. This parade, which was about a half-mile long, formed at the south end of Main Street and marched through the city six abreast. Each local union forming a separate unit, bearing their banners and various colors and uniforms halted at the flagpole. Mayor B. H. Harrison delivered an address of welcome to them.

July 19—Town Threatened By Burning Well. Blazing oil for several days threatened south end of town. It was too hot to approach. The solution was to dig a tunnel and use a blast of steam to extinguish the flame.

August 2—Paving on Highway 75 is complete between Wetumka and Weleetka.

August 9—It is announced that Holdenville will not get Highway 75.

August 2—Ten carloads of Seminole Indians on way to Washington, D. C.; Louis Dunzy, a Creek, is going as the official interpreter.

1930—January 10—Holdenville High School burns. Loss is $118,00 for five year old building.

January 23—School Report (Previous Six Weeks)-**Primary**, Flossie J. Allen, teacher, Number enrolled 64. Honor Roll-Turner Meadors, Busey Lee Jackson, Tommy Nolen, June Woford, Patty Ann Busey, Alice M. Rice, Marie Ussery. **First Grade**, Teacher Bertha Newton. Number enrolled 53, Honor Roll-Garrell Dunna, Billy Laport, Mildred Moore, Francis Williams, Eldon Osborn, Maudine Lowder, Lora Fisher, Richard Camplain. **Second Grade**, Number enrolled, 50, Teacher, Grace Klein, Honor Roll, **Third Grade**, Number Enrolled, 49, Teacher, Ruth Powell, Honor Roll, Virginia Hulsey, Francis Collins, Peggy McFall, Helen Brasher, Jo Woford, Geraldine Bowles, Raymond Kimbro, Mary Bell Fulks, Bobby Sheppard, Gaylor Vaughan, L. T. Case.**Fourth Grade,** Teacher, Gertrude Freeman, Number enrolled 55. Honor Roll Marthalu Switzer, Donald Fair, Bertha Beasley, Margaret Hardridge, Lucille Dillman, Dorothy Helen Harrison, Johnnie M. Jones. **Fifth Grade**, Teacher Ruth Murphy, Number enrolled 43, Honor Roll, Graham Diggs, Ruby Dipove, Freeman Moore, Bertha Aune-Ellison, Ben McFall, Jr., Ruby Kennedy, Glen Nolen, Winifred Knight, Dorthy Ann Barr, Evelyn Kolodny, Jane Baskin, Mary L. Nicks, Lavaca Bradburn, Bernice Ramsay, Maxine Williams, Lucille Taylor. **Seventh-B Class,** Honor Roll, Hazel Capps, Chess Williams, Jr., A. J. Gay, Sylvia Freeman, Alberta Parsley. **Grade 7-A,** Teacher Mattie Moses, Enrollment 42, Honor roll, Robert Bach, Kenneth Bennett, Lavern Bradburn, Elizabeth Chowins, Margaret Chowins, Alma Cline, Freida Collins, Ola Grimes, Reba Lewis, Jack Lucas, Florine Macy, Ivon Osborn, Foster Shackleford. **Grade 8-B**, Honor Roll, Elmo Benedict, Cleburn Wesson, Ruby England, Opal Osborn, Miriam Yourman. **Grade 8-A**, Teacher, Grace Lawrence, Number enrolled 32, Honor Roll, George Charon, Maxine Beasley, Kenneth Dipboye, William Jackson, Opal Osborn, Otis Rogers, Lucile Ramsey, Ruth Wilson.

May 30—Harry and Glenn Chowins dig 25 acres of potatoes. Out of 450 bushels they grade 195 as first class. Five carloads of potatoes already shipped from Wetumka this season.

August 8—The five miles of concrete paving on Highway 75 south of the city will be completed to city limits by Friday night.

November 21—A serious attempt is made to burn the High School. Fire started on second level fire escape and burned through door before it was discovered.

1931—January 30—John Madison Watkins (1864-1931), long time publisher of THE WETUMKA GAZETTE is dead.

1932—January 22—Sam Mc Kinney an Indian farmer, drowns when he falls from cable stretched across the North Canadian River just north of Harry Chowins' Farm.

January 22—Osteopath G. B. Trottman and wife and son and daughter, arrived here the first part of the week to make Wetumka their home.

March 25—Captain Jack Herring Dies.

February 11—J. R. Saxon announces for County Commissioner.

May 13—Lee Motor Company receives first Ford V-8 in Hughes County.

August 19—Wetumka Hospital to be opened Saturday. Miss

Emma Neeley, a nurse, has secured the entire upper floor of the American National Bank annex and will operate a hospital.

October 27—Sam and Josephine Proctor will hold their annual Rodeo at their ranch eight miles northwest of the city this Saturday and Sunday. Josephine Proctor is back in the saddle and will give roping exhibitions.

November 11—Julia C. Chowins, one of the first settlers of Wetumka, died in Los Angeles, California. Burial was in the Wetumka Cemetery.

November 23—Federal Emergency Relief Act (FERA) sewing room is in operation on Main Street.

November 14—Herman Darks announces for State Representative.

December 30—George Williams was married last Friday to Miss Mary Dickinson of Norman. She is a graduate of Oklahoma University with B. A. and M. A. Degrees, majoring in French and Spanish. She was also a member of Phi Beta Kappa. The couple will live at 305 South Washita Avenue.

October 15—Central School is severely damaged by fire.

December 31—Central School is completely destroyed by a fire shortly after midnight.

February 2—Glenn Chowins announces for County Commissioner.

April 16—Senator T. P. Gore and Congressman Will Rogers

advises that the Public Works Administration has approved a thirty-seven hundred dollar grant for the Wetumka school rebuilding project.

April 20—Schools to receive Federal funds. The Wetumka schools can expect to continue to a full nine months school term due to Federal funds. The teachers will receive their back pay since February 9th.

May 18—Cecil Kilgore, of Wewoka, purchases the Wetumka Bakery. He is an experienced bakery operator, having about seventeen years in the business and will move with his family to Wetumka next week.

In 1935, Oklahoma farms were 61% tenant operated-among the worst in the nation. (The sections where farm tenancy was highest were also highest in percentage of illiteracy. U. S. Census Bureau.)

January 25—Bob Wills and His Texas Playboys will play one engagement at local theatre.

February 7—Roly Canard, a descendant of Creek Chiefs is re-elected to his second term as principal chief.

March 22—Civil War Veteran is Buried. Rev. A. P. Ledbetter who recently moved from here to Dustin was 91.

April 26—Casket Factory is working at capacity. More than a dozen caskets are being turned out each week in the factory located at 400 South Main Street.

May 31—New law firm composed of Philip Jackson and Dan

Yahola has recently been formed.

July 19—The City Cemetery is to be improved by WPA projects. A stone fence along the front, all streets graded and graveled and set to bermuda. A 24 x 18 Chapel will be built and the access road to be improved.

August 16—125 Hughes County boys enter Conservation Service.

August 16—100 acres of onions are harvested and first carload will be shipped out soon.

September 13—Armory and street project approved by President Roosevelt.

October 25—$37,000 armory project for city started.

September 20—$290,000 is allocated for farm-to-market road improvement in Wetumka district (WPA).

September 20—$35,000 home of Mr. and Mrs. Terry Walker Completed; most expensive residence ever built near Wetumka. Will burn to the ground on January 15, 1937.

December 13—Five carloads of pecans are shipped out of Wetumka this season. Value was over $10,000.

January 17—Mrs. Otis Adams and Ruth Murphy to organized girl scouts in Wetumka.

August 7—Twenty-two buses stop in Wetumka daily. It is also a popular rest stop and there is a new restaurant at the Meadors

Hotel.

September 4—First steel body bus is added in Wetumka.

September 18—Construction of second wing is begun at Central School as armory nears completion.
November 27—New Road from Highway 75 to Fairview is nearing completion (WPA project.)

1937—May 7—Dustin Lake (22 acre WPA project) is completed.

June 18—Bob Willis and His Texas Playboys will play for dance in the new armory.

October 1—Dr. D. L. Wenrick opens his office in Wetumka. Had practiced in Dustin for three years. Dr. and Mrs. Wenrick are occupying the residence at 619 East Porter.

1938—January 6—Welfare clients to get oranges at Dustin, Lamar, Carson, Wetumka. The shipment arrived today.

January 20—The Wetumka junior high grades will be transferred to the High School. (Their places will be taken by students transferred from Mingo.) The new shop buildings (WPA project) are virtually complete.

April 28—SNOW WHITE and The Seven Dwarfs is showing locally at The Rogue Theatre.

May 6—"Wetumka Day" will be featured at the International Petroleum Exposition held annually in Tulsa. Host Badges have been received for Mayor Diggs, C of C Secretary Melton, and President Frank Breshears from W. G. Skelley, organizer of the event.

June 21—Wetumka's last Confederate soldier, Uncle Billy Freeman, will pack his fiddle and head to Gettysburg (Pennsylvania)
for a Union-Confederate reunion.

October 28—Wetumka High School is completely destroyed by
fire.

November 18—Okemahan carries every county except four to be
elected governor. Mr. Leon C. Phillips, who makes his home in
Weleetka and is well know locally, is the governor-elect in the
largest election majority ever carried by a candidate for governor
in Oklahoma.

December 23—Twenty-five thousand bushels of peanuts have
been marketed in Wetumka district bringing farmers over
$18,000.

1939—Color line to be established in Wetumka. The City Council is
studying proposed ordinance on an emergency basis after it was
learned that an offer had been made to sell property in section of
the city wholly populated by whites.

January 12—Wetumka Fire Department assists Weleetka in losing battle to save High School.

Lime from crushed limestone is available as soil additive from
State penitentiary at 40 cents a ton.

January 29—Dr. John Hemphill, pioneer Wetumka dies from
burns sustained when his robe caught fire as he was warming
himself.

March 1—Work to begin on South Main Street. Project is to

remove three blocks of center parkway.

March 8—WPA is assisting Indians in building road from Wetumka to Thlopthlocco tribal town and bridge across the North Canadian.

WPA is helping landscape streets in Henryetta that have subsided as much as sixty inches because of old mine workings.

April 4—Highway 9 is half completed, as a dirt road, between Dustin and Wetumka. ($85,605 was spent.)

June 2—Bass Moore, WPA supervisor, asks for election as constable.

July 10—Herbert L. Friend, Moss Teacher, defeats Clarence Hastings by 26 votes to be county treasurer.

July 31—Wetumka's two National Guard Companies are sent to Camp Pitkin, Louisiana.

September 20—Governor Leon Phillips, before a Congressional Committee, blames Oklahoma's migration problem on drought, freight rates and high farm tenancy rates.

October 3—Cotton crop looks better than in ten years. Expected to yield $1,000,000 or 20,000 bales for Hughes County's best year ever.

October 14—Jess Goodspeed, Wetumka's Champion Calf Roger, performs in New York's Madison Square Garden.

November 5—5,000 people see air demonstration at Boren Flying Field near Wetumka.

November 20—Cecil Kilgore, owner of the Wetumka Bakery, remains hospitalized in a Muskogee hospital after his leg was shattered in auto accident near Warner, Oklahoma. His auto was sideswipped by a truck. Mr. H. H. Darks was at the wheel.

January 10—Wetumka's population is 2,340 vs. 2,163 in 1030.

March 26—The University of Oklahoma's economics bulletins showed that The Great Depression had lessened somewhat in 1940. Building permits were up 58% over 1939. Farm income improved by 41% over the previous year. The weather may have had a role. The Wetumka gins reported that the cotton coming in "looked better" than anything they had seen in ten years.

April 11—Frightened Team Killed as They Plunge Into Moving Train-Barney Elam, a Colored Man living seven miles west of Wetumka said that his team became so frightened they broke loose and rain into the side of a fast train. They were so badly injured that City Marshal , Joe Bement, shot them at the request of their owner.

April 25—New Motor Car Firm Opens for Business in Wetumka. George Wilburn, brother-in-law of Cecil Kilgore begins Chrysler-Plymouth dealership. He had been a Ford dealer in Durant.

May 14—The increased economic activity may have some relation to the worst quarter for traffic accidents in Hughes county since statistics had been maintained. There had been 26 crashes in the county and every single one had resulted in at lease one serious injury or death. There had been 13 accidents inside cities and the same number outside cities. Sixteen of the crashes occurred during the daytime and ten at night. This was for the first three months of 1941.

May 25—Wetumka teachers are to receive a minimum of $75 per month; those with at least three years of college are eligible for $80. Those with a BA may get $90.

June 23—During flooding, U. S. 75 is undermined near the bridge as concrete rested on sandy soil.

July 3—Wife of Joe Louis (prize fighter) Marva Trotter Louis, daughter of Negro sharecropper from Wetumka, seeks divorce. She said he was "as handy with his fists at home as he was in the ring."

July 8—Harve Ball, has been county sheriff for ten years. Had been in Oklahoma since 1890s and in Holdenville from the beginning.

September 8—Sara Delano Roosevelt, FDR's mother, dies.

October 13—County Farm Agent reports decline in farm tenancy rate: from 74.3% to 68%.

October 31—Clarence Hastings and three passengers die in collapse of South Canadian bridge during flood.

October 31—Over 100 pieces of property in Wetumka Paving District 2 will be auctioned on courthouse steps.

November 24—The U. S. Supreme Court strikes down California's "Anti-Okie" law which tried to ban penniless transients at the border.

March 6—Betty Ferol Martin, daughter of early aviation enthusiast Clarence Martin, is the fifth girl to solo at Wetumka's Boren Field. She will become a Women's Air Service Pilot (WASP) to ferry planes from factories to air fields and replace men in non-combat flying.

April 23—The Federal government encourages farmers to grow as many peanuts as they can. Seed is available on a credit basis. Henry Bowles distributed 21,000 pounds of shelled peanuts for planting. Many farmers lacked faith in this type of seed as they had always planted peanuts in the shell. (The real problem will be a shortage of burlap sacks and warehouse space. Wetumka is given permission to use armory for peanut storage.)

May 11—McAlester is selected as site for naval ammunition depot; 40 million is rapidly invested. Holdenville is subject to rent control because architects and many workers live there.

May 24—Captain Glenn Chowins is with the Yanks in Ireland.

July 3—Wetumka opens Servicemen's Club on Main Street.

July 31—Twenty candidates for public office in county spent $1,051.47. Harve Ball was first at $167.70.

August 28—Boren Field is on the aviation map. Is used by cross country fliers.

September 13—Maudine Lowder and sister Faye are employed in Washington, D. C., FBI and Department of Labor, respectively.

October 29—Contingent of draftees (including Eldon Osborn) leave Holdenville.

December 12—Bill Stringfellow, 1941 WHS graduate is at Torpedo School at Newport, Rhode Island.

January 10—Hughes County had no fatal traffic accidents in 1942. It might reasonably be attributed to restrictions on tires and gasoline.

January 10—Miss Virginia Tomberlin leaves the junior high school faculty to be a WAAC.

January 15—Geneva Joe Davis, Moss, is the only woman high school principal in the county.

January 15—Lone Oak is the third instance of a whole school board moving away.

February 10—Miss Odie Tims, sister of Mrs. Stona Fitch, becomes a WAAC.

February 15—Civilian Pilot Training class of 15 cadets from Boston, Massachusetts arrive in Wetumka.

February 15—Army offers to buy all shotguns (for guard duty) in good condition.

July 19—Mrs. Jess Graves, 78, pioneer Wetumka matron, becomes confused or panic stricken and crosses in front of Frisco train. She was killed instantly. She was the mother of Wes Graves, café owner on Frisco Avenue and later caretaker at Wetumka lake.

October 3—Sgt. Eldon Osborn docks in New York.

1945—September—Sgt. Jack W. Bennett, Wetumka, said that he was aboard a plane that was able to fly over prisoner of war camps and drop bundles by parachute. (The Japanese air defense had been completely eliminated.) He said they were at 700 feet and he could see the men jumping up and down and turning summrsaults of joy.

September 18—Lieutenant Wallace Battles is aboard the Queen Elizabeth that docked in New York.

1946—Mach 20—T4 Haskell Brock sails from Calcutta, India, aboard the General Collins.
May 26—Bobby Jackson, son of Harry Jackson, serving with occupational forces in Japan.

March 1—Hughes county school enrollment has dropped 1,112 since 1942; Census Bureau says Hughes County has at least temporarily lost 4,000 residents.

March 25—Jim Ragland is made Wetumka School Superintendent. The Superintendent in Wetumka, Mr. Battles and Mr. Ragland did a job swap by recommending each other to their respective boards of education.

August 18—Two Ex-POWs of Hughes County give deposition of their treatment, atrocities and war crimes for the Tribunal in Tokyo.

January 16—Wetumkans attending Oklahoma University: Howard Aaron Anthony, Wida Mae Anthony, James Kenneth Bennett, Margurite Bicknell, George Charon, Stella Rose Chowins, Gregory Vance Clements, James Arthur Cowan, Afton C. Gille, James Arthur Harmon, James Jarrett, Moneer M. Rahhad, Harvey Leon Woford.

February 2—Mr. and Mrs. W. Arthur Spiller, formerly of Okemah, assume ownership of Nicks Funeral Home.

February 27—County school population decreases by 309 since 1946.

April 10—Farms in County have gone from nearly 3400 to around 2200 in the last ten years. (Today's figure is about 900 with 100 of them being less than 50 acres.) In 1940 2,635 farms had gross recepits of $1,181,238; In 1945, 2,091 farms had twice as much: $3,020,700.

April 24—Hughes County pays the sheriff, the county judge and county attorney $2,100 per year. All other elected officials earn $1,800.

May 13—Three of the five rural mail carriers in county are driving Army surplus jeeps.

July 23—Eldon Stout, former Wetumkan, is named Oklahoma Aviation Director.

September 28—Guardsmen promoted. Captain Albert C. Prucha, announced these promotions. To privates first class: Jack R. Allen, Windell Bachus, Raymond Basquez, James M. Carter, Richard Crowels, Carrol W. Folmer, Curtis L. Fuller, Chealy H. Hill, Wiley T. Little, Bob W. Murray, James E. Ramsey, Jack W. Ray, William E. Rogers, Dan B. Smith, Burks P. Sparks, Jack F. Spear, Bobby Towery and Ray G. Williams.

Promoted to technicians fifth grade were: Harold G. Massey and Forrest M. Poole. New corporals are: Bobby Brooks, Stona J. Fitch, Thomas A. Little, Martin M. Moore, Monroe L. Ray, Johnny Sheppard, Darrell V. Smith and Grady D. Williams.

Recently promoted to the ranks of sergeant were: Perry P. Kennedy, Jr., and William H. Marsh.

Charles L. Lucas was promoted to staff sergeant.

September 26—Body of Sgt. L. D. Conley, son of Mr. and Mrs. Shan Conley, Wetumka, is the first to arrive aboard an army funeral ship in New York. The war ended over two years before. From this date the bodies return in a steady procession until after Korean conflict.

February 1—Sheriff Harve Ball Retires. First elected in 1930 and served continuously except for two years. He beaten by Emet Petete, Holdenville Chief of Police, by two votes in 1944. Made comeback in 1946.

May 6—Gene Autrey campaigns in person, at Wewoka, for Senatorial Candidate Robert S. Kerr.

July 22—Wetumka Junior College will be discontinued. Was a casualty of benefits of G. I. Bill which enabled students to attend institutions some distance from home.

August 8—Mr. and Mrs. C. W. Duncan, have announced they are ready to open the Redskin Theatre.

August 8—Gopher Hill teacherage and Lone Star school building and its contents will be auctioned.

September 2—Mrs. Ida May Nichols, 83, a resident of Wetumka for 48 years dies. She was the mother of Charles and Glenn Nichols and had resided continuously in Wetumka since 1900.

September 22—3,000 attend fox and wolf hunt held three miles south and four miles east of Wetumka. Fifteen mounted judges officiated the event which drew over 600 dogs.

September 29—President Truman makes a stop at Holdenville with his special campaign train. He was well understood when he said: "Hello, I'm Harry Truman. I work for the government and I'm just trying to keep my job."

October 7—Governor Thomas E. Dewey, Republican candidate for President, makes stops in Holdenville and Calvin. He was the quintessential city slicker. Theodore Roosevelt's daughter, still very much alive, described him as "the little man on the wedding cake." It was said that this debonnaire New Yorker could strut sitting down. *And this is why I am totally amazed that this polished and poised New Yorker married a woman from Sapulpa, Oklahoma. His train held up a few days in Tulsa to let him get in some time with his in-laws.*

October 31—129 Hughes Countyans are receiving social security benefits. The latest Federal Consolidate Funds Report (1997) showed that 3,601 are presently receiving monthly benefits. This is one in four persons.

November 3—Truman beat Dewey in the county 5,792 to 1,676.

November 14—Two Wetumkans are killed at Weleetka train crossing. Mrs. George McCallie, 60, and her son Earl Clifton "Pete" McCallie died instantly at rural crossing. Mr. George McCallie was seriously injured.

November 14—Wetumka has county's first German war bride, Mrs. Reece Morgan.

Wetumka's only Confederate vet, Uncle Billy Freeman of Wetumka, is dead at 104. *Life* magazine (May 30, 1948) did a nationwide survey and found 68 veterans of the Civil War still alive. Two of them lived in Hughes County, "Uncle Billy" and George Grizzle of Holdenville. By the time the magazine was on the newsstands they were both dead.

January 17—George McClellan Kern dies. He was the father of Delbert and Francis Kern and came to the Wetumka area in 1889. He was one of the last persons who could honestly claim to have been a resident of both Old and New Wetumka.
June 6—There are only 267 mules being used on Hughes County farms.
June 14—New $228,000 North Canadian river bridge opens. The old bridge had washed out in 1945 and left Okfuskee County divided for almost five years.
June 8—County lost 8,540 population since 1940. Wetumka's official census figure is 2,012, down from 2,340.
July 9—Glenn Chowins is advanced from high school coach to high school principal at Wetumka.
October 1—Wetumka imposes a garbage fee of fifty cents a month. It is intended to pay for garbage pick-up, weed cutting ans spraying. Truman Smith drives first garbage truck which is a flat bed Chevrolet. Walter Meeks is in charge of spraying alleys with DDT.

October 9—Oklahoma's cotton crop is the smallest since records were started in 1896.

Wetumka's school enrollment is 730. (Grades 398, Junior High 125, high school 207).

September 23—All Wetumka schools show decrease. High School is 205; junior high 112, Central Grade School 384, Douglas High School, 34, Douglas Grade School, 73.

November 26—Assembly of God congregation begins $10,000 building fund drive.

October 21—Highway 9 is due $900,000 in improvements east of Wetumka which include new bridge and sixteen miles of grading and surfacing.

November 5—Bicknell's Drug Store will close after 25 years. For the previous 25 years it had been the Red Cross Drug and was located in space occupied by a tavern near the present Coast-to-Coast store.

November 13—Roley Canard, retired Creek Chief, dies of heart attack.

December 31—It is learned that 45th Infantry Division went into action after landing at Inchon on December 5. Had arrived in Japan on April 25 and trained for seven months. Chinese Communist radio made the first announcement as the American press was under a strict censorship order.

March 21—Herman Darks defeats Mayor Dalton Fuller, 450-

340. Unopposed councilmen were D. F. Burns, Bill Tankersley and Logan Walker.

June 14—Wetumka will enforce ordinance to remove all hog pens from within the city limits.

June 14—Wetumka's bonded indebtedness is $61,000; high point was $262,640.

September 25—The Choctaw Gin on Grand Avenue in Wetumka is dismantled and shipped to West Texas. Wetumka is left with one cotton gin. Weleetka has none.

December 31—$5,000 check from Ray Meadors in memory of his brother Frank, is presented by Stona Fitch to the Methodist church for their building fund. Mr. and Mrs. Julian Peixotto donated an organ in memory of their son. Church furniture to be manufactured in Holdenville by a small defense contractor (United Manufacturing) which made millions of tent poles during the war. Peace time conversion of this firm, located at the former Chestnut Lumber Yard, was first to building cedar chests and then church furniture than was distributed throughout six states.

January 22—Due to increased income from electricity distribution, Wetumka's bonded indebtedness has been reduced to $54,000.

March 10—Four Wetumkans in the 45th Infantry Division are undergoing hospitalization in Japan: Houston Hill, Richard Crowells, Bob Murray and M. L. Ray.

March 20—Wetumkans are awarded Combat Infantryman's

badge in Korea. They are Cpl. Jack R. Allen, son of Mr. and Mrs. Carl Herndon; SFC John W. Chastain, son of Mr. and Mrs. Lawrence Chastain; Sgt Richard Crowels, son of Mrs. Freeman Crowells; Pvt. Oren J. Davis, son of Mr. and Mrs. Bob Davis; Cpl. Donald Dyer, son of Mr. and Mrs. J. D. Dyer; Master Sergeant Julie O. Gammill; Cpl Edward Hall; Sgt. Billy J. Johnson, son of Mr. and Mrs. M. R. Johnson; Sgt. Tommy R. Kiser, son of Mr. and Mrs. Joe Kiser; SFC Wiley T. Little; SFC Burkes P. Sparks, son of Mr. and Mrs. Paul Sparks; SFC Nate Spears, son of Mr. and Mrs. S. M. Spears.

March 25—Wetumka Senior Class present drama. Players include Virginia Callison, Jo Dell Hall, Bill Gammill, David Peixotto, Faye Brown, A. B. Clement, Paul McBride, Norma Ruth Campbell, Ruth Lassiter and Ted Tankersley.

March 25—Dr. Roper Williams, is found dead in his dental office. A 45 caliber revolver is found nearby.

April 14—45th Division is arriving back in Seattle, Washington after rotation out of combat.

May 19—George B. Williams, brother of Roper Williams and propreitor of The Coin Store, dies after auto crash.

Had not regained consciousness after head-on collision with a bus south of Wetumka after midnight previous Saturday night. He was 45 years old.

May 23—Lightning strikes transformer and leaves Wetumka without power. For several days the movie theatres are shut down, and many businesses disrupted. Biggest inconvenience is that there is only one gasoline station with hand pump, Walter

Smith's at the city limits.

August 25—Dr. J. P. Gille, Wetumka dentist since 1908, dies after stroke.

October 2—Harry Askew, Oklahoma A&M College Senior, is student teacher at Wetumka. He will return in five years to be only the third Vocational Agriculture Teacher in the history of Wetumka schools.

November 13—Holdenville man, James Inman, is given ten year suspended sentence for suicide try.

November 15—Adlai Stevenson carries Hughes County with a margin of only 1,627 votes out of 7,757 cast. Herert Hoover, in 1928, carried the county: 3,937 to 3,169 for Al Smith who as a New Yorker, a "wet" and a Catholic was very unpopular in Oklahoma.

December 12—Herman Darks, the consummate politician, has an important weekend guest, Dr. George S. Long, brother of the assassinated Louisiana Senator, Huey P. Long, (and newly elected Congressman) is in Wetumka. Their freindship has spanned two decades.

December 25—Wetumka welder, Roy Rippy, is killed at Yukon when nearby gasoline drum explodes.

January 22—Dizzy Dean, former Spaulding farm boy, is youngest player ever inducted into the baseball hall of fame at Cooperstown, New York.

February 10—Group of Wetumkans are enroute to Wetumpka,

Alabama to help that town celebrate its 119th birthday. These group includes Mr. and Mrs. Jeff Biffle, Mr. and Mrs. Herman Darks, Don Darks, Bill Tankersley, Rev. D. F. Burns, J. Travis Watson, Haskell Brock, H. H. Loard, Charlie Conner, Elgie Absher, Jerry Ray, Frank McCoy, Tom Kirby, Roy Wilkerson, and Bill Johnson.

February 17—Wetumkans attending Oklahoma Agricultural and Mechanical College at Stillwater: Gene Chandler, Albert Clement, Ruth Davis, Tommie Davis, Bill Gammill, Millie Gammill, David Hall, Edward Hall, Richard Hall, John Hansford, Billy Johnson, Leon Lyle, C. Edgar McFarland, Robert Montgomery, William Mullins, Edward Scott, Elmer Shropshire, Donald Yahola.

May 1—Bertha Bloom, First Grade Teacher retires. Had taught little Wetumkans to read since 1928. Her parents had been among the first Wetumkans and operated a clothing store. Her widowed mother married their store manager, Nathan Lee, who sold the store and opened the Ford dealership in 1930 with Rebecca and Bertha as his partners. Miss Bloom never married and never learned to drive but she was one of the best educated teachers of her time. She would spend her retirement years in serious and purposeful world travel.

April 20—Donald Daniel Yahola, 46, dies after he and his brother Lyman were involved in a fight with three Okfuskee county men in Wetumka. Mr. Yahola was a graduate of Cumberland University Law School, Lebanon, Tennessee, and had practiced in Wetumka. He had been inactive for some time.

May 1—Bertha Bloom, 25 years a primary teacher in Wetumka, retires. Her parents were present from the earliest days of

Wetumka. Her father, Blair Bloom, had operated a dry goods store until his death. Their manager, Nathan Lee, married his widow. Miss Bloom, her sister Rebecca and brother David were partners with him in the Ford Dealership in Wetumka.

May 5—Raymond Jaggers Glen Chowins are notified that their Civil Service examinations and certification had expired. Bryan Nicsks is Acting postmaster.

June 11—Lumber Scott, member of county road crew, dies when he is pinned by the bed of his dump truck on a county road one-half mile south of Wetumka.

July 15—Retired Senator Tom Anglin, 71, dies at Holdenville.

August 27—Ruth Jett is Sucker Day Queen in fourth annual Sucker Day. The runner-up is Valerie Robinson.

September 27—20 Boxcars of Frisco trained are derailed in the Mission Bottom as tracks are ripped apart for 300 yards.

October 8—Wetumka's Main Street is given a three-inch over-lay of asphalt for the entire .8 mile length.

January 22—Huge fire at Grimes Gasoline Plant injures one person.

March 12—Darl Garrison Osborn (the author's father) is killed at Maud drilling site.

December 5—The Coin Store is sold to Dobson and Company.

June 25—Wetumka's school enrollment has declined from 922

in 1952 to 842.

July 29—Dustin's Main Street is paved by Highway Department.

August 13—Wetumka has new mercury vapor street lights that were installed by Charlie Baker and his crew.

October 2—Clyde Ray is in P&S Hospital with mangled hand that was crushed in a corn picker. Residents of nearby communities meet to harvest his 28 acres of peanuts.

January 2—Miss Faye Lowder holds birthday party for her uncle, H. H. Darks.

March 15—Wetumka's $75,000 bond election will fund additional playground room at Central School, a new high school athletic field and badly needed rapairs on the junior high school wing.

March 16—Wetumka's mayor, Herman Darks, gets twice as many votes as his nearest rival, Armand Gibson, who is also his cousin.

March 16—John Campbell was defeated by incumbent Chief of Police, J. T. McGibboney by just six votes. There was no legal mechanism for a recount in a city election.

May 24—Quarter horse sale at Darks ranch draws buyers from 20 states and nets $44,600. Catalogs had been distributed nationwide.

July 21—Fairview, due to its harvest schedule, is first school in county to achieve racial integration. Superintendent Raymond Willingham reports "everything is working out fine."

August 27—Sixth annual Sucker Day is held.

October 7—Spadework begins on Eufaula Dam.

November 17—Wetumka's new football stadium is near completion.

November 24—Mayor Herman Darks posts $500 bond after drunk driving charges were filed by County Attorney, Max Darks, his cousin. Mr. Darks, driving Chief of Police J. T. McGibboney's 1949 maroon Plyouth, collided with a car driven by Eckbert Jackson Early, the rural mail carrier.

December 1—Dustin nearly burns to the ground after failed attempt to burn "fire guard" in grassy area. Six business houses (a whole block) were burned after the volunteer fire department's fire truck wouldn't start. Hose was dragged a whole block but was frozen before it could be trained on the fire. Orville Gammill and Curtis Lowder took Wetumka fire truck to Dustin and prevented the fire from crossing the street.

December 3—Herman Darks, Wetumka's mayor, involved in head-on collision while trying to pass near Dustin. The wife of the vice-president of a Shawnee bank is killed and another person critically injured. Mr. Darks dies within a few hours. He was 47 years old.

December 5—Senator Robert S. Kerr is back in Wetumka for the last time. He addresses the annual Chamber of Commerce banquet which was held in the new cafeteria at Central School. Herman Darks was buried that day.

December 11—Bobby Goodspeed, son of Mr. and Mrs. Jess Goodspeed, is named 1955 world junior all-around cowboy at Fort Worth, Texas.

December 21—In a large voter turn out, J. W. (Bill) Nicks beats Mrs. Ora Jo Darks (the late mayor's widow) by a narrow margin of 53 out of 779 ballots cast.

0-595-21464-9

CPSIA information can be obtained at www.ICGtesting.com
Printed in the USA
LVOW040143231211

260826LV00001B/163/A